# Contemporary primary care

# Contemporary primary care

The challenges of change

Edited by
**Philip Tovey**

Open University Press
Buckingham · Philadelphia

Open University Press
Celtic Court
22 Ballmoor
Buckingham
MK18 1XW

e-mail: enquiries@openup.co.uk
world wide web: http://www.openup.co.uk

and
325 Chestnut Street
Philadelphia, PA 19106, USA

First Published 2000

A catalogue record of this book is available from the British Library

ISBN    0 335 20009 5 (pb)    0 335 20452 X (hb)

*Library of Congress Cataloging-in-Publication Data*
Contemporary primary care : the challenges of change / Philip Tovey
    [editor].
        p.      cm.
    Includes bibliographical references and index.
    ISBN 0–335–20452–X (hbk.). – ISBN 0–335–20009–5 (pbk.)
    1. Primary health care.  2. Community health services.  I. Tovey,
Philip, 1963–  .
RA427.9.C68  2000
362.1–dc21                                                    99–28982
                                                                    CIP

Typeset by Graphicraft Limited, Hong Kong
Printed in Great Britain by Biddles Ltd, Guildford and King's Lynn

# Contents

# ● Notes on contributors

**Jon Adams** is currently a lecturer in sociology at Napier University, Edinburgh. His main research interest is the use of complementary therapies by general practitioners.

**Lorna Arblaster** worked as a general practitioner for 12 years in a range of settings. Subsequently she returned to public health medicine where the effects of socio-economic conditions and social policy on health have been among the subjects of her work as a freelance researcher.

**Colin Barnes** is a senior lecturer in the Department of Sociology and Social Policy at the University of Leeds. He is the Director of the Department's Disability Research Unit, and Research Director for the British Council of Organisations of Disabled People (BCODP).

**Tony Dowell** is Professor of General Practice at the Wellington School of Medicine in New Zealand and a part-time general practitioner. His current interests include mental health research in general practice.

**Adrian Hastings** is a general practitioner in a group practice serving a deprived area of Leicester, and a lecturer in the Department of General Practice and Primary Health Care at Leicester University. His research interests include out of hours care, monitoring the quality of care and the evaluation of undergraduate medical education.

**Phil Heywood** is Professor of Primary Care Development at the University of Leeds. He is principally concerned to link teaching and research in the Leeds School of Medicine with moves towards a primary care-led NHS.

**Steve Iliffe** is a Principal in general practice in north-west London, and Reader in General Practice at the Royal Free & University College London Medical School, in the Department of Primary Care and Population Sciences. His main research interests are in the field of primary care for older people, especially mental health issues.

**Joanne Jordan** has a background in anthropology and is currently a lecturer in the School of Social and Community Sciences at the University of Ulster. Her research interests include assessing health needs in primary care, user involvement in health care, women's health, and research at the interface of health and social care.

**Satinder Kumar** is a Clinical Research Fellow at the University of Southampton, within the Primary Medical Care Group. He is currently completing his PhD; a qualitative and quantitative study of the impact of genetic advances on general practitioners.

**John Mellor-Clark** is Evaluation Manager for the Psychological Therapies Research Centre at the University of Leeds, where he is currently engaged in the development and national implementation of the CORE System; an initiative that attempts to standardize and centrally coordinate audit, evaluation and outcome measurement for the psychological therapies.

**Geoffrey Mercer** is a senior lecturer in the Department of Sociology and Social Policy, and a member of the Disability Research Unit, at the University of Leeds. He teaches and researches in the sociology of health and illness, and disability studies.

**Richard Neal** is a lecturer in primary care research at the Centre for Research in Primary Care, University of Leeds, and a part-time general practitioner in Leeds. His main research interest is frequent attendance to general practice.

**Philip Tovey** is Principal Research Fellow in the School of Health Care Studies, University of Leeds. His current research interests include complementary medicine, chronic illness and psychological well being.

**Alison E. Wilson** is Nurse Coordinator for Fisher Medical Centre, Skipton and Visiting Research Fellow at the School of Medicine, University of Leeds. Her research interests include primary care development and evaluation, general practice information systems and primary care nursing development.

# Acknowledgements

I would like to thank Tony Dowell and Phil Heywood for their comments on the original proposal for the book, and Waqar Ahmad for his observations on the introduction.

I am grateful to BMJ Books for permission to reproduce the tables in Chapter 4.

# List of abbreviations

| | |
|---|---|
| A&E | accident and emergency |
| ADL | activities of daily living |
| AGUDA | Association of General Practice in Urban Deprived Areas |
| BMA | British Medical Association |
| CBT | cognitive behavioural therapy |
| CIL | Centre for Independent (or Integrated) Living |
| CM | complementary medicine |
| CPC | counselling in primary care |
| CPCT | Counselling in Primary Care Trust |
| CPD | continuing professional development |
| DIAL | Disablement Information and Advice Line |
| FHSA | Family Health Services Authority |
| GMC | General Medical Council |
| GP | general practitioner |
| HIP | Health Improvement Programme |
| HTA | health technology assessment |
| ICIDH | *International Classification of Impairments, Disabilities and Handicaps* |
| NHSE | National Health Service Executive |
| NICE | National Institute for Clinical Excellence |
| NSF | National Service Frameworks |
| PCG | primary care group |
| PCT | primary care trusts |
| PHC | primary health care |
| PHCT | Primary Health Care Trust |
| RCGP | Royal College of General Practitioners |
| RCP | Royal College of Physicians |
| RCT | randomized controlled trial |
| SWT | social worlds theory |
| UDA | urban deprived area |
| WHO | World Health Organization |

 **Introduction**

Philip Tovey

Primary health care (PHC) is in the midst of substantial change. The reorganization of its form – the most visible and high profile dimension of this change – is being accompanied by an examination of a whole range of issues that constitute, or impinge upon, its content. And, of course, these are not developing in a vacuum but are intricately bound up with the prevailing political and social context. This book is an eclectic and critical exploration of primary care at this time of change.

Needless to say, the immediate political context has been dominated by the ongoing moves towards the 'primary care led NHS [National Health Service]' (Meads 1996). Although this was instigated under the then Conservative administration, and despite the fact that the election of a Labour government has brought change as well as continuity to plans for health care provision (Ham 1998), primary care remains central to the development of the 'New NHS' (Department of Health 1997). Indeed, a process of structural reconfiguration is now under way. This is seen, for instance, in the revisiting of established boundaries between primary and secondary care, and between primary and community care, as well as in the introduction of primary care groups as providers and commissioners of 'local' health care.

But although we must certainly pay close attention to such political shifts, we should avoid being drawn towards equating developments in primary care with responses to policy change alone. This is because arguably the greatest challenges faced by primary care are those relating to substantive areas of practice and provision, which have emerged as key issues independently of specific political initiatives. These issues are grounded in the complexities and dissatisfactions of contemporary society and the challenges and pressures for change that they induce.

There is an essential interplay between these issues and the social context within which they have emerged. They are issues and dilemmas for primary care, but they are not simply primary care issues. Provision for, and involvement of, marginalized groups, concerns about the validity of experts and established systems of expertise, questions about the impact of new technologies, and the acceptability and personal impact of socio-economic inequalities are of direct importance to our discussions here, but have a resonance that extends throughout our social, political and cultural institutions. Thus, the climate of change fostered by political initiatives on (primary) health care may well serve to facilitate debate in these areas, but it has certainly not been its cause.

## About the book

The aim of this book is to bring together critical and thought provoking pieces on a diverse set of issues of relevance to the evolving shape and character of primary care; in the main these are research informed. What is important to clarify at the outset is that contributors and contributions were not included in order that a consensus might be reflected or produced; either on the type of primary care that may be seen as the desired outcome of change, or, in fact, on the angle from which themes are addressed. Instead each chapter has been written on the basis of what excites or interests the author: what each contributor takes to be a particularly pressing issue in their area of interest. This has resulted in the production of pieces with very different starting points and terms of reference: methodological, political, and professional. Thus, each chapter can, and should, be read as a stand-alone piece.

However, having noted the independent nature of the pieces, each chapter does contribute to one of three distinct parts of the book: the challenges of context and organization; the challenges of practice; and the challenges of research. Although this separation provides a useful way of grouping chapters with related emphases, there is inevitably considerable overlap between the three parts; for instance, virtually all the contributions in Parts 1 and 2 are grounded in research, and those of Part 3 inevitably address practice related issues.

The opening contribution to Part 1 has been written by Tony Dowell and Richard Neal, both academic general practitioners, with the intention of revisiting existing 'visions' of primary care (such as that grounded in Socialist principles) and working towards the identification of the component parts of a new one, which draws on, but transcends, those that we already recognize. It can perhaps be regarded as the logical starting point for critical assessment of PHC, in that it necessitates an initial stepping back from practicalities in order to ask questions about the meaning and purpose of primary care at a fundamental level. In so doing the relationship between PHC and broader systems of thought (for instance Socialism) can be highlighted. It is essentially a think piece; and is regarded by the authors themselves as a partial account, and one that should form the basis of critique from those with competing (or complementary) visions, especially when these are informed by other disciplines.

Whether or not it actually ties in with a consistent vision in any meaningful sense, or is the result of political and managerial expediency, the *form* of primary care necessarily impinges on its capacity to deliver health care. The framework around which provision is delivered is more than a neutral base; it acts to shape both priorities and possibilities. Phil Heywood (Chapter 2) provides an examination of some of the cornerstones of recent changes in the organization of service delivery. For instance, fundholding is reviewed in terms of its impact on services, prescribing and costs. The move to primary care groups (PCGs) is discussed in the context of the broader reforms of the NHS. The author pays particular attention to new mechanisms of quality assurance that have emerged as a part of the reform process, against the background of an apparent failure of self-regulation in specific high profile cases.

The structural limitations or possibilities of a service depend, in no small measure, on who is included and who is excluded from performing therapeutic (and managerial) tasks, and the capacity of those involved to shape as well as respond to agendas. In other words the nature of team working, and the character of the interprofessional relationships on which teams are established, are pivotal. This is, of course, an issue that has brought with it a good deal of rhetoric and naïve expectation in recent years. It has again been brought to prominence by changes such as the enhanced role for nurses that is currently in vogue, and notably the (limited but required) involvement of nurses and others in the running of PCGs. As well as tracing the history of team working in primary care, Alison Wilson (Chapter 3) critically appraises the relevance of non-clinical literature on teams against a background appreciation of the particular dynamics of primary care settings. She also provides an 'evidence based' review of the nature of team working as it currently is; and, attempts to synthesize knowledge with the intention of presenting a picture of what could be achieved in the future.

Having covered both the philosophical and organizational bases of primary care, attention (in Part 2) shifts to substantive areas of challenge relating to primary care practice. Diversity is, of course, an essential feature underlying that practice. Patient populations reflect social, cultural and demographic differences and these result in varying patterns of expectations and needs. In Chapter 4, Steve Iliffe provides the first of two chapters that are concerned with the nature of provision for a particular group of patients. Given that both groups – older people and people with impairments – can be regarded as marginalized or inappropriately served by existing arrangements, it is important that both chapters include discussion of the assumptions that inform that provision. In the first of these chapters older people are the focus of discussion. It is argued that the prevailing assumption of a rapidly ageing society is a myth; that the way in which older people are characterized is inappropriately negative; and that primary care, rather than acting as a facilitator of improved health amongst older people, is actually structured in a way that acts as a barrier to the achievement of that objective. Major change to both policy and practice is advocated.

Geoffrey Mercer and Colin Barnes (Chapter 5) discuss the problematic nature of provision for disabled people. The chapter is based on the distinction between two quite different models of disability: the medical model, which might reasonably be seen as the conventional or established approach;

and the social model, which brings the extent to which activity is restricted by the organization of society and its institutions to the centre of analysis. The authors use the social model as the basis of a critical review of the appropriateness of current primary care organization; in particular highlighting how existing initiatives fail to deliver the kinds of services that are consistent with the needs of service users.

The subject of disability is inextricably linked with the 'new genetics', the topic covered by Satinder Kumar in Chapter 6. Perhaps as much as in any other single area, there is potential here for competing interpretations of both the key issues, and of the nature of the approach that should inform analysis and practice. The approach taken by Kumar is explicitly general practitioner (GP) centred. The author considers the role of GPs in relation to science, their perceptions of disease and their involvement in risk assessment. The multi-dimensional character of this topic is reflected in coverage that develops within a sociological, psychological, epistemological and ethical context, as well as a biomedical one.

It was noted earlier how many of the issues facing primary care pre-date its current high profile position. Indeed, by way of contrast to, say, the 'new genetics', some have been near constant concerns during the historical evolution of the service. This is certainly the case with the subject of Chapter 7: the socio-economic context of provision and in particular the enduring reality of poverty. The study of the interrelationships among poverty, health and health care provision is perhaps the archetypal illustration of the necessity to 'socially locate' analyses. Taking the inverse care law as a starting point, the authors, Lorna Arblaster and Adrian Hastings, bring this perennial issue up to date by looking at recent socio-economic trends and the nature of contemporary responses, mindful throughout of the limitations of interventions that cannot address the rather broader causes of health inequalities.

The number of subjects competing for attention in Part 3, Challenges of research, far exceeded the space available to cover them. The section could have justifiably included chapters on ethnicity and health care, women's health, the currently emerging area of men's health, the diagnosis and treatment of medically unexplained symptoms, matters of ethics, and so on. The three chapters that have been included will hopefully be of interest for the way in which they touch upon themes of enduring and cross-topic relevance for the coming period of research in PHC: the relationship between research evidence and service provision; the adoption of a pluralist approach to methodology against the background of the continuing perception of the 'randomized controlled trial' (RCT) as the gold standard; and the potential application of social science theory as well as methodology.

With the introduction of PCGs, the imperative for locality planning, which became a part of the organizational framework for the delivery of primary care during the 1990s, is being given an additional impetus. In the opening chapter of part three, Chapter 8, Joanne Jordan draws on the evidence from a number of recent pieces of research to examine the potential for using the (in theory, wide ranging and valuable) data held in primary care as the basis of an informed approach to the purchasing and planning of local health care. Specifically, answers to two questions are sought: how is this resource to be accessed; and once that access has been achieved, how useful is the information provided?

Part 3 is completed by two chapters that look at relatively recent inclusions in the primary care treatment portfolio (counselling and complementary medicine) and ask, in rather different ways, how we might most effectively establish knowledge about them. These are treatment options that can bring with them bodies of knowledge, styles of working, conceptions of successful outcomes and beliefs about how these might be gauged that are at odds with established practice in the surgery. The number of questions raised by their incorporation is therefore substantial.

It is the lack of a credible evidence base for the utilization of counselling in primary care that forms the basis of the chapter by John Mellor-Clark (Chapter 9). This is a particularly timely commentary in view of the enormous expansion of counselling provision in recent years and the likelihood that it will remain an integral feature of provision during the current changes. The author argues that the lack of an evidence base to support this expansion contradicts established NHS policy. He then goes on to question the reliance on the RCT in pursuit of that evidence base.

As with counselling, there would appear to be a trend towards an increasing role for complementary therapies in a reshaped primary care system. Jon Adams and Philip Tovey (Chapter 10) note that this integration is occurring in a variety of ways, including, for instance, referral to outside practitioners and the use of different therapies by general practitioners themselves. Central to the argument presented here is that although such trends are frequently acknowledged, we actually know very little about the nature of grassroots activity: the coming together of modes of thought, as well as of individuals. This is because research has to date tended to shy away from the potentially difficult task of exploring what is actually happening at practice level, rather than what is said to happen or what representative bodies pronounce should happen. In Chapter 10 the authors present one means by which such research can be undertaken: through use of the framework and concepts of a hitherto under used sociological theory.

To summarize, unresolved issues, dilemmas and challenges are to be found at all levels of PHC: the conceptual or philosophical, the organizational and the operational. In turn, a range of methods and frameworks are available for the analysis of these issues. This book has been written with a view to both reflecting, and encouraging, that diversity of focus and approach.

## References

Department of Health (DoH) (1997) *The New NHS: Modern – Dependable*, Cm 3087. London: The Stationery Office.

Ham, C. (1998) Foreword, in M. Baker, *Making Sense of the New NHS White Paper*. Abingdon: Radcliffe Medical Press.

Meads, G. (ed.) (1996) *A Primary Care Led NHS: Putting it into Practice*. Edinburgh: Churchill Livingstone.

# Part I
# Challenges of context and organization

# ❶ Vision and change in primary care: past, present and future

Tony Dowell and
Richard Neal

## Introduction

In this chapter we explore the identity and culture of general practice and primary health care from a historical perspective. This is a reflective paper, combining our interpretation and analysis of changes and visions in primary care over the past century, and drawing from this the key elements of a new vision. In doing so, we outline the degree to which it has been possible historically to articulate a vision for general practice and primary care. We then discuss the demarcation between vision and cultural stereotyping, and explore the relationship between vision and change. The chapter concludes with an outline of the key elements of a contemporary vision, and a discussion of the utility of such a vision.

There are many definitions of general practice and primary health care. They have in common the provision of comprehensive care from a community base as a starting point and an emphasis on sustaining holistic relationships. What is less clear is how well these definitions apply to the past and whether their rhetoric can be translated into present day practice. If these definitions are accurate then their essence should be visible to observers outside primary care and promulgated as part of any visionary statements made by those within. For example, Fry (1993: 3–4) describes the characteristic features of UK general practice as 'the single port of entry into the NHS, with the exception of A&E [accident and emergency] and special clinics . . . 24 hour availability [for] first contact care, co-ordination and manipulation of local medical and social services . . . gate keeping and protection of hospitals . . . [and] long term and continuing generalist personal and family care'.

The Alma Ata declaration (World Health Organization/United Nations Children's Fund 1978: 2) describes primary health care as essential health care made universally accessible to individuals and families in the community by means acceptable to them, through their full participation and at a cost that the community and the country can afford. It forms an integral part both of the country's health system of which it is the nucleus and of the overall social and economic development of the community.

The National Health Service Executive (NHSE) in its recent report of research and development in primary care (National Health Service Executive 1997: 8) defines primary care as 'first contact, continuous, comprehensive, co-ordinated care provided to individuals and populations undifferentiated by age, gender, disease or organ system'.

These definitions provide different emphases with which to assess the identity of primary health care. Fry accentuates the personal role of the GP with responsibilities to provide 24 hours a day care. The Alma Ata declaration identifies the need to provide care that is universally accessible and the NHSE emphasizes the management imperative.

Our background as GPs provides us with a view that is to some degree parochial. We firmly believe that the future of general practice is inextricably linked with the continuing development of the primary health care team and acknowledge the impact of broader societal factors on health and disease. We believe that it is the GP who has provided the most enduring picture and stereotype of the primary health care professional. We thus see our own analysis of the state of primary care as incomplete and look to colleagues in other primary care disciplines to provide complementary visions.

### Vision and the process of change

Change is a constant accompaniment to professional life. It is a paradox that health care practitioners are often conservative by nature and yet health care is perceived by our patients and by society as being in the constant grip of rapid progress. A doctor's duty is to intervene, and to be the natural enemy of the entropy and order of nature. This striving for intervention and change produces a medical culture that is inherently dynamic and adapts to new practices and technology (Smith 1998). At the same time many doctors, and more recently other health care professionals, seem to have a duty to be a 'pillar' of society, and to develop practices that can endure and be trusted. Although change is thus an important feature of health care, professionals are generally ambivalent about change and until recently little thought was given to how change occurred, let alone how it might be managed. It is possible to discern various epochs of change in primary health care, but much more difficult to decide is whether those periods were driven by a 'vision', or whether they 'just happened'. We define two broad types of change in primary care: that arising as a result of a vision (for example by 'leaders' from within, wider visionary political initiatives or individual 'visionaries'), and that occurring as a result of 'imposed bureaucratic change' often as a result of political change imposed without the support of those within primary care; although we recognize that they are not fully mutually exclusive.

Doctors and health care workers are subject to a wide range of different pressures that will promote or impede change. Clinical habits are influenced by past experience, patient pressure, the activities of pharmaceutical companies and government edict. What is less clear is how these forces interact and to what degree a clear vision has been a major driver of change. Currently, one of the most widely accepted models of change is that developed by Prochaska and DiClemente (1986), which embodies the concepts of 'diffusion of innovation' and the 'pre-contemplation to action' cycle. Key features of these are that only relatively small numbers of individuals will be innovatively seeking change at any time, and that when a change is proposed it is likely to be promulgated first by early adopters of new ideas and later by the silent majority.

The impact of wider political and social change on health care is often profound and produced by complex series of events. The roots of the present changes in health care in the UK have their origins in the vision of the post-war welfare state, but have been modified as each political era has come and gone. For example, it is interesting to speculate how primary care might have been shaped if prevailing social policy in the past 20 years had been driven from the centre left rather than the right of the political spectrum.

Significant changes in the direction of general practice may be promoted by either individuals or organizations. The nature, process and driving forces for change can be described and defined in a number of different ways. Lawrence (1993) suggests that the demand for change is led by: accountability; patients with needs; a profession dedicated to assuring quality; and a society that sets targets for efficient and effective care, where possible justified by research. Scott and Marinker (1993), however, take the view that change necessitated by circumstances is acceptable in primary care, and that change willed and enforced by others is considered arbitrary. Furthermore they believe that the fashions prevalent with twentieth-century general practice (for example educationalism, screening, health promotion and performance review) have largely been driven by a small number of enthusiasts. Al-Shehri *et al.* (1993: 101) state that 'People with vision sense signals emerging from the present which point to the nature of change and combine them in order to make a meaningful, if theoretical, construct of the future', and that 'more relevant for most organizations than the visionary individual is a collective vision developed by the stakeholders in the organization'.

Few of the key participants in the recent history of primary care have been explicit about a wider purpose or motive behind their actions. Many of those who have produced the greatest change in primary care have done so from a narrow professional perspective. They have sought, for example, better working conditions for professionals or incremental improvements in patient care driven by a deep clinical experience in general practice. Julian Tudor Hart was an exception in linking his vision of *A New Kind of Doctor* (Tudor Hart 1988) to broader political initiatives.

## What has gone before?

*Models of cultural identity*

This section examines models of primary health care throughout this century from a UK perspective. The inspiration for primary care development flowed through a number of major themes or 'visions', which we attempt to define. These models, or cultural stereotypes, are caricatures of the people who were best suited, personally or politically, by the systems in which they were working; they were the people for whom the time was right. They were not necessarily visionaries, rather individuals who were agents of that vision, and typical of the innovators of their generation. Sociologically they represent 'ideal types', constructed by emphasizing certain traits of a given social item that do not necessarily exist anywhere in reality. These traits are defining, and are not necessarily desirable ones (Giddens 1993). General practice has long been expert at defining itself from a 'folk' rather than professional taxonomy perspective; these descriptions are part of that process. Although in their time visions and visionaries may be regarded by their own peer groups as belonging to a 'golden era' it seems likely that other groups within society view the models differently. A vision depends on the perspective of the visionary and generally the public has had less excitement for these models than the professionals may have done.

*The first half of the twentieth century*

Present day primary care has its origins in the feuds between apothecaries and physicians in the seventeenth century. As the apothecaries began to work in poorer communities the tradition evolved of family doctors living among their patients and providing family orientated medicine with a degree of continuity of care. These goals of local and continuing care have provided perhaps the most sustaining vision of general practice, and a framework for care still present today.

Two political initiatives dominated general practice development in the early half of the twentieth century. Lloyd George's National Health Service Act of 1911 (Parliament 1911) introduced health and medical insurance for employees, and was part of a global trend towards providing primary health care as a basic service of a modern democratic state. The Dawson Report of 1920 (Ministry of Health 1920) set out future plans for health centres and primary and secondary care, although few such centres were developed at that time.

The 'Peckham Experiment' began in 1926, led by two 'visionaries', George Scott Williamson and Innes Pearse, who set out to test the hypothesis that 'health is more infectious than disease'. Families were invited to join and attend for 'healthy activities' at the Pioneer Health Centre (an architect-designed glass building years ahead of its time), during which they underwent periodic health checks. Despite receiving accolades and visitors from all over the world, the centre failed in its ultimate goal of reducing illness and morbidity in its members, and few of its ideas were adopted at the time. The population preferred health centres to be 'sickness shops', as they still do today; the way in which people used the GP in the East End of London in this way in the late 1980s is graphically described by Widgery (1991).

During this time primary health care was virtually the sole domain of (predominantly male) GPs, who were generally regarded as inferior to their hospital colleagues, yet largely copied them in their style of medicine. Doctors practised 'science' in the guise of expertise, diagnostic equipment, chemical tests and drugs. According to Porter (1997), the more primary care physicians prescribed science however, the more they ran the risk of intimating that practitioners other than themselves were the true experts. This era drew to a close with the Beveridge Report (Parliament 1942), which set up the welfare state, and led to the formation of the NHS in 1948, with Aneurin Bevan as the first health minister.

### The 'traditional GP': 1948–mid 1960s

At the time of the setting up of the NHS, GPs objected fiercely to the idea of a salaried service and clung to the right to be 'independent contractors'. In 1948 GPs brought into the NHS their 'panel' of patients and the tradition of independent practice. This was then tailored to the bureaucratic structure of the infant welfare state. Two 'visionary' strands can be identified as developing from this early experience with the NHS. The first is the collective identity of doctors whose experience of war, and the formation of the NHS, had left them searching for stability and tranquillity; and the second is the vision of the early pioneers of the College of General Practitioners, who defined the intellectual independence of the profession.

The NHS became very popular largely because it combined the traditional values of family medicine with universal accessibility. The doctors generally worked alone or in small practices. There were very few attached district nursing staff. These were under the control of medical officers for health in geographical areas, and GPs were slow to realize the potential of working together, as they were wary of developments (Swift and McDougall 1964). Few practice nursing posts existed before 1966. This was largely due to finance; employing nurses did not make economic sense as there was no reimbursement to the GP. The large numbers of health centres that had been expected to flourish in this era failed to materialize.

The majority of these 'benign patriarchs' settled with comfort into the new Elizabethan age. They seemed to work very hard, battling with increasing success against infectious disease and bringing the new resources and technology of the NHS to the individuals and families under their care. They practised medicine in more or less the same way as the generation before them, and for most doctors, or indeed any of the practice staff, the long hours and influenza epidemics left little time for any other activity. The stereotype from this era, the sometimes gruff, cuddly, avuncular and largely unaccountable male GP has persisted, at least in the minds of cartoonists. Patient expectations were low, despite the 'liberation' of the free NHS, and GPs seemed to retain the universal respect and affection of their patients.

However a small number of GPs did have time for visionary zeal and reflection, and their efforts led to the formation of the College of General

Practitioners in 1952, which subsequently directed much of its work into developing a secure infrastructure from which to develop patient services (Royal College of General Practitioners 1994). The 1966 Charter for general practice heralded the real beginnings of the group practice and the primary care team, and was the beginning of the end of the era of the family doctor immortalized by A.J. Cronin in Dr Findlay (Cronin 1978). Towards the end of this era many family doctors were beginning to be influenced by the development of general practice as a 'speciality', quite distinct from hospital medicine, and by some understanding of behavioural and social science. It was also around this time that the first university departments of general practice were being founded.

### The 'Golden Age' of general practice: 1969–1979

The 1970s are regarded by many GPs as a 'Golden Age' (Marsh 1998). General practice was accorded a new degree of respect and resourcing with the introduction of group practices and primary health care team working. The 1966 Charter allowed up to 70 per cent of the cost of staff (nurses, receptionists, secretaries and managers) to be reimbursed. This led to changing roles for the GP and the delegation of tasks from GP to nurse (Hasler 1994).

In this period a new generation of professional leaders and thinkers consolidated the efforts of a few pioneers. General practitioner academics in the new departments of general practice expressed a vision in which research and education were the pillars of new professional confidence. Byrne and Long (1976), and Pendleton and colleagues (Pendleton *et al.* 1984), along with others, identified the central importance of the consultation and an energized College of General practitioners provided a new intellectual impetus. More medical graduates positively opted for general practice and in the wake of widespread social and political emancipation a new strand of radicalism emerged. This new social and sometimes 'socialist' vision of general practice attracted those who felt that a legitimate role for the GP was to act politically for both individual patients and local communities. Some of its proponents had been influenced by work or travel in developing countries, while for some women doctors the successes of feminism provided the inspiration to challenge the prevailing male middle-class world of general practice. One visionary of this era was Julian Tudor Hart, who used his work in a poor, Welsh valley mining community as a platform to carry out first class general practice and epidemiological research, and to champion the cause of his patients.

Organizations such as the Socialist Medical Association, the Medical Practitioners Union and more recently the Association of General Practice in Urban Deprived Areas (AGUDA) provided organizational frameworks for likeminded individuals, while women's rights and the increasing nuclear threat provided causes around which these health workers could rally. Although politically active doctors remained small in number, the impact on the profession was significant, with larger numbers of liberal minded colleagues able to subscribe to one, or more, aspects of change and the new radicalism.

As in society generally during this time, there was a feeling that the previously rigid codes of hierarchy, status and even dress for health professionals were becoming more relaxed. It became acceptable for doctors to be concerned about community health issues and the sandal-wearing, muesli-eating, cycling doctor became a potent figure in general practice mythology, and an enduring cultural stereotype of the era. This decade saw significant experiments in general practice team-working and community development, particularly in the inner cities. Despite any outward show of radicalism, the GPs continued to lead the developing primary health care teams, and function as the direct employer and paymaster to most of its members.

The emancipation ideologies of the late 1960s and 1970s caused some doctors to question their relationship with patients and the idea of the patient as a partner in health care began to develop, as epitomized by the description by Tuckett *et al*. of the consultation as a 'meeting of experts' (Tuckett *et al*. 1985). This generation of doctors became heavily influenced by Hungarian psychologist Michael Balint, who, by making doctors focus more on their own personality and style of consulting, led many to adopt a more patient centred approach (Balint 1957); later developed by Stewart *et al*. (1979). Practitioners also began to embrace other models of working, such as those provided by the complementary therapies, outside the traditional medical model, partly as a result of the work of Illich (1977) and McKeown (1979) in highlighting the limitations of the medical model. Patient participation groups were initiated, although with limited success (Richardson and Bray 1987).

*The GP as pragmatic manager: 1980–1997*

During the 1980s, the Thatcherite policies of privatization and apparent disregard for public services eroded the confidence of those visionaries who had promoted a community based approach to general practice. In their place arose a 'vision' based on a political dogma that redefined 'health' as a commodity, rather than as a right. Opposing intellectual and political tensions in health care delivery were to some extent resolved by the introduction of the Health Service changes and the new general practice contract of 1990 (Secretaries of State for Health, Wales, Northern Ireland and Scotland 1989). The development of fundholding, together with rapid changes in information technology and the perceived value of business acumen, led to the emergence of a third cultural stereotype in general practice and primary care.

The new contract offered significant opportunities to those prepared to adopt a more commercial and market style approach to patient care. Although unused to purchasing and contracting, the first wave of fundholders found themselves dealing with large budgets, a major increase in administrative workload, and a burgeoning use of computers and mobile phones. This new breed of GP had parallels in a new businesslike attitude in academic departments and the Royal College of General Practitioners (RCGP), and in the creation of new advisory and managerial posts in Health Authorities and Trusts. There were parallels in the other primary care professions; practice managers (often upgraded from receptionists, secretaries and administrators) became commonplace in most practices, and nurses, midwives and health visitors all took on more managerial roles and found themselves working in a more managed workforce.

For many, however, this new highly pressured managerial approach held little appeal, and the new contract and health 'reforms' were associated with a marked decline in the morale of general practice and primary care. Although the 'market' in general practice was to a large extent artificial, savings made on fundholding budgets strengthened the notion of the GP entrepreneur. Many patients, after generations of 'family doctoring', appeared to find the prevailing culture disagreeable, felt more disenfranchised, and felt that the NHS was more interested in numbers than names.

Primary care was supplied with a vision for the future very different from those that had gone before. Successive cabinet ministers under Thatcher's leadership provided the clearest guidance and policy directive for primary care since Bevan. This vision was imposed from without and the leaders within general practice and primary care seemed to be engaged in working to modify the prevailing policy rather than to actively promote it. This modifying policy may be deemed to have been successful since the ground was laid for the increasing prominence given to primary care with the concept of a 'Primary care led NHS' (National Health Service Executive 1994). This concept represents a compromise between politicians who saw it as a way to save money from expensive secondary care budgets and the subdued remnants of those within the profession who hoped that a strengthened primary health care sector would lead to more justice and equity.

## Towards the reality of a primary care led NHS: 1997 onwards

Change continues in primary health care. Tony Blair's Labour Government came into power in May 1997, seemingly on a tide of great public relief rather than expectancy. Within primary health care a White Paper (Department of Health 1997) has already set the tone for change, although this appears to have been met by an atmosphere of hope tempered by trepidation, and may go some way to truly develop the notion rather than the rhetoric of a primary care led NHS. Many of the concepts introduced by the market driven changes of the 1980s have survived intact. The purchasing of health as a commodity and an insistence on efficiency remain. Primary care is deemed, however, to be underpinned by values and principles such as 'quality', 'fairness', 'accessibility' and 'responsiveness' (Leeds Health Authority 1997). An evolutionary vision appears to have been produced seamlessly by committees. There is much to applaud in the present state of primary care and if there is less passion and thunder than in previous epochs perhaps that represents a maturity within a profession where more can participate and contribute. It is harder to define cultural identity in a society where so much seems eclectic and transient. If primary care and its leaders retain a vision it is complex and not articulated easily by any one individual; it must provide solutions for the challenges that tax both primary care professionals and their patients.

We believe that the enduring stereotype of primary care in this era is a GP, but a very different one from before. The 'clinical governor' has less time commitment to the practice than previous generations, and is likely to delegate out of hours working to a cooperative or a deputizing service, even in rural areas. This trend has developed despite an increasing demand to be seen out of hours, and may be a reflection of the '24-hour society' combined with lack of contact with a family doctor, who knows the patient and their problems. The ideals of the 1980s have been replaced by a return to (superficially) more caring and compassionate values, addressed on a public health rather than an individual basis, through involvement with locality commissioning and primary care groups. The GP spends time carrying out clinical governance, 'a system through which NHS organizations are accountable for continuously improving their services and safeguarding high standards of care by creating an environment in which excellence will flourish' (Scally and Donaldson 1998).

The focus of work is still the consultation, where clinical decisions are based upon sound scientific evidence in a more explicit way than in previous generations. Although this may be empowering, and provides valuable ongoing professional education, many of the GP's clinical difficulties will never be resolved by 'evidence based practice' due to their inherent complexity. Modern day clinical practice is very different from that in secondary care. More people are seen with fewer symptoms, and there is a steady increase in demand (the 'doing better, feeling worse' syndrome; Porter 1997), despite falling rates of common and fatal diseases. For these reasons, and others, there is an uneasy truce between patient expectation and professional workload, and patients are complaining more. A prevailing theme of the 1990s has been that of social disintegration, most marked among the disempowered and disenfranchised. Apparent pressure from dissatisfied 'excluded' individuals, for example by increasing demands for out of hours visits, is met with a tendency to scapegoat and marginalize, creating a vicious circle where these groups make more demands as a result.

The career structure for the 'clinical governor' has changed too. He or she is likely to have a sequential or portfolio career, work in more practices and other places for shorter periods of time, and may work as a salaried GP. Colleagues in nursing, management and professions allied to medicine are also likely to have portfolio careers. The doctor or nurse who grows old with their patients is becoming an endangered species, fundamentally challenging one of the foundations of general practice – the long-term relationship between doctor and patients.

General practice and primary care at the present time is thus composed of a complex set of structures, initiatives and patient interactions. The main drivers for the present situation are the continuing hand of political interference and an increasingly professional group of leaders and managers. If there are visions they are specialized: GP academics lead research policy initiatives; and the RCGP provides guidance on GPs' professional development, as do nursing bodies and practice managers' associations for their own constituents. The General Practitioner's Committee (formerly the General Medical Services Committee) and the Local Medical Committees continue to protect GPs' livelihoods, and various other groups provide 'vision' in their respective fields (for example out of hours care, and non-principals).

*Can past visions guide future development?*

Do these past visions or caricatures provide the elements for a future vision for primary health care for the first decade of the new millennium? Many of the changes that have led to our present 'state of care' would seem to be the result of imposed and bureaucratic processes. Fundholding, for example, was introduced as part of a political imperative rather than as a necessity. Potentially visionary changes, such as models of nurse-led community development instigated following the Cumberledge Report (Department of Health and Social Security 1986), were challenged and overtaken by fundholding. Perhaps the boldest visionary statement of intent in primary care, the Alma Ata declaration, underwent development by trial and error for ten years in the Third World before its impact was felt in UK general practice. We contend that the current eclectic meld of professional initiatives and managerial directives does not constitute a true vision of primary care. Something is missing. It is also our contention that each successive change, although providing general practice with renewed vigour at its inception, loses momentum and direction so that the future is then left without sustainable inspiration from within; each visionary period expires and fizzles out in a way that could not have been predicted by its proponents at the time.

## Principles of a new vision

Many individuals and organizations can star-gaze and describe their vision for the future. We present the key elements of our vision here, while acknowledging that it is, by its very nature, an incomplete one. We believe that by drawing on themes from the past and beginning to understand how 'vision' may or may not drive further development of primary care, we have provided a structure that will be of value and applicability to 'users', planners and providers of primary health care. A vision for primary care must reflect current trends and set an agenda for future trends. If primary care is to thrive long into the next millennium, we believe there are certain principles, initiatives and ideas that the new model practitioner will need to adopt.

*An appropriate timescale and context*

Our examination of past identities suggests that new visions are near to expiry within a decade. It seems likely that, in keeping with other 'millennium syndromes', visions developed now should be designed to self-destruct before the end of the first decade of the new millennium. This is the first principle of a new vision: the short term is an integral part of primary care. There is much to be said against this concept. It undermines continuity and stability and leaves health professionals uncertain about their futures. It seems none the less to be part of current global health care and societal trends. Visions may also only be applicable in relatively small and well defined geographical and cultural locations.

*Reflecting on enduring values*

Low morale, disillusionment and poor recruitment may have made many people question the vitality of present role models and role definitions. A new vision of primary care, therefore, must engage in a number of paradigm shifts that draw on the successes and achievements of the past 40 years.

*Getting rid of unhelpful 'baggage' and accepting the past*

The past decade has been painful for many health professionals. Rapid changes of policy have left many demoralized and disillusioned. A new vision must envisage health professionals who can be relaxed about past struggles and accepting of an uncertain status quo. Although it may seem illogical, there seems to be a real opportunity for all in the present situation; socialist and feminist health crusaders can join forces with the zealots of fundholding, certain in the knowledge that past collective efforts have been found wanting.

*An appreciation of societal values and attitudes*

Changes in society as a whole affect how people perceive and react to health and illness, and how they seek help. As practitioners many of us are insufficiently involved in changes that affect the way in which society determines its values and attitudes. These include ethical dilemmas (for example, euthanasia, cloning, the new genetics, termination of pregnancy), as well as the way in which health, illness and health care are valued by individuals and by society. The healthier a society gets the more health care it seems to demand; there may be an urgent need for primary care to consider ways of reversing this trend.

*Patient empowerment and participation*

Patients and consumers play an increasingly important role in care. Recent increases in consumer demands are linked to more widespread coverage of health issues in the popular media and rapid expansion of access to the Internet and the seemingly infinite amount of health related information it contains. This amount of information being available to the public may lead to patients being both more empowered and more confused as to the nature of their problem and where to seek help. One consequence of this may be a move towards increasing specialization in general practice. This development, which is already a feature of many GP systems abroad, should be assessed carefully. It is likely to disempower the GP in the role of gatekeeper, and lead to the patient choosing to have several different primary care providers.

Primary care desperately needs to embrace the potential of information technology, an area it has been very slow to harness to date. There is now the real possibility of reliable and fast links to other professionals and organizations. Shared records and results can improve quality and reduce workload rather than create further layers of bureaucracy.

The visionary health worker must also accept that there is a strong culture of 'rights without responsibilities', fuelled by the current political trends for charters. Although aspects of this have undoubtedly led to improvements in care, a climate that encourages criticism if standards are not met will inevitably lead to more litigation and the development of more defensive practice. A new culture of rights with responsibilities is urgently needed.

### Redesigning the consultation

The fundamental 'unit' of primary care workload will remain the consultation. In the UK consultation times are still short compared to many other developed countries and this, together with the large number of house calls, has led to a perception in the profession of overwork, incompatible with high quality care. A first visionary step would be to re-evaluate the most appropriate style, duration and content of the consultation. Whether this would lead to longer consultations, fewer patients or an increased degree of 'specialization' is unclear, but this must be done if satisfaction is to return to the doctor–patient relationship. Although the role of both parties in the consultation has changed, tensions remain. Practitioners have recognized the concept of patient rather than doctor centred consultations and there are tentative moves towards a consultation being a partnership between doctor and patient. Furthermore, in both the UK and abroad a small proportion of patients accounts for a large proportion of all the consultations (Neal *et al.* 1998), little of which can be directly related to medical 'need'. A more radical, but in time pragmatic, change for UK general practice would be to consider an end to unlimited free access to the GP or primary health care team. Other systems, based on health insurance or charges for consultations and home visits, successfully combine high quality general practice with a managed workload. The UK system, however, remains in many people's eyes the most successful model of primary care delivery in the industrialized world.

### The practitioner's role

Over the past three decades, roles within primary care have evolved and developed. The roles of GPs overlap with the nursing, therapy and management professions; aspects of the traditional GP roles (for example, advocate, physician, friend, and adviser) may legitimately be taken on by other more skilled or trained professionals. The GP may develop other roles in, for example, management, specialist clinical care, teaching, and research and development. In a new vision of primary care there needs to be a sophisticated partnership between different professions, with equal allocation of power, and clear demarcation of roles. The new GP may inherit the role of the general physician, although in the community rather than a general hospital ward. In order to adapt to this role a degree of specialization will be required; a trend already developing in larger group practices. A further role is that of GP as the public health doctor for primary care in each locality. With the advent of new information technology and new methods in epidemiology, this role is one that GPs could adopt. Linked to this is the GP as the manager of primary health care, who determines the balance between primary, community and secondary care.

*Teamwork at last*

A new vision for primary care would see a re-evaluation of the success and failure of teamwork. There are some areas of practice, for example GP obstetrics, where doctors may have to relinquish long traditions of service and care and allow other professionals to replace them. The new GP will not be able to do all things well but will acknowledge the contributions of others more easily. The new vision will have to overcome the existing divide between employing organizations of practice and community nurses.

A more radical vision would be to question the ongoing validity of GPs' independent contractor status and to ask whether primary care may be better with a more accountable, managed and salaried service. Mirroring the way in which GPs have moved away from doctor centred consulting, there is a need to move away from doctor centred teamwork, although there are few signs of this happening at present (Royal College of General Practitioners 1996; Wright 1996).

*Professional development and education*

The standard career pathways of all primary care professionals is changing. At present much postgraduate learning is essentially voluntary; it seems likely that this will become less so. Mandatory accreditation and re-accreditation are already the norm in some countries and are likely to be introduced in the UK in the near future. The widespread acceptance of evidence based practice may provide a focus for self-directed and lifelong learning, but only if the appropriate model evidence based practice in primary care can be found (Gill *et al.* 1996). There have also been significant changes in the workforce. For some time female GPs have been demanding and creating more flexible careers; a wish that is beginning to be expressed by their male colleagues. The visionary will have to adjust to the changes this will bring in workforce planning and clinical care.

*Models of clinical practice*

There are a number of current alternative themes and models of clinical practice. Enthusiasts for each of them promote the advantages of their model, often to the exclusion and detraction of the alternatives. Guidelines and evidence based practice have had a major impact on clinical thinking. Methods of critically appraising evidence have provided the tools with which clinicians can use the results of research to benefit patient care. The importance of this change should not be underestimated. Much thought has been expended in adapting evidence based guidelines for the real world of primary care, and the visionary must be happy to work with the sometimes uncomfortable compromise between evidence based practice and the responses and needs of the individual patient.

A further balance that must be sought is that between the biomedical reductionism that general practice has copied from laboratory inspired hospital practice, and an art or evidence based expert generalism that takes its

origins from the holistic nature of family practice (Pietroni 1990). One practical expression of the resolution of this tension is the Marylebone Health
Centre in London. The original idea behind this project was to explore and
evaluate ways in which primary health care can be delivered to an inner city
area. The 'new' approaches include a holistic component, comprising an
educational self-help model with a complementary medical model. The health
centre runs a 'standard' NHS general practice alongside provision of a variety
of other health and educational services. The involvement of patients, or
users, underpins much of their work and great investment is made in the
personal and professional development of staff. The practice successfully
integrates use of the standard medical model alongside Chinese medicine
and a range of other therapies.

*Understanding the system*

GPs have found it easy to be insulated from the realities confronting many
other sections of society. The healing imperative often took precedence over
economic trends and health service managers were regarded primarily as
administrators. The past decade has seen a rude awakening from clinical
isolation. The visionary must be sympathetic to the wider influences on health
care trends and be able to accommodate chaos, complexity and uncertainty
in the planning of primary care; and must be aware that economic and health
care trends are cyclical, and that politicians have to tailor their promises and
their agendas to these wider trends. There are long-term trends that transcend
party politics. Health care budgets are now explicitly finite, and primary care
infrastructure will be linked to cost–benefit analyses. Visionaries must also
encompass ways of working more effectively with those who manage services.
Part of the vision, however, is the realization that however imperfect the
vision is, most of those working in health care do have the same goals.

## A folk caricature for the new millennium

We have used the presence of enduring stereotypes to support the development of principles for a new vision. A human incarnation of that vision
might answer to the following description. Vision is not limited by gender,
class, race or age; those battles have been fought and, hopefully, won. The
new model practitioner is aware of professional history and recognizes the
enduring values that history has created. A trend towards graduate entry to
medical school will equip our practitioner to view medical education and
practice more broadly and to value experience or qualifications in management and public health. More important than dress code will be a working
style that is comfortable with changes of pace and direction in a career
lifetime. Enthusiasm for information technology and research evidence will
be a character trait, as will a recognition that these trends will bring new
rights and responsibilities to the doctor–patient relationship. There will be
little room for cynicism or burnout in a scenario where many of the structural and clinical challenges of primary health care have been resolved.

The practitioner will have to specialize, but the choice of area will be from an embarrassing richness of options. The GP of the future can be the reincarnation of the general physician, a holistic practitioner of complementary medicine, a primary care community physician with skills to support effective community action or a primary care manager. These caricatures may sound part fantasy and part impossibility, but we believe there are sufficient role models in the present and the past from which to gain inspiration. Other primary care professions will also see increasing specialism in their roles.

*First steps to reality*

In order to realize this vision there are a number of responsibilities and obligations that must be accepted by practitioners, patients and government. The first requirement for a sustainable vision is a reasonable acceptance of the scale of the tasks, and the time required to achieve them. At present the NHS remains under funded not just in terms of money but in terms of the goodwill that health professionals have given to nourish it since its inception. As a re-evaluation of the present situation gets under way all aspects of care should be scrutinized. The most important change may be at individual practitioner level.

Inherent in the debate for the future is a theme that is echoed several times throughout this book: the status quo is not an acceptable option. Change in primary health care will continue and it is preferable that this change takes place with energy and vision from those caring for patients. The central pillar of any future vision is the principle that primary health care is universally accessible health care for individuals and families. The blending of the art and science of family medicine into the provision of essential health care, which has characterized the work and lives of our 'ideal types' and past visionaries, will be central to this.

## References

Al-Shehri, A., Stanley, I. and Thomas, P. (1993) Developing an organizational vision in general practice, *British Medical Journal*, 307: 101–103.
Balint, M. (1957) *The Doctor, his Patient and the Illness*. London: Pitman.
Byrne, P.S. and Long, B.E.L. (1976) *Doctors Talking to Patients*. London: HMSO.
Cronin, A.J. (1978) *Short Stories from Dr Finlay's Case Book*. London: Longman.
Department of Health (DoH) (1997) *The New NHS*: Modern – Dependable, Cm 3087, London: The Stationery Office.
Department of Health and Social Security (DHSS) (1986) *Neighbourhood Nursing: A Focus for Care. Report of the Community Nursing Review in England* (Cumberledge Report). London: HMSO.
Fry, J. (1993) *General Practice – The Facts*. Oxford: Radcliffe Medical Press.
Giddens, A. (1993) *Sociology*, 2nd edn. Cambridge: Polity Press.
Gill, P., Dowell, A.C., Neal, R.D. *et al.* (1996) Evidence based general practice: a retrospective study of interventions in one training practice, *British Medical Journal*, 312: 819–21.

Hasler, J. (1994) *The Primary Health Care Team*. London: Nuffield Provincial Hospitals Trust.

Illich, I. (1977) *Limits to Medicine: The Expropriation of Health*. Harmondsworth: Penguin.

Lawrence, M. (1993) Caring for the future, in M. Pringle (ed.) *Change and Teamwork in Primary Care*. London: BMJ Publications.

Leeds Health Authority (1997) *Changing the Face of Primary and Community Care in Leeds*. Leeds: Leeds Health Authority.

Marsh, G.N. (1998) 50 years of the National Health Service – the 70s – a golden age, *British Journal of General Practice*, 48: 1362–3.

McKeown, T. (1979) *The Role of Medicine: Dream Mirage or Nemesis?* Oxford: Blackwell.

Ministry of Health (1920) *Interim Report on the Future Provision of Medical and Allied Services (Chairman Lord Dawson)*, Consultative Council on Medical and Allied Services. London: HMSO.

National Health Service Executive (1994) *Developing NHS Purchasing and GP Fundholding: Towards a Primary Care-Led NHS*. EL (94) 79. Leeds: NHSE.

National Health Service Executive (1997) *R&D in Primary Care – National Working Group Report*. Leeds: NHSE.

Neal, R.D., Heywood, P.L., Morley, S., Clayden, A.D. and Dowell, A.C. (1998) Frequency of patients' consulting in general practice and workload generated by frequent attenders: comparisons between practices, *British Journal of General Practice*, 48: 895–8.

Parliament (1911) 1 & 2 Geo 5 chap. 55. *An Act to Provide for Insurance Against Loss of Health for the Prevention and Cure of Sickness and for Insurance Against Unemployment and for the Purposes Incidental Thereto*.

Parliament (1942) *Social Insurance and Allied Services. Report by Sir William Beveridge*. London: HMSO.

Pendleton, D., Schofield, T., Tate, P. and Havelock, P. (1984) *The Consultation: An Approach to Learning and Teaching*. Oxford: Oxford Medical Publications.

Pietroni, P. (1990) *The Greening of Medicine*. London: Victor Gollancz.

Porter, R. (1997) *The Greatest Benefit to Mankind. A Medical History from Antiquity to the Present*. London: HarperCollins.

Prochaska, J.O. and DiClemente, C.C. (1986) Toward a comprehensive model of change, in W.R. Miller and N. Healther (eds) *Treating Addictive Behaviours: Process of Change*. New York: Plenum.

Richardson, A. and Bray, C. (1987) *Promoting Health through Participation: Experience of Groups for Patient Participation in General Practice*. London: Policy Studies Institute.

Royal College of General Practitioners (1994) *Forty Years On. The Story of the First 40 Years of the Royal College of General Practitioners*. London: RCGP.

Royal College of General Practitioners (1996) *The Nature of General Medical Practice. Report from General Practice 27*. London: RCGP.

Scally, G. and Donaldson, L.J. (1998) Clinical governance and the drive for quality improvement in the new NHS in England, *British Medical Journal*, 317: 61–5.

Scott, M.G.B. and Marinker, M. (1993) Imposed change in general practice, in M. Pringle (ed.) *Change and Teamwork in Primary Care*. London: BMJ Publications.

Secretaries of State for Health, Wales, Northern Ireland and Scotland (1989) *Working for Patients*. London: HMSO.

Smith, R. (1998) Imagining futures for the NHS, *British Medical Journal*, 317: 3–4.

Stewart, M.A., McWhinney, I. and Buck, C.W. (1979) The doctor–patient relationship and its effect upon outcome, *Journal of the Royal College of General Practitioners*, 29: 77–82.

Swift, G. and McDougall, I.A. (1964) The family doctor and the family nurse, *British Medical Journal*, 1: 1697.

Tuckett, D., Boulton, M., Olson, C. and Williams, A. (1985) *Meetings Between Experts: An Approach to Sharing Ideas in Medical Consultations*. London: Tavistock.

Tudor Hart, J. (1988) *A New Kind of Doctor*. London: Merlin.
Widgery, D. (1991) *Some Lives! A GP's East End*. London: Simon and Schuster.
World Health Organization/United Nations Children's Fund (1978) *Primary Health Care*. Geneva: World Health Organization.
Wright, A.F. (1996) GP 2000 – A General Practitioner for the New Millennium, *British Journal of General Practice*, 46: 4–5.

# 2 The changing character of service provision

Phil Heywood

## Introduction

General practice has seen a century of change in service delivery. Some changes have primarily affected the organizational structure and context of practice; others have addressed the nature of the services delivered. However, improvement in the quality of service to patients may have been coincidental to many of those changes, and some organizational changes may have worsened the care on some measures.

This chapter has selected a few of the shifts in service delivery and seeks to define their purposes, explore their success in achieving those purposes, and describe some of the unplanned effects of the changes.

The terms 'general practice' and 'primary care' are often used interchangeably. General practice was originally used to describe the context in which a GP worked and what the GP did. As team-working increased, an alternative description for the discipline, not focused on a single professional group, became desirable. There was also a belief that the organization and style of the new general practice would be so different from the existing general practice that it required a new name (British Medical Association 1970). However, the move from the old fashioned, 'poor' general practice to the new 'good' primary care has been evolutionary, so it was never possible to define a time when the discipline changed from general practice to primary care.

In this chapter I use primary care to mean the community based health services that provide preventive, primary, personal and continuing care to patients and their families, including responsibility for the practice population as well as individuals. It is mainly a partnership between general practice and personal community health services but includes some other contractor services. I use general practice to mean the discipline and context of the GP, and it is therefore part of primary care.

These definitions are confused by another definition of 'primary care'. The six components of general practice are said to be primary care, preventive care, continuing care, family care, domiciliary care and personal or holistic care. Primary care is here used to describe care given at the point of first contact with a patient; within this definition departments of urogenital medicine and accident and emergency departments are both offering primary care. Hence, in one definition, general practice is part of primary care and, in the other definition, primary care is part of general practice.

## A century of change

Throughout the twentieth century the pace of change faced by general practice and primary care has accelerated. The first half of the century was characterized by moves to make the services available to all; the second half by attempts to improve quality and to reduce the isolation of general practice. Some of these changes have been mentioned in Chapter 1. However, as those occurring during the 'NHS period', in particular, constitute an important context for ongoing organizational change, a brief (and rather differently focused) review is in order here.

During the fifty years of the NHS, general practice has changed in two ways, both of which reduce the GP's isolation. Firstly, GPs have worked increasingly in teams; and secondly, general practice has taken up a position of responsibility for the whole NHS, ensuring that patients receive the highest possible standards of care.

General practitioners have worked less and less in single handed practice. The number of partnership groups, and the size of groups has increased; simultaneously co-working with other health care professionals has increased. Until now, teams have usually been groups within practices, but the latest reforms will lead to even greater networking between practices as members of primary care groups (Department of Health 1997).

At the inception of the NHS, general practice was organizationally peripheral to it; influence rested with the local health authority, which had several consultant but few GP members; power and influence was vested in the hospitals. Until eight years ago, health authorities worked with hospitals, managing care as provider organizations; in future, through the Health Improvement Programme, they will work with primary care on commissioning. The latest reforms have made primary care central, responsible for the commissioning and provision of primary care and the commissioning of secondary care.

The first two decades of the NHS was a time of increasing disaffection of GPs. Taylor (1954) and Collins (1950) had reported variable and unsatisfactory standards of provision. The factors that contributed to the disaffection included perceived reduction in status, relative to hospital doctors feeling like 'the poor relation of the consultant' (Honigsbaum 1979: 310). There were problems in recruitment and retention of GPs, possibly exacerbated by emigration (Seale 1962; Ash and Mitchell 1968). General practitioners reported deterioration in the attitudes of some patients (Hadfield 1951), and many were unhappy with the methods of finance and remuneration that disadvantaged those who wanted to provide more services for their patients. There was increasing personal demoralization and professional militancy, which resulted in the government negotiating with the profession about a 'charter' for family doctors (British Medical Association 1965).

This resulted in a new contract for general practice in 1966, which introduced a new method of payment and gave increased levels of remuneration. General practitioners were encouraged to work in groups. Some of the costs of adequate premises and employing appropriate ancillary staff were reimbursed. The new contract rewarded vocational training and continuing medical education and encouraged the development of appropriate out of hours services by paying for night work.

After a further two decades, concern was expressed again at the quality of service provided to patients and the government stated its intention to 'raise the general quality of these services nearer to that of the best' (Department of Health and Social Security 1986: 14) and 'give patients the widest range of choice in obtaining high quality primary care services' (Department of Health and Social Security 1987: Foreword). A new contract for the provision of primary care services was imposed, against the wishes of many GPs, which was intended to reward good practice and reduce the financial benefits to poorer practice (Health Departments of Great Britain 1989). It made health promotion and disease prevention an explicit responsibility of general medical services; and it rewarded GPs who undertook child health surveillance, minor surgery, health promotion clinics and continuing medical education. It introduced a supplementary allowance to doctors who provide services in deprived areas.

At almost the same time another White Paper was redefining the relationship between primary and secondary care by introducing general practice fundholding (Department of Health 1989b). It also introduced the expectation that GPs will undertake medical audit and was a further attempt to control the costs of prescribing. Fundholding largely affected contracting for secondary services, but included control of budgets for prescribing and for employment of staff (National Health Service Review 1989). The changes were intended to lead to improved cost containment and cost effectiveness, quality of care, patient choice and empowerment.

Less than a decade later, there are plans for further major changes to primary care, ultimately giving it responsibility for commissioning primary and secondary services and providing primary care services.

Since the inception of the NHS there has been a continuing concern about the quality of general practice services received by patients. There were few objective reviews of quality before Collins's (1950) damning report, and his conclusions were, themselves, challenged for their subjectivity. Two influences that have had an undoubtedly huge, but unmeasurable, effect on quality in general practice were the establishment of the Royal College of General Practitioners in 1952 and the introduction of mandatory vocational training for general practitioners.

## A patient-led NHS?

The major issue that recurs is how to reconcile what patients are judged to need with what patients want. For example, in circumstances when governments are clear what the population needs, such as health promotion, is it accept-able to the people (Department of Health 1991; Department of Health 1998a)? In other circumstances when it appears clear what patients want, is the system willing or able to offer it? Many of the changes introduced by governments are to give patients a better service. However, in the mid-1980s, the Consumers' Association (1983) reported a survey of what patients wanted from general practice. The percentage of patients requesting each option were:

| | |
|---|---|
| More time explaining about illness | 91 per cent |
| More time listening to patients | 89 per cent |
| Free general health check-ups | 89 per cent |
| More information about hospitals/specialists | 84 per cent |
| More time explaining about drugs | 82 per cent |
| A more helpful receptionist | 80 per cent |
| Shorter waiting times at the surgery | 79 per cent |
| A choice of which hospital to go to | 77 per cent |
| A nurse at the surgery | 71 per cent |
| More home visits | 71 per cent |
| More convenient surgery hours | 69 per cent |
| Minor surgery at the surgery | 68 per cent |

In introducing the health service changes in the early 1990s, the Secretary of State for Social Services (Department of Health and Social Security 1986: Foreword) promised 'good quality services which are sensitive and respons-ive to the needs of the patient' and the Prime Minister pledged, 'We aim to extend patients' choice' (Department of Health 1989b: Foreword). The changes, in fact, offered free health checkups (in some circumstances); more informa-tion for patients about GPs and their practices, but not about hospitals or specialists; extended availability of GPs; and minor surgery. The other health service changes were in danger of reducing GPs' availability for routine con-sultations and may thus have resulted in less time being available for GPs to listen to patients and to talk with them.

There may be hypocrisy in the treatment of the public, the issue being one of the exercise of power. Few are brave enough to give to patients the power to manage their own health and health care. There is a risk involved in giving patients the power to do what they wish about their health – they may choose to look after themselves in ways that clinicians, public health specialists, health service managers and politicians do not want. The rhetoric of 'the new patient-led NHS' (Audit Commission 1995) soon changed to a 'primary care-led NHS' (National Health Service Executive 1995).

During the 1980s and 1990s there was a move to equate poor health with poor health care, even though the report of the Research Working Group into inequalities in health in 1980 (the Black Report) had clearly shown the relationship between health and social issues (Department of Health and Social Security 1980). Even within health care, the Black Report recommended a series of resource shifts, many of which are still awaited nearly 20 years later. Services to be given a higher priority included: the health and welfare of mothers and children, by supporting midwives, health visiting, family planning, school health, day nurseries, welfare food and boarding out; family practitioner services, excluding pharmacy; services for the care of disabled people in their own homes through home nursing, chiropody, home help, meals, day care, aids and adaptations; and services for disabled people. In parallel they recommended smaller priority to be given to: acute in-patient and out-patient services; pharmaceutical services; in-patient and out-patient facilities for people with mental health problems and learning difficulties; and residential care for elderly people.

If the determinants of health are accepted as lying in the environment and in people's lifestyles, it is appropriate that the health care agencies should enter into partnerships with others to influence health. Such partnership working has been a feature of the more recent approaches to health policy, and to the new position that primary care is invited to occupy.

Health Action Zone status and Healthy Living Centres (Ramm 1998) both require evidence that health authorities and the health care providers are working in partnership with the local authority (including social services, education and housing) as well as with the voluntary sector, local businesses and, where appropriate, police, probation and legal organizations. These affiliations will be inherited by primary care groups when they take over the local responsibility for commissioning.

In 1948, general practice was organizationally separate from other medical services, GPs being in contract with an Executive Council. The employment situation of 'independent contractor' was carried through to the attitude of many GPs as independent within the NHS. Continuing features of general practice have been its distance from the remainder of the health service and the distance of one GP from another. There has been continuing professional isolation, although those distances have shortened with each organizational change.

The Family Doctors' Charter was the instrument that allowed the primary health care team to become a reality, although it had first been suggested as a model of working 46 years previously (Ministry of Health 1920). The primary health care team was inevitably multi-disciplinary in nature, with different professional groups and different employment status. General practitioners were self-employed independent contractors; practice nurses, practice managers and reception staff were directly employed by the GPs; and health visitors, district nurses and midwives were employed by the district health authority and on secondment to the practice. The health centre building programme brought GPs from premises they owned themselves, often attached to their homes or in lock-up shops, into purpose designed premises owned by health authorities (Wofinden 1967; Leese and Bosanquet 1996). The cost rent scheme allowed GPs themselves to build imaginative and innovative premises.

Vocational training schemes brought the teachers of GP registrars together to plan teaching by examining their own work, but they constituted only a minority of practitioners. Postgraduate medical education brought GPs together, although the content of such sessions was often based on hospital views of GPs' educational needs. More recently, research has been the lever to bring together a few, well motivated primary care practitioners from several different disciplines; although much remains to be done to improve the research networking and the research output of primary care (Heywood 1998).

There was an increasing interest by GPs in medical audit in the late 1980s. Practices wished to make judgements about the quality of the various services they offered to patients. To achieve this they required standards against which to judge themselves. This led increasingly to joint working between practitioners and practices. Ultimately, medical audit was made an objective for general practice in the implementation of *Working for Patients* (Department of Health 1989b).

During the past decade, further joint working has been necessary to produce and implement local guidelines for the management of common conditions (Grimshaw *et al.* 1995). Each step has increased both the possibility and the necessity for joint working between practices. Clearly some practices have been more involved than others in these developments. One criticism of the many changes has been that, although the intention is always 'to bring the standards of all practices nearer to that of the best' (Department of Health and Social Security 1986: 14), the actual outcome has sometimes widened the gulf between the best and the least good practices.

## Continuity of care

One of the unique features of general practice is continuity of care. It has been hailed as a unique contribution that the GP can make to medical care (Freeman and Hjortdahl 1997). It combines three separate notions:

- the enduring clinical responsibility for an individual who is one of a registered population; the period of responsibility may or may not be punctuated by separate episodes of ill health;
- the ongoing care of a patient's condition, which may be a chronic illness, established disability, or a physiological state such as pregnancy;
- the patient builds up knowledge of the doctor over time and the doctor builds up knowledge of the patient in his or her setting; a relationship develops between the patient and the doctor, which is central to the care provided.

The importance given to the continuing personal relationship has diminished as it has been disrupted by gradual changes in the organization and delivery of care, while the care of common chronic illness has become systematized, and improved in consequence. Relationships often build quickly from shared emotional experiences. When the GP's 24-hour responsibility was exercised by 24-hour availability, the doctor shared many of a patient's life experiences. General practitioners and community midwives were formerly more involved in childbirth, rather than just prenatal and postnatal care. More emergencies were treated by the patient's registered GP when each doctor was on call more frequently; hence the GP would have more involvement with families, at the moment of death of a family member. Team care has led to patients meeting a sea of faces when previously they could expect to see their own doctor, due to: group practice; more doctors in training; and less involvement in out of hours provision through the use of rotas, out of hours cooperatives and deputizing services.

General practitioners are continuously responsible for their patients' medical needs for 24 hours a day, unless the patient is in hospital or away from home. If a GP plans to be away, they must make arrangements for the care of their patients in their absence. This is not merely the provision of a deputy to provide care. It also requires the proper use of case notes and computerized records to hand over the day to day care of individual patients, and it requires the adoption of routine ways of handling common conditions so that patients receive consistent care, irrespective of whom they see. This has been greatly assisted by practices generating and adopting management guidelines.

At the same time, continuity of care has been affected by changes in society: people are more mobile; many leave home for education, training or work; the breakdown in families and relationships can lead to relocation. All of these can interrupt a continuing relationship with the GP.

### A primary care-led NHS? – fundholding

General practice fundholding was introduced into the UK with the NHS re-organization of 1990. It was the first radical attempt to make an organizational engagement between general practice and the remainder of the health service, to complement the long-standing clinical engagement. The intention was to make GPs more aware of, and responsible for, their use of secondary care services by giving them a budget with which to purchase some of these services. The scheme only included about a quarter of the money spent in secondary care; the rest remained a responsibility of the health authority. Fundholding practices were mainly responsible for the costs of out-patient services and a number of listed procedures and investigations. They also managed their staff budget, a prescribing budget and a management allowance.

Judging the effects of introducing fundholding has faced several problems (Petchey 1995; Smith and Wilton 1998). The purposes of introducing fundholding were more implicit than explicit, although there were overall objectives of improved cost containment and cost effectiveness, improved quality and greater patient choice and empowerment (Audit Commission 1996). No formal evaluation was built into the process from the beginning, and certainly there was no collection of baseline data from practices before they took on fundholding. Opinion and evidence seem to differ in that many GPs believe that fundholding has been good for patients (Newton et al. 1993; Bain 1994; Leese and Bosanquet 1996), but no large body of research evidence strongly supports the opinion.

Several other changes in general practice and the health services took place simultaneously with the introduction of fundholding, making it impossible to judge fundholding as the sole cause of any observed change. A large group of non-fundholders in Nottingham was able to deliver greater service changes than many fundholders have achieved in other areas (Black et al. 1994). It has often been difficult to know what is a consequence of the fundholding status and what a consequence of the pre-existing characteristics of the practices that were granted fundholding status. To be accepted, practices were required to have minimum list sizes, and be judged able to manage budgets with adequate administrative support and information technology (IT) and information systems (National Health Service Review 1989).

Fundholding practices have received more resources than non-fundholding practices. Some of this additional resourcing has been explicit, such as the fundholding management allowance and higher level of reimbursement for fundholding IT investment. There has been a more general belief that fundholding practices have been better resourced than health authorities for the services purchased from the budget. One study of routinely collected data in one NHS region showed the cost per patient in non-fundholding practices for in-patient work was 59–87 per cent that of fundholders' patients, and for out-patient care 36–106 per cent (Dixon *et al.* 1994); however, these observations may have been based on poor quality data. The implication was that fewer resources were spent per capita on patients from non-fundholding practices.

Evaluating the consequences of GP fundholding on service provision has proved equally difficult. The areas that warrant evaluation include: services purchased outside the practice; services not previously provided by the practice but introduced because of fundholding; and services normally provided by the practice, including prescribing. Have they changed and improved?

*Services*

Concurrent with the introduction of fundholding there has been a steady and substantial increase in acute admissions to hospital. The extent to which this might be a consequence of fundholding has been questioned. There are cost advantages for fundholding practices, since they do not pay for emergency treatments (Capewell 1996; Keeley 1997). Nevertheless, the increase in emergency admissions has affected admissions from both fundholding and non-fundholding practices, and there is no good evidence that fundholders are substantially different from non-fundholders (Mays 1997).

General practitioners may have entered into fundholding with the primary intention of having a greater choice of secondary care providers for their patients (Pritchard and Beilby 1996), fearing the imposition of restrictions by health authorities. The early evidence from England and Scotland differed. In Oxford little difference was demonstrated between the referral behaviours of fundholders and non-fundholders before and after the reforms (Coulter and Bradlow 1993), whereas an uncontrolled Scottish study suggested a decreased use of hospital services by fundholders (Howie *et al.* 1993).

About two-thirds of fundholding doctors believed that fundholding had led to better access to in-patient services, an improvement in patient services and shorter waiting times (Leese and Bosanquet 1996). There is a consistent demonstration of better access to secondary services and shorter waiting times for the patients from fundholding practices (Samuel 1992; Dowling 1997). A study of orthopaedic services demonstrated a slower increase in referral rate by fundholders, and that the patients of fundholding practices were seen faster (Kammerling and Kinnear 1997). These effects on access to secondary services are the basis for the system being called a two tier system.

There is consistent evidence that fundholding has been used to develop new practice based services for patients, frequently shifted from secondary care; these include counselling, physiotherapy, chiropody, dietetics, specialist outreach clinics and near patient testing. Attempts to evaluate the consequences of shifting these services have faced several issues. Firstly, some of these services, such as counselling (Clark *et al.* 1997), have been developed in both fundholding and non-fundholding settings. Secondly, evidence may be equivocal on how useful and effective the services are, whether or not related to fundholding; for example counselling (King *et al.* 1994), and near patient testing (Hobbs *et al.* 1997). Thirdly, although the effects of locating the service in the fundholding practice may have been observed, there have been few attempts to observe the effect of removal on their previous location.

Specialist outreach clinics are the archetypal example of the shift of services from secondary to primary care, in which hospital specialists hold their outpatient clinics in general practice settings. They are found increasingly in both fundholding and non-fundholding practices, providing quicker access to specialist care for patients (Bailey *et al.* 1994; Perrett 1997). It remains unproven whether they offer equivalent or better quality than hospital based clinics (Harris 1994), whether they are an efficient use of resources, and what their impact is on other primary and secondary care services, or on the teaching and research functions of hospitals and general practice. Concern has been noted on the possible adverse effects of fragmenting services (Corney and Kerrison 1997).

There is little useful comparative evidence on the effect of fundholding status on the continuing provision of general medical services, apart from extensive studies of prescribing. One study compared the clinical care of patients with joint pain in six practices before and after the introduction of fundholding. No changes were found in the duration of consultations nor in the proportion of patients prescribed analgesics; although there may have been worse understanding and coping by patients after the introduction of fundholding (Howie *et al.* 1994). There is an almost unanimous view from general practice that fundholding has increased, or considerably increased, the administrative workload of the practice (Leese and Bosanquet 1996), but how this might have affected the clinical services of the GPs is unmeasured.

*Prescribing*

One of the expressed reasons for introducing the changes of *Working for Patients* (Department of Health 1989b) was to increase efficiency. The prescribing costs of GPs account for about 10 per cent of total NHS expenditure. During the 1980s ways had been considered to reduce the costs of prescribing; it was therefore to be expected that the general practice fundholding scheme would include some means of reducing prescribing costs. The measure chosen was for fundholding practices to keep any savings they made from prescribing, to invest into improved services for their own patients.

Early evidence showed that prescribing costs in fundholding practices were apparently increasing more slowly than in non-fundholding practices – 10 per cent versus 15 per cent in 1991; 8 per cent versus 13 per cent in 1992, and 8 per cent versus 11 per cent in 1993 (Audit Commission 1995). The significance of these findings was disputed but similar data have been observed elsewhere and have tended to be associated with a move by practices to reduce prescribing costs by increased generic prescribing during their early years in fundholding (Bradlow and Coulter 1993; Dowell *et al.* 1995). A significant study by Wilson *et al.* (1996) showed that fundholding did not make a major contribution to differences in total prescribing costs between practices, such differences being best explained by deprivation, training status and partnership status. In contrast, differences in the rise in total prescribing costs were best explained by fundholding status. It remains problematic how much of this effect is a direct consequence of fundholding. Some non-fundholding practices have also been able to contain prescribing cost increases; fundholders may have intentionally delayed cost reduction until after they attained fundholding status; cost differentials due to generic prescribing will be eroded as a higher proportion of non-fundholders move towards generic prescribing; and initial cost differentials between fundholders and non-fundholders may erode with time (Stewart-Brown *et al.* 1997).

*Costs*

It is not the purpose of this review to assess the cost effectiveness of fundholding, nor its success at cost containment. Nevertheless, there was considerable investment into the scheme and in the absence of fundholding those resources could have been used for direct patient care. It is therefore significant to note that it has been difficult to judge whether fundholding has been a success economically. The actual implementation costs of fund-holding in 1993–94 of £38 million per annum far exceeded the estimated costs of £15.6 million per annum (Petchey 1995). Perhaps a fragmented and decentralized administration might be expected to carry higher trans-action costs than a more centralized system of commissioning and purchas-ing (Dixon and Glennerster 1995).

The move to fundholding made explicit the GP's responsibility for a de-fined (registered) population, as well as for individual patients. Purchasing decisions involved the GPs in choices between different types and levels of provision, which potentially would benefit some patients and disadvantage others. This was the first experience for most GPs of explicit prioritizing, or rationing (few realized that almost every decision about practice develop-ment and use of time is itself prioritizing and therefore giving more to some patients and rationing others). Nevertheless, setting priorities for the whole population, and living with the consequences of those decisions for indi-vidual patients led to disquiet (Ayres 1996) and ethical concerns. In Ayres's study the GPs expressed a view that rationing decisions should be made away from the consultation with individual patients; the decisions should be explicit and should be made by a group representing clinicians, managers and probably public representatives.

## A primary care-led NHS? – primary care groups

In his foreword to *The New NHS: Modern – Dependable* (Department of Health 1997), the Prime Minister emphasized such details as a round-the-clock nurse-led help line, and IT to link surgeries to specialist centres. However, the White Paper contained changes of much greater potential importance than those he cited. These included:

a service that is fairer, distributes resources more equitably, eliminates two tierism, is needs led, better integrates health and social services, is based on co-operation rather than competition, reinstates strategic planning, emphasizes quality, addresses health inequalities, promotes better health and involves the public.

(Chisholm 1998: 1687)

Two features of the White Paper will be of particular importance for primary care. The first is a series of mechanisms to improve quality. The second is a continuation of the shift in the responsibility, from secondary to primary care, to decide the configuration of services.

*Improving quality*

Self-regulation within the medical professional was deemed to have failed in the high profile Bristol paediatric surgery case (Klein 1998; Treasure 1998). There were three areas of failure: professional competence; the quality of communication between doctors; and information about risk given to patients (or their parents) (Klein 1998; Smith 1998). Although these issues arose in a surgical speciality, they have repercussions for primary care. The General Medical Council (GMC) had already made explicit the high standards to which all doctors should aspire (General Medical Council 1995). It has brought in new procedures for dealing with doctors whose performance gives rise to concern (General Medical Council 1997). The president of the GMC has described how professional self-regulation implies firstly a responsibility to the public (Irvine 1997). All doctors have a duty to maintain good practice; patients must be protected from poor practice; where appropriate, dysfunctional doctors should be helped back to practice; and there must be openness about doctors' performance.

The GMC procedures are mainly appropriate when local mechanisms for improvement have failed. Until now, local ways to manage quality in primary care have been poor. Where practitioners have wished to improve their services, they could be supported. Where they didn't, the health authority has had few levers of influence. Failure of a contractor to perform to his or her terms of service (Department of Health 1989a) could lead to a Service Committee hearing. However, following publication of the report of the Wilson Committee, *Being Heard* (Department of Health 1994), practice based complaints procedures have been established and consequently hearings to consider breaches in terms of service have reduced in frequency.

The White Paper gives local mechanisms to enhance quality, and national structures to which the local mechanisms for quality will relate. The main mechanism by which quality will be assured and standards of clinical care improved in primary care, as well as in hospital trusts, is through clinical governance. In the same way that corporate governance is about financial and managerial probity and accountability, so clinical governance is about clinical probity and accountability (Donaldson 1998).

More details of these mechanisms for improving quality were given in a further White Paper, *A First Class Service: Quality in the New NHS* (Department of Health 1998b). It brings together existing and new mechanisms to define acceptable standards of practice; it describes structures to monitor these standards; and it proposes remedies to improve standards. The main standard setting structures will be the National Institute for Clinical Excellence (NICE) and National Service Frameworks (NSF). Standards will be monitored locally through the clinical governance framework and a Commission for Health Improvement. Standards will be improved through clinical governance and continuing professional development.

Trusts, primary care groups and individual practices are all expected to achieve improvement in clinical quality by many and various means. There is an underlying assumption that quality will become everybody's responsibility and everybody's concern. Every trust and primary care group will appoint a senior professional (who may be a doctor or a nurse) to take responsibility for clinical governance in the organization. In primary care this person will be expected to lead on clinical standards and professional development. *The New NHS: Modern – Dependable* (Department of Health 1997) additionally described how every practice would be required to identify a senior professional to develop the quality issues within the practice, but this role has not been expanded in later publications.

It is only by using appropriate evidence to underpin professional actions that patients will receive the best standards of care (Sackett and Rosenberg 1995). It is disputed how much current practice is evidence based, in either hospital practice (Ellis *et al.* 1995) or in general practice (Gill *et al.* 1996). There is an expectation that current moves towards evidence based practice by doctors and nurses will increase. The improved NHS networking of IT is intended, in part, to make access to electronic databases more ubiquitous. However, the data that are used to assess the quality of care must have the confidence of government, health service professionals and managers (Black 1998).

If professional self-regulation is to continue, it is to be built on explicit performance review. Previously there has been a reluctance to share the process and outcomes of clinical audit with non-clinical managers, even though it is an essential part of clinical effectiveness. It is intended that, in future, clinical audit will be undertaken with the addition of both internal and external scrutiny. Any past tendency to ignore or trivialize untoward events will disappear. There must be explicit assessment of the risks of untoward events developing, and strategies developed to minimize those risks. In addition there will be robust systems in place to investigate adverse events, so that existing trusts and the new primary care trusts will be expected to learn lessons from poor performance. This process of learning from examples of poor performance will be balanced by attempts to identify and build on good practice (Scally and Donaldson 1998).

At a national level there will be two new structures to set quality standards, the National Institute for Clinical Excellence and National Service Frameworks. NICE will be set up as a health authority with the task of developing national guidance based on clinical evidence and cost effectiveness. Its clear authoritative guidelines on clinical and cost effectiveness will offer support to doctors, nurses and midwives. By establishing NICE, government is taking responsibility for assessing which patients will and will not be helped best by particular treatments. NICE will produce the clinical guidance, but it will not monitor performance.

It is intended that there will be universal desktop access to NICE to ensure guidance reaches the right people, including patients, and produces appropriate action. NICE will provide a focus for reviewing clinical behaviour and practice through existing means of implementation, including local prescribing policies and formularies, guidelines, audit programmes and lifelong learning.

NSFs are mechanisms for assessing performance. Best evidence of clinical effectiveness and cost effectiveness will go into the frameworks, as well as users' views. The aim is to reduce unacceptable variation in care and standards across the NHS. An expert reference group will develop NSFs to set national standards and define service models; they will put in place implementation support programmes, and then measure improvements in performance against a timescale. Progressively more detailed information will be published, comparing each unit's performance for a range of conditions. In addition to quantity and cost, six main areas of quality and outcomes are mentioned. These are improvements in health; fair access to services; effective delivery of appropriate health care; efficiency; patient and carer experience; and health outcomes of NHS care. NSFs will address whole systems of care, applied either to major care areas, initially mental health, or to major disease groups, initially coronary heart disease.

The White Paper sees programmes of continuing professional development (CPD) as the means of underpinning clinical governance. It is overtly linked with professional self-regulation, with the explicit intention of meeting the learning needs of the health professionals, inspiring public confidence and meeting the wider service development needs of the NHS. It is intended that programmes for CPD will be publicly accountable for nationally set standards and maintenance of those standards, be open to public scrutiny and be responsive to changing clinical practice and service need. Clearly CPD will no longer be haphazard, but will be a managed process.

The final means for maintaining standards is an expectation that clinicians will be expected to 'blow the whistle' when they detect unprofessional conduct or performance in colleagues, if the colleagues themselves will not take appropriate professional steps to correct their deficits.

### The influence of primary care

For many decades GPs had felt outside the mainstream of medical practice, and of medical influence. The creation of the NHS and the establishment of the Royal College of General Practitioners started the movement of general practice towards the mainstream. But the feelings of professional alienation, and the first efforts to create a college or academy for GPs, go back to the mid-nineteenth century (McConaghey 1972).

The original structure of the NHS was tripartite, separating general practice from hospital practice and from public health. *Working for Patients* (Department of Health 1989b) was the greatest step towards integrating general practice into the management structures for providing healthcare; but the changes still mainly involved general practice, rather than primary care. The opportunities for GPs to purchase services and, subsequently, groups of practices coming together to commission services, altered the traditional relationships they had with secondary health care providers.

*The New NHS: Modern – Dependable* (Department of Health 1997) takes these changes further. The shift that is likely to have the most effect in the long term is the acceptance that primary care is more than just general practice. The membership of primary care group boards will include either one or two nurses, a social worker, a manager and laity, in addition to GPs. Doctors and nurses are required explicitly to work in partnership in PCGs. As nurses have taken the preventive role within practices, they are likely to have greater responsibility for health needs assessment in primary care groups.

## Postscript

The NHS has reached a state of continuous development as an organization. The need to provide increasingly good standards of care will continue. The organizational distance of primary care has gone. The recognition that primary health care requires joint working with community health and social services is recognized, and the new NHS is trying to create the necessary links. There is a clear acknowledgment that health encompasses a greater range of agencies than merely health care. Two challenges remain. The first is to make such a complex network of relationships work. It is easy to recognize that they are essential, but difficult to ensure that they work in practice. The second is to have clarity about how much power should be given to patients, and equally how to ensure that they are given appropriate means to exercise their rights.

## References

Ash, R. and Mitchell, H.D. (1968) Doctor migration 1962–4, *British Medical Journal*, 1: 569–72.

Audit Commission (1995) *Briefing on GP Fund-holding*. London: HMSO.

Audit Commission (1996) *What the Doctor Ordered*. London: HMSO.

Ayres, P.J. (1996) Rationing health care: views from general practice, *Social Science & Medicine*, 42(7): 1021–5.

Bailey, J.J., Black, M.E. and Wilkin, D. (1994) Specialist outreach clinics in general practice, *British Medical Journal*, 308: 1083–6.

Bain, J. (1994) Fund-holding: a two-tier system? *British Medical Journal*, 309: 396–9.

Black, D.G., Birchall, A.D. and Trimble, I.M.G. (1994) Non-fund-holding in Nottingham: a vision of the future, *British Medical Journal*, 309: 930–2.

Black, N. (1998) Clinical governance: fine words or action? *British Medical Journal*, 316: 297–8.

Bradlow, J. and Coulter, A. (1993) Effect of fund-holding and indicative prescribing scheme on general practitioner prescribing costs, *British Medical Journal*, 307: 1186–9.

British Medical Association (1965) *A Charter for the Family Doctor Service*. London: BMA.

British Medical Association (1970) *Primary Medical Care*, Planning Unit Report No. 4. London: BMA.

Capewell, S. (1996) The continuing rise in emergency admissions, *British Medical Journal*, 312: 991–2.

Chisholm, J. (1998) Primary care and the NHS white papers, *British Medical Journal*, 316: 1687–8.

Clark, A., Hook, J. and Stein, K. (1997) Counsellors in primary care in Southampton: a questionnaire survey of their qualifications, working arrangements, and case-mix, *British Journal of General Practice*, 47(423): 613–17.

Collins, J.S. (1950) General practice in England today, *Lancet*, 1(6604): 555–85.

Consumers' Association (1983) GPs, *Which?*, June: 254–8.

Corney, R.H. and Kerrison, S. (1997) Fund-holding in the South Thames Region, *British Journal of General Practice*, 47: 553–6.

Coulter, A. and Bradlow, J. (1993) Effect of NHS reforms on general practitioners' referrals, *British Medical Journal*, 306: 433–6.

Department of Health (DoH) (1989a) *Terms of Service for Doctors in General Practice*. London: Department of Health.

Department of Health (DoH) (1989b) *Working for Patients*, Cm 555. London: HMSO.

Department of Health (DoH) (1991) *The Health of the Nation: A Consultative Document for Health in England*, Cm 1523. London: HMSO.

Department of Health (DoH) (1994) *Being Heard: The Report of a Review Committee on NHS Complaints Procedures*. London: Department of Health.

Department of Health (DoH) (1997) *The New NHS: Modern – Dependable*, Cm 3087. London: The Stationery Office.

Department of Health (DoH) (1998a) *Our Healthier Nation: A Contract for Health*, Cm 3852. London: The Stationery Office.

Department of Health (DoH) (1998b) *A First Class Service: Quality in the New NHS*. London: Department of Health.

Department of Health and Social Security (DHSS) (1980) *Report of the Working Group on Inequalities in Health*. London: DHSS.

Department of Health and Social Security (DHSS) (1986) *Primary Health Care: An Agenda for Discussion*, Cm 9771. London: HMSO.

Department of Health and Social Security (DHSS) (1987) *Promoting Better Health: The Government's Programme for Improving Primary Health Care*, Cm 249. London: HMSO.

Dixon, J., Dinwoodie, M., Hodson, D. *et al.* (1994) Distribution of funds between fund-holding and non-fund-holding practices, *British Medical Journal*, 309: 30–4.

Dixon, J. and Glennerster, H. (1995) What do we know about fund-holding in General Practice?, *British Medical Journal*, 311: 727–30.

Donaldson, L.J. (1998) Clinical governance: a statutory duty for quality improvement, *Journal of Epidemiology and Community Health*, 52(2): 73–4.

Dowell, J.S., Snadden, D. and Dunbar, J.A. (1995) Changes to generic formulary: how one fund-holding practice reduced prescribing costs, *British Medical Journal*, 310: 505–8.

Dowling, B. (1997) Effect of fund-holding on waiting times: database study, *British Medical Journal*, 315: 292.

Ellis, J., Mulligan, I., Rowe, J. and Sackett, D.L. (1995) Inpatient general medicine is evidence-based, *Lancet*, 346(8972): 407–10.

Freeman, G. and Hjortdahl, P. (1997) What future for continuity of care in general practice?, *British Medical Journal*, 314: 1870–3.

General Medical Council (1995) *Duties of a Doctor: Good Medical Practice*. London: General Medical Council.

General Medical Council (1997) *The New Performance Procedures: Consultation Document*. London: General Medical Council.

Gill, P., Dowell, A.C., Neal, R.D. *et al.* (1996) Evidence based general practice – a retrospective study of interventions in one training practice, *British Medical Journal*, 312: 819–21.

Grimshaw, J., Freemantle, N., Wallace, S. *et al.* (1995) Development and implementation of clinical practice guidelines, *Quality in Health Care*, 4(1): 55–64.

Hadfield, S.J. (1951) A field survey of general practice 1951–2, *British Medical Journal*, 2: 683–706.

Harris, A. (1994) Specialist outreach clinics, *British Medical Journal*, 308: 1053.

Health Departments of Great Britain (1989) *General Practice in the National Health Service: the 1990 Contract.* London: HMSO.

Heywood, P. (1998) Research and development in primary care, in M. Baker and S. Kirk (eds) *Research and Development for the NHS.* Oxford: Radcliffe Medical Press.

Hobbs, F.D., Delaney, B.C., Fitzmaurice, D.A. *et al.* (1997) A review of near patient testing in primary care, *Health Technology Assessment*, 1(5): 1–229.

Honigsbaum, F. (1979) *The Division in British Medicine.* London: Kogan Page.

Howie, J.G.R., Heaney, D.J. and Maxwell, M. (1993) Evaluation of the Scottish shadow fund-holding project: first results, *Health Bulletin*, 51(2): 94–105.

Howie, J.G.R., Heaney, D.J. and Maxwell, M. (1994) Evaluating care of patients reporting back pain in fund-holding practices, *British Medical Journal*, 1994: 705–10.

Irvine, D. (1997) The performance of doctors. II. Maintaining good practice, protecting patients from poor performance, *British Medical Journal*, 314: 1613–15.

Kammerling, R.M. and Kinnear, A. (1997) The extent of the two tier service for fund-holders, *British Medical Journal*, 312: 1399–1401.

Keeley, D. (1997) General practice fund-holding and healthcare costs, *British Medical Journal*, 315: 139.

King, M., Broster, G., Lloyd, M. and Horder, J. (1994) Controlled trials in the evaluation of counselling in general practice, *British Journal of General Practice*, 44(382): 229–32.

Klein, R. (1998) Competence, professional self-regulation, and the public interest, *British Medical Journal*, 316: 1740–2.

Leese, B. and Bosanquet, N. (1996) Changes in general practice organization: survey of general practitioners' views on the 1990 contract and fund-holding, *British Journal of General Practice*, 46(403): 95–9.

McConaghey, R.M.S. (1972) Proposals to found a Royal College of General Practitioners in the nineteenth century, *Journal of the Royal College of General Practitioners*, 22(124): 775–88.

Mays, N. (1997) Fund-holding seems not to be implicated in rise in emergency admissions, *British Medical Journal*, 315: 749.

Ministry of Health (1920) *Interim Report on the Future Provision of Medical and Allied Services.* Consultative Council on Medical and Allied Services (Dawson Committee). Cmnd 693. London: HMSO.

National Health Service Executive (1995) *Developing NHS Purchasing and GP Fund-holding: Towards a Primary Care-led NHS.* Leeds: Department of Health.

National Health Service Review (1989) *Practice Budgets for General Medical Practitioners*, Working Paper no. 3. London: HMSO.

Newton, J., Fraser, M., Robinson, J. and Wainwright, D. (1993) Fund-holding in the Northern Region, *British Medical Journal*, 306: 375–8.

Perrett, K. (1997) Specialist outreach clinics in Sheffield: a faster tier of out-patient provision for the patients of fundholding GPs?, *Journal of Public Health Medicine*, 19(3): 347–53.

Petchey, R. (1995) General practitioner fund-holding: weighing the evidence, *Lancet*, 346(8983): 1139–42.

Pritchard, D.A. and Beilby, J.J. (1996) Issues for fundholding in Australian general practice, *Medical Journal of Australia*, 164(3): 215–19.

Ramm, C. (1998) A healthy living centre in the community, *Nursing Times*, 94(12): 52–3.

Sackett, D.L. and Rosenberg, W.M.C. (1995) On the need for evidence-based medicine, *Health Economics*, 4(4): 249–54.

Samuel, O. (1992) Fundholding practices get preference, *British Medical Journal*, 305: 1497.

Scally, G. and Donaldson, L.J. (1998) Clinical governance and the drive for quality improvement in the new NHS in England, *British Medical Journal*, 317: 61–5.

Seale, J. (1962) Medical emigration from Britain 1930–1961, *British Medical Journal*, 1: 782–6.

Smith, R. (1998) Renegotiating medicine's contract with patients, *British Medical Journal*, 316: 1622–23.

Smith, R.D. and Wilton, P. (1998) General practice fund-holding: progress to date, *British Journal of General Practice*, 48(430): 1253–7.

Stewart-Brown, S., Surender, R., Bradlow, J., Coulter, A. and Doll, H. (1997) The effect of fund-holding in general practice on prescribing habits three years after introduction of the scheme, *British Medical Journal*, 311: 1543–7.

Taylor, S. (1954) *Good General Practice*. London: Oxford University Press.

Treasure, T. (1998) Lessons from the Bristol case, *British Medical Journal*, 316: 1685–6.

Wilson, R.P., Hatcher, J., Barton, S. and Walley, T. (1996) Influences of practice characteristics on prescribing in fund-holding and non-fund-holding general practices: an observational study, *British Medical Journal*, 313: 595–9.

Wofinden, R.C. (1967) Health centres and the general medical practitioner, *British Medical Journal*, 2: 565–7.

# 3 The changing nature of primary health care teams and interprofessional relationships

Alison E. Wilson

## Introduction

The importance of the team relationship in primary health care has increasingly occupied a central place within health service policy. Yet despite the rhetoric, which insists that team working can only be a good thing (Lambert 1991), inherent tensions remain between professional groups. Although there are examples within the literature of 'successful' team initiatives, anecdotally, primary care providers describe their experience of teamwork as somewhat frustrating. They cite poor communication; medical dominance; lack of commitment; and inequalities in pay, conditions, status, autonomy and responsibility as responsible for poor team-working. Furthermore, none of these issues have been adequately addressed by health policy or the structures within which health service providers work.

Although the literature contains many examples of attempts to improve team-working, these tend to be descriptive and applicable in only very particular circumstances, thereby failing to provide generalizable evidence to support team approach in primary health care (Pearson and Spencer 1997). However, this lack of generalizable evidence is not surprising, given that the study of relationships within teams has to deal with issues of some complexity. These issues include professional tribalism; gender and political influence, which are fashioned by changing societal structures; cultural awareness; fears of rising consumerism; technological advance; and, increasingly, health economics.

Common sense, however, suggests that team-working and professional collaboration should be important in a health care environment. This is particularly the case in one that is striving to provide high quality care from a multi-disciplinary pool of providers with diverse knowledge and skills; and with limited health care resources, and, consequently, competing priorities.

## Team characteristics

Teams have been defined as a collection of individuals who have an explicit reason for working together, and are in need of each other's different abilities and skills (Wilson 1994). They cooperate to carry out joint tasks (Argyle 1973); make different contributions towards achievement of a common goal (Pritchard 1981); but satisfy the individual need for personal fulfilment (Adair 1986); as well as their social needs (Morgan 1986). Characteristics demonstrated by so called 'effective' teams include having a common purpose with a clear understanding and respect for roles and responsibilities; sharing responsibility for outcome; and being able to work in an autonomous group (Gilmore *et al.* 1974; Belbin 1981). It is my contention that such criteria present an over simplification of the elements of team success and, given the changing nature of primary health care itself and the complexity of interprofessional relationships, it is not surprising that it is increasingly difficult to achieve a level of teamwork that we do believe to be successful. Indeed, we may need to shift our perceptions of what level of team effectiveness we wish to strive for.

In consideration of interprofessional relationships and team dynamics, therefore, it is important to contextualize the issues. What may be influential are formative historical developments in society, social policy, and the professional development of the individual disciplines within the team, which have consequentially led to the cultural norms and structural arrangements that exist today. The delivery of primary care, which is shaped by the workforce, workload, and roles and boundaries between primary care providers, presently consists of two core professional groups: general practitioners and the nursing disciplines (Jenkins-Clarke *et al.* 1998). Each has experienced sustained changes over the years in their educational requirements to practise, their role and responsibilities, their ability to recruit and sustain a skilled workforce, and the organizational framework within which they work.

This chapter will, therefore, review the historical development of the primary health care team, concentrating in particular on: the development of the role of the GP; the influence of health and social policy on team structure; the impact of nursing development on interprofessional relationships; and the tensions that arise within the process of team-working that affect the team's ability to work effectively. The final section will reflect on what the author believes to be the emerging issues for the workforce and workload in primary care and will include a discussion of the challenge of an evidence based future for interprofessional collaboration and appropriate team development.

## Establishing the general practitioner within the primary health care team

The World Health Organization (WHO) is a major influence on our philosophy of health care in Western society, promoting health in its widest sense, including physical, mental and social well being (World Health Organization 1984). Primary care is the population's first point of contact with health services, and a broad multidisciplinary team approach, where team members play an equal role in improving health for all, is acknowledged by primary care professionals and managers to be an appropriate model of service delivery (Department of Health and Social Security 1981; Department of Health 1996a, 1996b, 1997b). Primary health care in the UK is, conversely, orientated around general practice, and consequently remains dominated by the GP.

The professional status afforded to general medical practitioners has its roots in the eighteenth and nineteenth centuries. The increasing organization of 'healers' into distinct professional groups – physicians, surgeons and apothecaries – resulted in the formation of a distinct professional body; the British Medical Association (BMA). The BMA guaranteed basic standards of medical qualification and practice for both hospital and community based doctors (Allsop 1984). With the creation of the NHS in 1948, patients were given the right to register with one GP, who provided access to other medical specialities, acting as a 'gatekeeper' to NHS services and other resources. GPs, keen to maintain their independence from the specialities and from alternative health care disciplines, successfully negotiated a contract with the NHS, which maintained their independence from the NHS, and created the 'contractor' status, still in existence today (Gorden and Pampling 1996). This act of separation from mainstream NHS policy and financial management, significant in strengthening the independence and autonomy of the GP, also established the 'generalist' practitioner as a somewhat 'poor relation' in the 'pecking order' of medical practice. And yet it was these generalist practitioners who, during the 1950s and 1960s, began to establish a theoretical basis for family medical practice (Balint 1957) and to develop a professional culture of their own, involving vocational training and the development of quality standards (British Medical Association 1965; Royal College of General Practitioners 1972) long before their hospital counterparts.

Such developments, while remaining voluntary, substantially strengthened the notion of independent practitioner status, which, it was argued, was necessary to safeguard clinical freedom. This clinical freedom, however, consequently led to unacceptable variation in practice (Gordon and Pampling 1996), and resulted in a succession of health reforms during the 1980s and 1990s, which were intended to deliver improvements in the quality of clinical care in *all* practices, and in so doing establish some semblance of managerial control and accountability. One of the most significant of these was the new GP Contract, which, for the first time, forced GPs to comply with a way of working that, if ignored, would substantially reduce practice income (Department of Health 1989a).

Much of the individualism and tribalism rooted in early medical practice continues to characterize medicine and the culture of family practice today, despite the attempts of every major report and primary care reform, from the 1920 Dawson Report (Dawson 1920) to the present 1997 White and Green Papers (Department of Health 1997a, 1997b), to support the notion of teamworking and interprofessional collaboration. The struggle to maintain independence and clinical autonomy has continued to exert its influence. Thus GPs have established for themselves a somewhat unique position, both 'within' and yet 'apart' from the team.

## The influence of health policy on team structure and development

Although Collins (1950) emphasized the coordinating role of the GP in relation to other primary care professionals such as nurses, social workers and technicians, it wasn't until the family doctor charter (British Medical Association 1965) that a structure was introduced to support team development. A system of ancillary staff reimbursement (which involved financial support for the employment of reception, administrative, and nursing staff by the GP), provided a positive lever for changes in working practice and substantially expanded the 'practice' based team. In 1974, district nurses and health visitors ceased to be employed by local authorities and became health service employees, attached to GP practices, although not in the direct employ of GPs. Although the Harding Report of 1981 (Department of Health and Social Security 1981) promoted improvements in *doctor and nurse* collaboration (with the aim of producing better outcomes for patients), there has been little concern for, or evidence to support, a broader multidisciplinary team approach (Jones 1992; Stanley and Hatcher 1992). Indeed, the Cumberledge Report (Department of Health and Social Security 1986) recommended 'neighbourhood' nursing teams, thus weakening links between practices and community nurses. This report, however, was never popular and practice-attached nursing teams were quickly reinstated.

The NHS reforms of the late 1980s and early 1990s also attempted fundamental changes in the organization and financing of health care, the like of which had not been experienced since the inception of the NHS in 1948 (Ham 1991). Reforms such as *Promoting Better Health* (Department of Health and Social Security 1987) and the new GP contract (Department of Health 1989a) began to more specifically dictate the content of the GPs' work, placing greater emphasis on health promotion and disease prevention, information and patient choice. The nature of these services, which became a necessary part of general practice, encouraged a wider team approach. The GPs, while complaining bitterly that health promotion was best done elsewhere (Smith *et al.* 1994), recognized the contribution the nursing professions, in particular, could make in providing health advice to their practice populations. This left *them* relatively free to concentrate their efforts on the more traditional activities of diagnosis and management of disease, without fundamentally making changes to their role or losing clinical freedom. The incentive of payment to undertake health promotion activity somewhat softened the blow of diminished autonomy and increasing managerial control. It also provided the financial and structural flexibility to directly employ practice nurses to undertake these tasks. There was a consequent increase in nursing staff employed by practices to around 17,500 in 1990 from only 3,500 in 1983 (Department of Health 1990).

*Working for Patients* (Department of Health 1989b) introduced a further significant reconfiguration of health services provision. It attempted to increase accountability of GPs through medical audit, while giving them greater control over the management of NHS resources, in the new health care 'market' created by a 'purchaser/provider' split. Working within either 'fundholding' practices or in 'commissioning groups', GPs, while remaining 'providers' of health services, also became 'purchasers' of secondary care, and alternative primary care services. It soon became clear that fundholding, which was introduced under the auspices of 'devolved management', offered opportunities for greater diversity in the content and location of primary health care services, and greater flexibility over who provided the service. Coupled with the increasing sophistication of information systems, administration and management, the totality of primary health care practitioners began to broaden. Primary health care teams might now include practice managers, fundholding managers, IT specialists, counsellors, physiotherapists, pharmacists, psychologists, chiropodists and complementary therapists, either 'contracted' to, or directly 'employed' by, the GP. This substantially expanded the 'primary health care team' under the management of the GP (Pringle 1992). Therefore, although the reforms effectively destroyed vertical integration across secondary and primary health care, 'horizontal' integration (structurally at least) was enhanced.

Hanney *et al.* (1992) and Usherwood *et al.* (1995) examined the changing make up of the primary health care team, observing that although there were increases in numbers of whole time equivalent practice staff, these were most likely to be practice nurses, receptionists and administrative staff associated with fundholding. Some professional groups, previously thought to form part of an 'extended' primary health care team, such as social workers and psychiatric nurses, appeared to have left the direct primary health care team altogether.

## Shifting roles and power within the team

Despite the apparent expansion in multidisciplinary care, inequalities in professional relationships persisted, the GP being responsible for placing contracts, deciding on resource priorities and being accountable through health authorities for budget allocations. They remained, therefore, a controlling force within the multidisciplinary team, continuing to strengthen their own professional power, particularly as less time (given their new managerial status) was available to develop good working relationships with all members of the new team.

Responsibility for planning *community* services on the other hand, was given to local authorities who should, the White Paper suggested, work in collaboration with other health and social care agencies to secure the appropriate provision of services for the population they served (Department of Health 1989c). Working across sector boundaries, as well as dealing with alternative professional values, would prove to present one of the greatest challenges to the primary health care team (Soothill *et al.* 1995).

The integration of services attempted as a result of the NHS Community Care Act (Department of Health 1989c) soon revealed profound differences in the way professionals viewed the same problem (Rowbottom 1992). Each professional group uses its own language and vocabulary, and works from quite different ideologies and philosophies from the other groups, often in conflict with them. Not only do population health needs differ according to the individual or community in question, but so do the philosophy and value system of each primary care discipline (Thomas and Corney 1993), thus increasing the likelihood of different professional groups operating within their own specific treatment paradigm (Dorwick 1997). Lack of consensus about the objectives of primary health care teams (Bennett-Enslie and MacIntosh 1995; West and Field 1995), the outcomes of team working, or the appropriate composition of the team itself (Poulton and West 1993; Wiles and Robinson 1994) would all influence the professional's ability to collaborate effectively. These have consequently continued to present difficulties for working together more closely (Webb and Wistow 1986).

Further recent policy changes may present an even greater challenge to the primary health care team, particularly the GP. In 1997 the government commissioned an experiment in deregulating the provision of personal medical services, in the form of the 'Primary Care Act Pilots' (Department of Health 1997c). Primary care providers were encouraged to consider alternative, efficient and effective ways of providing primary health care. These projects were to include the use of other community based professional groups to provide what had previously been known as 'general medical (or dental) services', or services presently provided by, or under the direction of, a GP. Some proposals were more radical than others. In one such project (Vanclay 1998) highly skilled nurse practitioners were contracted by the health authority to provide personal medical services to an urban, deprived population, and a GP was offered a part-time post within the unit as a salaried employee. Such changes (although actually resulting from a shortage of GPs to provide general medical care to certain groups of the population, particularly those located within the inner city), represent a breakthrough for professions allied to medicine, emphasizing the importance of alternative providers in primary care. Present legislation, and financial and procedural barriers that obstruct the development of roles within the primary health care team will be wiped aside, and the new law, if implemented, will effectively end the GP monopoly of general medical services (Coulter and Mays 1997). These projects are viewed with suspicion by some Primary Health Care Trust (PHCT) members, and evaluations are yet to emerge. However, they may prove to be a significant stage *en route* to breaking down historical professional barriers.

The publication of the white paper *The New NHS: Modern – Dependable* (Department of Health 1997a), which creates primary care groups (PCGs) and Primary Care Trusts (PCTs), demonstrates how the present government is prepared to further influence the constituents of the primary health care team, and the relationship between those concerned with providing and supporting primary health care. GPs will be expected to collaborate with other GP partnerships and nurses, along with representatives of social services and patient groups, who have been given a place on the PCG Board. Other professions allied to medicine (such as occupational therapists and physiotherapists) are conspicuous by their absence; although the board is expected to provide leadership, and those working at the 'coal face' are encouraged to participate in the context of Health Improvement Programmes (HIPs). Although boards are presently dominated by GPs this development could signal an opportunity to develop joint working and collaboration in a more equal relationship.

The greatest threat to medical dominance of the primary health care team in this decade, however, may not, in fact, be that posed by structural reform, but may come from challenges within the team itself. This can be illustrated by exploring the changes taking place in nursing as a result of role development.

### Nursing development and its impact on interprofessional relationships

Given the historical development of the GP role and the influence of health policy on the structure of primary health care, it is not really surprising that the GP has played a dominant role. Acting as a filter for access to services, the GP has effectively controlled health service costs, despite attending to their own business interests.

The team, however, consists of a range of different disciplines, the largest of which is nursing. The core primary health care team consists of GP employed nurses (usually practice nurses or nurse practitioners), and Health Service Trust employed staff, including community or district nurses, health visitors, midwives and psychiatric nurses. Each discipline from within this group of nurses is either employed by the practice or is attached to it, and although each possess their own unique set of skills and responsibilities, they increasingly overlap in their day to day activities (Jenkins-Clarke et al. 1997).

Nursing development within primary care has largely been influenced by the same NHS policy changes that have affected the organization of medical care in the community. While the Dawson Report (1920) and the family doctor charter (British Medical Association 1965) significantly changed the structure of primary health care to incorporate nurses, the Harding Report (Department of Health and Social Security 1981) and the reforms of the 1980s emphasized the unique contribution nursing could make to the quality and diversity of care required to meet the needs of an increasing primary care workload and exponential growth in costs.

### The pursuit of nursing autonomy

There have been other significant developments within nursing itself in which nurses have 'reflected consciously' on the nursing role (Witz 1994: 30), and challenged previously accepted philosophies, status and relationships with other primary care providers. Since the reorganization of nursing structures as a result of the Salmon Report (Ministry of Health and Scottish Home and Health Department 1966), the nurse has been concerned with the uniqueness of the role; one that is complementary to the patient, rather than subservient to the doctor (Savage 1992). The pursuit of greater autonomy for nurses has developed hand in hand with the pursuit of a theoretical basis for nursing and the control and development of nurse education

(United Kingdom Central Council for Nursing, Midwives and Health Visitors 1986; Rhead and Strange 1996). The nurse as an 'autonomous practitioner' is further supported by the professional code of conduct of the United Kingdom Central Council (UKCC) for Nursing, Midwives and Health Visitors (1996), which emphasizes competency, judgement and responsibility for their own actions. However, despite specific attempts radically to reconstruct the primary care nurse, the pursuit has until recently been somewhat unsuccessful.

Although it has already been suggested that the Cumberledge Report (Department of Health and Social Security 1986) acted to weaken links between the two main professional groups, the report proposed an increase in nursing autonomy and responsibility, for which the medical profession was unprepared. Although the concept of the 'nurse practitioner and public health nurse' being responsible for a 'neighbourhood' of clients, put forward within the report, was philosophically sound, it was strongly resisted by doctors, on the grounds that nurses could not possibly work so autonomously (Delamonthe 1988). The GMC took a rather conservative view of doctors sharing or delegating responsibility for patient care, and recommended the retention of ultimate responsibility for patients by doctors (General Medical Council 1992). The Cumberledge Report was never implemented, and the subsequent expansion of *GP-employed* nurses has enabled GPs to control primary care nursing development by supporting the development of skills that they needed in order to meet the requirements of the new GP contract (Atkin and Lunt 1996). In so doing, they have avoided the need to negotiate with the managers of community nurses at the expense of community nurse development (Robinson 1990).

*Roles and boundaries*

Fundamental to this issue is, of course, what appropriately remains the doctors' role and what becomes the domain of nursing. The more traditional demarcations between doctor and nurse based on 'cure' and 'care' are becoming blurred and this poses a challenge to the supremacy of the medical profession (Beardshaw and Robinson 1990). Furthermore, it also presents increasing dilemmas for nursing. On the one hand there is a wish to uphold traditional values, to claim patient 'advocacy' as integral to the nurses' role (Witz 1994; Mallik 1998), and to look towards the coming together of nursing disciplines in the form of 'integrated nursing teams' (Gerrish *et al.* 1998). On the other hand, there is an attempt to reconstruct nurses as 'professionals' of care, asserting autonomy, accountability and responsibility for decision making, creating new professional groups in the form of 'clinical specialists' and nurse practitioners (Gerrish *et al.* 1998).

It is interesting to note that although early attempts at introducing the nurse practitioner were thwarted, the escalation in primary care workload – resulting from a change in focus from secondary to primary care – has necessitated the development of a nursing role, not only *complementary* to the GP, but as an *alternative*. Evaluations carried out by the Department of Health, while limited in their focus, have demonstrated an acceptance of the role by patients, who appreciate the additional information and education provided by nurse practitioners, helping with both the understanding and management of their condition (National Health Service Executive 1996). Indeed, subsequent studies have demonstrated patient satisfaction with a nurse consultation as an alternative to one with a GP.

Availability and access to a credible alternative may be what is important for patients. Jenkins-Clarke *et al.* (1997) found that nurses could be seen more quickly than a doctor and those with previous experience of the nurse consultation were more likely to use the nurse practitioner and be satisfied with the care they received. GPs themselves, it seems, are also becoming more supportive of an advanced role for nurses, reporting not only the advantages of delegating aspects of their work to 'suitably trained' nurses but also aspects of nurse effectiveness (Murphy *et al.* 1992; Marsh and Davies *et al.* 1995; Fall *et al.* 1997; Jenkins-Clarke *et al.* 1997; Lattimer *et al.* 1998). It is also notable that such developments have occurred mainly as a result of training *practice nurses* to develop their skills, whereas the *community* nursing workload has been increasing to such a point that district nurses and health visitors have reported a consequent dissatisfaction with their role (Wade 1993; Seccombe and Patch 1994). There is potential for the primary care nursing workforce to help meet the present and future demands of an increasing workload; and while nursing suffers a similar crisis of recruitment to that of doctors (Seccombe and Patch 1995) the imperative to recruit, train and deploy nurses with the appropriate 'mix' of skills has never been greater.

Thus, given the historical and policy influences on the primary health care team that have conspired against the individual struggles of different disciplines to define their role and to be equally valued members of the team, why should these professions strive towards more effective teamwork, and what can be done to make primary care teams more effective?

## Improving the process of team-working

*Individual or group decisions*

West and Poulton (1997) contend that research indicates that groups are more effective than individuals when committed to achieving a common goal. However, there is also research evidence that demonstrates that certain individuals may achieve more when operating alone rather than negotiating within a group, particularly in answering questions and making decisions (Handy 1985; Morgan 1986). Groups, after all, take longer to make those decisions. Much of primary care activity requires immediate decision making. Patients consulting with the doctor, and to some extent the nurse, 'expect' immediate decisions even if they include a decision to 'wait and see' or to refer. Doctors are trained to make independent clinical decisions on a one-to-one basis with their patients. There is a notion of personal responsibility and accountability, over and above an organizational response, that is embedded in the values of the Hippocratic Oath, which each medical practitioner has sworn to uphold. Allowing others to contribute in an equal way to decision making within the primary health care team would require restructuring of the way 'family medicine' is delivered. Giving other primary care providers the responsibility for a similar level of decision making would require devolved responsibility to another health care provider, and trust on the part of both the GP and the patient. The relationship between the GP and patient, although significant for the patient in relation to expectations of confidentiality (Wells *et al.* 1999) may, as already discussed, be of less importance than concerns about accessibility (National Health Service Executive 1996).

Whereas GPs maintain that individual patients require individual relationships with their doctor, some have also suggested that the 'doctor–patient relationship' is an ideological construct through which GPs gain a sense of professional identity and a means of exercising and maintaining medical power (Dorwick 1997). Delivering an appropriate outcome for both, however, may be inextricably linked to each set of expectations. The notion of 'vicarious liability' for the health care of *'their patients'*, despite the individual accountability of other professional groups involved in that patient's care, such as nurses, continues to be upheld by the GMC, and therefore mitigates against shared or devolved responsibility. Prescribing used to be the exclusive responsibility of the doctor, but changes are now occurring that legitimize the right of nurses to prescribe certain medicines and supplies (Royal College of Nursing 1997). Although limited at present, future extensions to nurse prescribing may further challenge the power and authority of the medical profession. It will be interesting to observe how the relationship between patient and doctor, or doctor and other primary care provider changes when GPs are no longer the only group with the power to prescribe or refer.

Group decisions, then, may not be appropriate in all circumstances, but could be desirable in planning the development of services and agreeing roles and responsibilities. The appropriate sharing of responsibility for planning and development could result in improvements in team collaboration and decision making. Field and West (1995) suggest that this would require GPs to become more 'facilitative', prior to giving their own view. Although this might avoid such phenomena as 'groupthink' (described originally by Janis (1972), where a lack of conflict and questioning in group decision making leads to constraints on action or innovation), clearly in the development of team collaboration there are issues of more profound importance. This action alone is unlikely to change fundamentally the nature of team working given that team members do not have equal stakes in the outcome.

*Measuring team effectiveness*

West and Poulton (1997) have looked in some detail at the effectiveness of primary health care teams, comparing dimensions of team functioning with teams in other organizations. Primary health care teams score more poorly on each dimension than the other teams included. As observed by the authors themselves, however, primary health care teams are often *whole organizations* rather than functional teams *within* an organization.

The dimensions of team effectiveness they put forward are:

• task effectiveness – extent to which the team is successful in achieving its task related objectives;
• mental health – well being, growth and development of its members;
• team viability – probability of continuing to work together and function effectively;
• social reflexivity.

They contend that if team performance indicators are precise, the team is more likely to improve its performance and inhibit 'social loafing' (Poulton and West 1993) i.e. that team effectiveness depends on the measurement tool.

Hackman (1987) suggests that effective performance in teams is a joint function of: the effort of the group members; the knowledge brought to the task; task appropriateness; and the processes operating within the group. Similarly Deutsch (1991) described the functional roles adopted in teams as 'task' or 'maintenance'. Team members have specific skills and experience or expertise to apply to the task, but the team also requires 'nurturing' to function most effectively. Without this care the team has difficulty in communicating, maintaining motivation and becoming a cohesive group. Multidisciplinary primary health care teams characteristically do not protect time to work together, do not appoint someone as team coordinator and tend to work reactively. The level of activity generated by team members is huge but little time is made available for reflection, planning or celebration when things go well, or, indeed, commiserating when they go badly (Speigal et al. 1992).

Reflection or collaboration is, quite simply, not part of the culture. Similarly, diverse management structures (often striving towards different rather than common goals) and the independent contractor status of GPs, who do not share the same status or reward system, are major threats to interprofessional collaboration and team effectiveness.

## Facilitating effective group processes

Achieving team cooperation may therefore require not only structural changes to the system, but also changes in the culture of general practice and primary care, as well as specific support from an external source. Pendleton (1995) advocates the help of a 'professional development consultancy', which addresses the needs of the individual and those of the organization. The 'Teamcare Valleys project' (Teamcare Valleys 1993) in Wales used part-time 'clinical fellows' to work on specific projects to encourage and support practice based teams. However, the outcomes of this ambitious project are not clear. They report that team cohesiveness was improved by group education and the inclusion of a wider constituency in certain defined project tasks, but the 'business' of primary health care continued to 'get in the way' of team communication. Thus a project coordinator was relied upon to communicate with individuals who essentially worked alone on their 'part' of the project. Similar models of teamwork 'facilitation' have been tried in order: to improve team-working on health promotion in primary care

(Lambert 1991); to change the culture of general practice; to develop individuals, organizations and systems to promote the principles of 'Health for All' (Thomas 1994); and more recently to develop integrated nursing teams (Gerrish *et al.* 1998).

Clearly, as development projects, Teamcare Valleys and the Liverpool Facilitation project (Thomas 1994) appear to have been successful in stimulating activity. Regeneration of the Valleys, for example, took place through a process of interprofessional collaboration and joint working, but in order to do that a significant external investment was required, as was the political will to bring about change.

Did any of this fundamentally change entrenched beliefs about the process of interprofessional relationships and teamwork? The evaluations at the time were positive, but given the significant financial input and political support, some degree of success was virtually inevitable. Several years on, it would be interesting to discover how things have subsequently developed. Significantly, there are no reports in the literature of studies that explore long-term changes in professional behaviour following efforts to improve teamwork in primary care.

### Towards an evidence based future

So, what can we learn from the past, and what are the emerging issues for the future? If we are not merely to experience an explosion in new activity, involving changes in the provision of care and provision of the carer, which is manipulated by those with the greatest power and influence, careful evaluation of activities and research into the best configuration of services for the future must go hand in hand.

The methods used to undertake any research must be appropriate to the particular research question, and yet the generally accepted concept of a hierarchy of 'evidence' described by Sackett *et al.* (1997) evolves from a belief that there is a standard hierarchy of *research methods*. The emphasis on a positivist 'experimental' method, clearly regarded as the 'best' approach in medical research, may be inappropriate for the study of team function because of the number of variables and the dynamic and complex nature of the developments therein. If teamwork development involves dimensions of individual role, services and systems, then similarly so must the evaluation (Thomas and Graver 1997). At each point in the process of development, behaviour and attitudes will change, thus revising the participants' views of the world and their role within it. The research method, must, therefore, be sensitive to each of these aspects; and while remaining focused on outcomes, must be able to identify fully all antecedents of the final picture captured within the process of change.

The strength of the particular method may be judged by those within primary care teams who accept what has been found to be true or untrue. The interpretation of such studies by those involved in primary care teams and wishing to learn from the research is as valid as the interpretation by the researcher (Najman *et al.* 1992). A mixture of qualitative and quantitative methods will produce different insights into the effect of any given intervention or development. And indeed such a mix may provide a way of addressing the different priorities of the various stakeholders (Beattie 1991), including change at the level of individual professional practice, and broader organizational structures and processes (Hart and Bond 1995). Action research is a useful approach in that it: enables an evaluation of dynamic and complex systems with multiple agendas; enables evaluation of unexpected outcomes resulting from the processes involved; and promotes change through ownership and feedback (Thomas and Graver 1997). Researchers, therefore, should be immersed in the culture of primary health care, but have the insight to explore objectively each avenue of team development that emerges, and must find different ways for multiprofessional team members to work constructively together.

## What are the issues for future team development?

I have described the changes in health and social policy responsible for shaping the form of primary care in the UK and, as a consequence, the structure of the primary health care team. I have endeavoured to demonstrate the significance of historical events both imposed upon, and influenced by, two of the main professional groups within the primary health care team. However, given the present state of flux within the system, the changing composition of primary health care teams, and the redefinition of roles within the team, other primary care providers may emerge as significant in influencing how teams communicate and collaborate in the future.

As demographic changes and technological advances continue to impact on society and health service provision, the ability of existing structures and alliances to meet demand in primary care must be questioned. The shift from secondary to primary care continues to gather speed. More diagnostic investigations are taking place in primary care and more patients are being discharged from hospital early, the population is ageing and the chronic sick and disabled are surviving into old age; all these dictate an efficient and effective use of health and social care resources. Finding appropriate ways to configure new services does not simply require new structures and technology; it will require major thought about which skills will be appropriate for the future and who are the most appropriate professional groups to fulfil health and social care needs. No single professional group can possibly do the job alone. A major challenge will be to decide on the best *mix of skills* to provide the most *cost effective* care.

Patients' expectations are changing. Patients want more say in how they are treated and who manages their care. Contact with a family doctor is being replaced by speedy access to less expensive health care providers, although if costs are to be contained some method of 'filtering' the workload will have to continue. If it is not to be the GP, then consideration will need to be given to who the 'gatekeeper' might be. 'NHS Direct' is one solution (Department of Health 1997b), thus extending the 'team' well beyond usual geographical boundaries.

Changes in policy and new methods of providing care continue to be introduced without the precursory evaluation, with the consequent changes in public expectation. Changes in team configuration will most certainly result from the new PCGs and subsequent PCTs. The multidisciplinary primary health care team may become something of the past as each professional group defines its area of expertise and skills, which will be offered to the 'network' of services, fashioned to meet national priorities and local needs. Individuals within such networks may have some difficulty identifying and defining the primary health care team. Networks of health service professionals, as well as those of voluntary and commercial organizations, will however, be required to communicate and collaborate in ways they have never done before if patients are to receive 'integrated' packages of care. Devlin (1998) asserts that although most health professionals consider private involvement in public organizations to be inappropriate there are several good examples where private finance has improved care to individual patients, and the conditions of health care providers themselves, for example out of hours services, information systems and chronic disease patient care programmes. The question is not *should* the private sector become involved, but rather *to what extent* should it? And when it does, what impact will this have on communication across professional groups?

Furthermore, with the investment in education for nurses and professions allied to medicine these disciplines are developing a stronger academic base, challenging the supremacy of the doctor, and existing boundaries and roles. Multidisciplinary education has at last become a possibility, supported by the nursing and general practice professional bodies (CAIPE 1996a). Evaluations of projects concerned with developing interprofessional collaboration, by joint educational initiatives, are already underway (CAIPE 1996b) and appear to be successfully breaking down the barriers that have led to a lack of understanding of roles, values and abilities.

As primary care team members we can challenge all the assumptions of the past and begin to create the sort of team, and the method of team-working, we find most useful in providing high quality care to our patients. The research community can assist the transition by providing evidence on strategies for successful team-working and improved interprofessional collaboration.

## References

Adair, J. (1986) *Effective Team-building*. London: Gower.

Allsop, J. (1984) *Health Policy and the National Health Service*. Harlow: Longman.

Argyle, M. (1973) *Social Interaction*. London: Tavistock.

Atkin, K. and Lunt, N. (1996) Negotiating the role of the practice nurse in general practice, *Journal of Advanced Nursing*, 24: 498–505.

Balint, M. (1957) *The Doctor, His Patient and the Illness*. London: Pitman Medical.

Beardshaw, V. and Robinson, R. (1990) *New for Old? Prospects for Nursing in the 1990s*. London: King's Fund Institute.

Beattie, A. (1991) The evaluation of community development initiatives in health promotion: a review of current strategies, in *Roots and Branches*. Buckingham: Open University Press.

Belbin, R.M. (1981) *Management Teams: Why they Succeed or Fail*. London: Heinemann.

Bennett-Enslie, G. and MacIntosh, J. (1995) Promoting collaboration in the primary health care team: the role of the practice meeting, *Journal of Inter-professional Care*, 9(3): 251–6.

British Medical Association (1965) A charter for the family doctor service, *British Medical Journal Supplement*, 1: 89–91.

CAIPE (Centre for the Advancement of Inter-professional Education) (1996a) Conference Report: *Collaboration in General Practice*. Paper 2, March.

CAIPE (Centre for the Advancement of Inter-professional Education) (1996b) *Developing and Evaluating Local Inter-professional Educational Initiatives – The RCGP Education Fellowship Scheme*. Report to the NHSE.

Collins, J.S. (1950) General practice in England today, *Lancet*, 1 (6604): 555–85.

Coulter, A. and Mays, N. (1997) Deregulating primary care, *British Medical Journal*, 314: 510–13.

Dawson, B. (1920) *Report on the Future Provision of Medical and Allied Services*, Cmd 693. London: HMSO.

Delamonthe, T.D. (1988) Nursing grievances IV: not a profession; not a career, *British Medical Journal*, 296: 271–4.

Department of Health (DoH) (1989a) *General Practice in the NHS. A New Contract*. London: HMSO.

Department of Health (DoH) (1989b) *Working For Patients*, Cm 555. London: HMSO.

Department of Health (DoH) (1989c) *Caring for People: Community Care in the Next Decade and Beyond*, Cm 849. London: HMSO.

Department of Health (DoH) (1990) *Health Care Parliamentary Monitor*. London: HMSO.

Department of Health (DoH) (1996a) *Choice and Opportunity in Primary Care: The Future*, Cm 3390. London: HMSO.

Department of Health (DoH) (1996b) *Primary Care: Delivering the Future*, Cm 3512. London: HMSO.

Department of Health (DoH) (1997a) *The New NHS: Modern – Dependable*, Cm 3807. London: The Stationery Office.

Department of Health (DoH) (1997b) *Our Healthier Nation: A Contract for Health*, Cm 3852. London: The Stationery Office.

Department of Health (DoH) (1997c) *Personal Medical Services Pilots and the NHS (Primary Care) Act*, EL (97) 27: April 1997.

Department of Health and Social Security (DHSS) (1981) *The Primary Health Care Team: Report of a Joint Working Group of the Standard Medical Advisory Committee and the Standing Nursing and Midwifery Advisory Committee* (Harding Report). London: DHSS.

Department of Health and Social Security (DHSS) (1986) *Neighbourhood Nursing: A Focus for Care. A Report of the Community Nursing Review in England* (Cumberledge Report). London: HMSO.

Department of Health and Social Security (DHSS) (1987) *Promoting Better Health: The Government's Programme for Improving Primary Health Care*, Cmnd. 249. London: HMSO.

Deutsch, M. (1991) A theory of co-operation and competition, in J. Hayes (ed.) *Interpersonal Skills, Goal Directed Behaviour at Work*. London: HarperCollins.

Devlin, M. (1998) *Primary Health Care and the Private Sector*. Oxford: Radcliffe Medical Press.

Dorwick, C. (1997) Rethinking the doctor–patient relationship in general practice, *Health and Social Care in the Community*, 5(1): 11–14.

Fall, M., Walters, S., Read, S. *et al.* (1997) An evaluation of a nurse led ear care service in primary care: benefit and costs, *British Journal of General Practice*, 47: 699–703.

Field, R. and West, M.A. (1995) Teamwork in primary healthcare; perspectives from practices, *Journal of Interprofessional Care*, 9: 123–30.

General Medical Council (1992) *Professional Conduct and Discipline: Fitness to Practice*. London: GMC.

Gerrish, K., Pollard, J. and Ross, B. (1998) The community nursing facilitators' role, *Primary Health Care*, 8(8): 12–14.

Gilmore, M., Bruce, N. and Hunt, M. (1974) *The Work of the Nursing Team in General Practice*. London: Central Council for Education and Training for Health Visitors.

Gorden, P. and Pampling, D. (1996) Primary health care – its characteristics and potential, in P. Gorden and D. Pampling (eds) *Extending Primary Care*. Oxford: Radcliffe Medical Press.

Hackman, J.R. (1987) The design of work teams, in J.W. Lorsh and C. Ham (eds) *Handbook of Organizational Behaviors*. Englewood Cliffs, NJ: Prentice Hall.

Ham, C. (1991) *The New NHS*. Oxford: Radcliffe Medical Press.

Handy, C. (1985) *Understanding Organisations*. London: Penguin.

Hanney, D.R., Usherwood, T.P. and Platts, M. (1992) Practice organisation before and after a new contract: a survey of general practitioners in Sheffield, *British Journal of General Practice*, 42: 517–20.

Hart, E. and Bond, M. (1995) *Action Research for Health and Social Care: A Guide to Practice*. Buckingham: Open University Press.

Janis, I.L. (1972) *Victims of Groupthink*, 2nd edn. Boston, MA: Houghton Mifflin.

Jenkins-Clarke, S., Carr-Hill, R., Dixon, P. and Pringle, M. (1997) *Skill Mix in Primary Care. A Study of the Interface between the General Practitioner and other Members of the Primary Health Care Team. A Final report*. York: York Centre for Health Economics, University of York.

Jenkins-Clarke, S., Carr-Hill, R. and Dixon, P. (1998) Teams and seams: skill mix in primary care, *Journal of Advanced Nursing*, 28(5): 1120–6.

Jones, R.V.H. (1992) Teamwork in primary care: how much do we know about it? *Journal of Inter-professional Care*, 6: 25–30.

Lambert, D. (1991) Developing primary health care teams, *Primary Health Care Management*, 12: 2–3.

Lattimer, V., George, S., Thompson, F. *et al*. (1998) Safety and effectiveness of nurse telephone consultation in out of hours primary care: randomised controlled trial, *British Medical Journal*, 312: 1054–9.

Mallik, M. (1998) Advocacy in nursing: perceptions and attitudes of the nursing elite in the United Kingdom, *Journal of Advanced Nursing*, 28(5): 1010–11.

Marsh, G.N. and Davies, M.L. (1995) Establishing a minor illness nurse in a busy general practice, *British Medical Journal*, 310: 778–80.

Ministry of Health and Scottish Home and Health Department (1966) *Report of the Committee on Senior Nursing Staff Structure* (Salmon Report). London: HMSO.

Morgan, G. (1986) *Images of Organisation*. London: Gower.

Murphy, E., Kinmonth, A. and Marteau, E. (1992) General practice based diabetes surveillance: the views of patients, *British Journal of General Practice*, 42: 279–83.

Najman, J.M., Morrison, J., Williams, G.M. and Anderson, M.J. (1992) Comparing alternative methodologies of social research, in J. Daly, I. MacDonald and E. Willis (eds) *Researching Health Care. Designs, Dilemmas, Disciplines*. London: Tavistock/Routledge.

National Health Service Executive (1996) *Nurse Practitioner Evaluation Project: Final Report*. London: Coopers and Lybrand.

Pearson, P. and Spencer, J. (eds) (1997) *Promoting Teamwork in Primary Care. A Research Based Approach*. London: Arnold.

Pendleton, D. (1995) Professional development in general practice: problems, puzzles, paradigms, *British Journal of General Practice*, 45: 377–81.

Poulton, B.C. and West, M.A. (1993) Measuring the effect of team-working in primary health care. Paper presented at 'Audit for Teams in Primary Care' Conference, Royal College of Physicians, London.

Pringle, M. (1992) The developing primary care partnership, *British Medical Journal*, 305: 624–6.

Pritchard, P. (1981) *Manual of Primary Health Care*, 2nd edn. Oxford: Oxford University Press.

Rhead, M. and Strange, F. (1996) Nursing lecturer/practitioners: can lecturer/practitioners be music to our ears? *Journal of Advanced Nursing*, 24: 1126–72.

Robinson, G. (1990) The future for practice nurses, *British Journal of General Practice*, April: 132–3.

Rowbottom, J. (1992) *Seamless Services – A Stitch in Time: Care in the Community*. London: Institute of Health Service Management.

Royal College of General Practitioners (RCGP) (1972) *The Future General Practitioner. Learning and Teaching*. London: RCGP.

Royal College of Nursing (RCN) (1997) *Extension of Prescribing Powers to Nurses*. RCN Factsheet 2, Sept 1997.

Sackett, D.L., Richardson, W.S., Rosenberg, W. and Haynes, R.B. (1997) *Evidence-based Medicine. How to Practise and Teach EBM*. London: Churchill Livingstone.

Savage, J. (1992) The new nursing: empowering patients or empowering nurses?, in J. Robinson, A. Gray and R. Elkan (eds) *Policy Issues in Nursing*. Buckingham: Open University Press.

Seccombe, I. and Patch, A. (1994) Workloads, pay and morale of qualified nurses in 1994. Report 272, in S. Jenkins-Clarke, R. Carr-Hill and P. Dixon (eds) (1998) Teams and seams: skill mix in primary care, *Journal of Advanced Nursing*, 28(5): 1120–6.

Seccombe, I. and Patch, A. (1995) *Recruiting, Retaining and Rewarding Qualified Nurses in 1995*. (Report 295). London: Institute for Employment Statistics.

Smith, N., Wilson, A. and Dowell, A.C. (1994) Better Living – Better Life. Evaluation report to the Department of Health (unpublished).

Soothill, K., MacKay, L. and Webb, C. (1995) *Inter-professional Relations in Health Care*. London: Arnold.

Speigal, N., Murphey, E., Kinmonth, A. *et al.* (1992) Managing change in general practice: a step by step guide, *British Medical Journal*, 304: 231–4.

Stanley, I. and Hatcher, P. (1992) The PHCT: Realising the Myth, *Good Practice,* April: 17–19.

Teamcare Valleys (1993) *University of Wales College of Medicine, 1990–1993, Overview Report*. Teamcare Valleys. Cardiff: Welsh Office.

Thomas, P. (1994) *The Liverpool Primary Health Care Facilitation Project 1989–1994*. Liverpool: Liverpool FHSA.

Thomas, R.V.R. and Corney, R.H. (1993) Teamwork in primary care: the practice nurse perspective, *Journal of Inter-professional Care*, 7(2): 47–55.

Thomas, P. and Graver, Z. (1997) The Liverpool intervention to promote teamwork in general practice: an action research approach, in P. Pearson and J. Spencer (eds) *Promoting Teamwork in Primary Care. A Research Based Approach*. London: Arnold.

United Kingdom Central Council for Nursing, Midwives and Health Visitors (1986) *Project 2000, A New Preparation for Practice*. London: UKCC.

United Kingdom Central Council for Nursing, Midwives and Health Visitors (1996) *The Scope of Professional Practice*. London: UKCC.

Usherwood, T., Barker, S. and Joesbury, H. (1995) Primary health care teams in Britain. Unpublished report to the Department of Employment, Sheffield, and the NHSE, Leeds, in P. Pearson and J. Spencer (eds) *Promoting Teamwork in Primary Care. A Research Based Approach*. London: Arnold.

Vanclay, L. (1998) Team working in primary care, *Nursing Standard*, 12(20): 37–8.

Wade, B. (1993) The job satisfaction of health visitors, district nurses and practice nurses working in areas served by four trusts: Year 1, *Journal of Advanced Nursing*, 18: 992–1004.

Webb, A. and Wistow, G. (1986) *Planning Need and Scarcity: Essays on the Personal Social Services*. London: Allen & Unwin.

Wells, M., Hassey, G.A., Wilson, A. and Pearson, D. (1999) Diabetic registers – a practice survey of patients' attitudes, *Health Informatics Journal*, 4.3/4.4: 250–4.

West, M. and Field, R. (1995) Teamwork in primary health care. Perspectives from organisational psychology, *Journal of Inter-professional Care*, 9(2): 117–22.

West, M. and Poulton, B. (1997) Primary health care teams: in a league of their own, in P. Pearson and J. Spencer (eds) (1997) *Promoting Teamwork in Primary Care. A Research Based Approach*. London: Arnold.

Wiles, R. and Robinson, J. (1994) Teamwork in primary care: the views and experiences of nurses, midwives and health visitors, *Journal of Advanced Nursing*, 20: 324–30.

Wilson, A. (1994) *Changing Practices in Primary Care*. London: Health Education Authority.

Witz, A. (1994) The challenge of nursing, in J. Gabe, D. Kelleher and G. Williams (eds) *Challenges to Medicine*. London: Routledge.

World Health Organization (WHO) (1984) *Health for All*. Geneva: WHO.

# Part 2

## Challenges of practice

# 4 Commissioning services for older people: make haste slowly?

Steve Iliffe

## Introduction

Our society is not ageing rapidly, nor is the older population an increasingly problematic burden for the community. Doctors and nurses now entering the commissioning process need not fear the impact of demography on their future tasks as both providers and purchasers of services. On the contrary, the older population is an enormous public resource that already underpins social and health care, and that has potential for making even greater contributions to civil society. The problems facing commissioners lie more within the existing structures, attitudes and skills of health services than with supposed patterns of population ageing.

As those of us who work in primary care become both providers of community services and ultimately purchasers of specialist care we will need to know what our populations need, how much better we can deliver services in the community, and how to judge the quality, effectiveness and value of specialist care. How good are we at assessing the needs of the older population, which makes the greatest use of specialist care and has the most complex problems? How expert are we in primary care in developing new approaches and methods that deliver better quality care for older patients? How much experience have we acquired in getting research into practice, and collaborating across professional boundaries, for the benefit of older people?

The answers are not comforting (Wilkinson and Murray 1998), but the opportunities for promoting successful ageing and health in later life now arising through primary care commissioning are huge, if we can grasp them. This chapter argues that the current organization of the NHS and of social care is inappropriate to the needs of a twenty-first-century community, and that British primary care is both obsolescent and, in its present configuration as a demand-led service with limited capacity for teamwork, an obstacle to development of health care for older people. General practice has failed to develop a level of competence in the care of older patients comparable to that acquired by hospital based geriatric medicine in the 1970s. As we shall see, the programme of 75 and over checks imposed on general practice in 1990 has foundered for lack of a scientific basis, and also for lack of basic support from health authorities. Fundholding has also failed to promote the developmental and innovative culture in general practice (Audit Commission 1996) that would be needed to transform the quality of primary care for older people.

The potential for fundamental change of our health services, through the emergence of primary care commissioning, needs careful and cautious exploration, given the risk for primary care workers of neglecting the 'core business' of general medical care when diversifying into public health issues (Baines and Couper 1998). This is the task facing GPs and community nurses, who may find that focusing on the needs of older people in their community helps them to understand and respond to complex issues around needs *and* wants, dependence *and* autonomy, citizens' preferences *and* populations' priorities, both at individual and locality level.

### The myth of the rising tide

Since 1981 there has been no increase in the proportion of the population aged 65 and over, currently standing at 16 per cent of the total population, and this age group will probably rise to only 17 per cent by 2011 (Arber 1996). The projected rate of increase among those aged 60 or more during the 1990s is 0.08 per cent per year, about a quarter of that projected for those under 60, whereas the number of those aged 65 to 74 is likely to fall by half a million. Only the 85 and over group will grow in size. We are living through a pause in the process of demographic ageing, and probably face only a modest increase in the size of the older population in the first quarter of the twenty-first century, with a projected increase among those aged 60 and over from 20 per cent to 24 per cent (Warnes 1989). Sweden experienced such a change in the middle of this century, and became one of the most stable and successful societies in Europe, able to provide expanding welfare services to all age groups while also redistributing domestic and paid work between men and women and increasing citizen participation in government (Secretariat for Future Studies 1984).

The ageing of British society occurred during the middle decades of this century and was accommodated without hugely damaging effects on social structures or the economy. Projected increases in the proportion of older people in the population at the beginning of the next century are neither new nor unprecedented, and they will be significantly less than increases in under developed countries (Timaeus 1986). Anxieties about the ageing of the British population and the effect of demography on provision of health and social services are, therefore, less to do with the absolute numbers of older people than to do with heightened expectations among service providers, policy makers and politicians about the character and costs of such care.

The 'rising tide' of dependent and disabled older people may be little more than a ripple, but for a society where provision is approaching minimalist levels, it appears to professionals and politicians as a threat. This threat can be felt already in primary care, and as primary care professionals move into commissioning status and confront rationing problems it will be experienced with increasing intensity.

It need not be, with a little preparation and forethought. The older population is an important economic and social resource for the whole community, exhibiting its own dynamic in the expanding social networks of the older population and the increases in family commitments across the generations. In 1977 a third of those aged 75 or over had no children, but by the early 1990s this had fallen to nearer 16 per cent (Timaeus 1986). Mutual support has grown between older people and their children and grandchildren, contrary to the myth that children neglect and abandon their ageing parents. The result is that older people provide over a third of the so-called informal care of ill and disabled individuals, act as a major source of childcare for the increasing proportion of working mothers and provide the backbone of voluntary support in the health service and in voluntary organizations that contribute on a broad scale to health and social care (Wilkinson and Murray 1998).

These patterns of provision may be obvious to primary care workers with long experience of communities and frequent, albeit brief, encounters with families over long periods of time. Where staff turnover is high and the work operationalized as tasks, not constructed around reciprocal relationships, the patterns may be hidden, allowing stereotyped and negative views of older people's health needs to emerge.

The relationship between older people and their children, friends and neighbours is not one of simple dependency of young on old or vice versa, but a complex relationship of reciprocity that shifts only gradually – and then only sometimes – towards the younger becoming the predominant givers. When these relationships fail, family doctors, community nurses and social workers are called upon to solve difficult problems, sometimes at times when services are at their least responsive, and it is through these experiences that distorted perspectives of ageing and the needs of older people can arise.

The major contribution of older people to family and local economies can occur because we are not only living longer, but remain healthier for longer too. Life expectancy for women is currently 79 years, and 74 for men, with projected figures of 83 for women and 78 for men by the year 2021 (Baines and Couper 1998). Instead of a pandemic of disability and dementia, most of the gain in life expectancy seems to be occurring without disability (Robine and Ritchie 1991). A woman of 65 with 17.6 years life expectancy will remain fit and active for nine or ten years, and a man of the same age, with a life expectancy of 13.7 years, for seven or eight years. American studies of cohorts of older people during the 1980s showed that the decline in disabling conditions was most pronounced for disorders of the heart and circulation (Manton *et al.* 1995). In these studies the probability that a person aged 85 or over remained free of disabilities increased by nearly 30 per cent during the 1980s. The impact of improving health can be seen in the recent review of findings from the 1991 Census and seven other national surveys of older people (Jarvis *et al.* 1996), which showed that:

- among those aged 60–79, 57 per cent of men and 40 per cent of women had taken part in some sporting activity in the previous month; the percentages were 21 per cent and 12 per cent respectively for the 80 and over age group;
- 59 per cent of men and 64 per cent of women aged 60–79 had no limiting long-standing illness;
- among those aged over 65, 80 per cent had no difficulty with any personal care, 68 per cent had no difficulty with any domestic task and 69 per cent had no difficulty with any locomotor task;
- in 1987 one in six of those aged 60 or more had done some voluntary work in the previous year, as had 8 per cent of those aged 80 to 84.

Refocusing on the better health of the older population does not mean that illness and disability have been vanquished. The theory that morbidity is being compressed into the last few months of life (Fries 1980) with an active, fit existence suddenly turning into disability and fatal illness over a short period of time has not yet been realized for the whole population. A significant minority of older people have major, disabling problems that require medical, nursing or social support to maintain a good quality of life, and the prevalence of major neurological and musculoskeletal causes of disability, like stroke, cardiac failure, the dementias, Parkinson's disease, osteoarthritis and osteoporosis leading to fractured neck or femur, is likely to rise among the very old (Tallis 1992), even if their incidence falls. These problems do constitute a challenge to health and social services and those engaging in primary care commissioning will have to face them, but chronic disease management is only one dimension of the commissioning task, because successful ageing will produce its own medical problems, which will demand attention, potentially on a large scale.

For example, how will older citizens know about their fitness to drive, who will advise them and what medical constraints will be imposed upon them? Although the number of older drivers, especially those over 80, is increasing rapidly, the crash rate per driver among those aged 65 and over is low, probably because older drivers tend to drive shorter distances, and avoid driving at night, in heavy traffic or in bad weather. However, the crash rate per mile driven for older drivers is higher than that for younger adults, and is lower than only one other group; teenagers. Right-of-way and turning accidents occur particularly frequently, and may be due to age related changes in vision that cause problems with:

- merging traffic streams;
- vehicles appearing unexpectedly in the peripheral vision;
- judging own speed and that of approaching vehicles;
- and reading poorly lit road signs or dim vehicle information displays (Waller 1991).

It is not clear how much these problems can be overcome or ameliorated, and the tendency of many older people is to avoid driving in situations that put them at most risk. This may not be practical for some, especially if they do have a significant social role in collecting children from school, working for voluntary bodies or even in maintaining paid employment. Successful ageing increases the demands on the older population, while the increase in the pace and density of modern traffic puts older drivers at a disadvantage. This may diminish as a generation that learned to drive relatively late in life gives way to one that grew up in an automotive society (Kline *et al.* 1992) but those commissioning secondary care services may have to think as much about consequences of the healthiness of their older population as the individual GP must think about judging competence to drive.

## The poverty of planning

Geriatric medicine was developed to correct the neglect of older people's health that the NHS faced in the immediate post-war period. It became effective and successful as a discipline within medicine because it identified old age as a problem period needing particular responses from the NHS. As the health of older people improved, this solution itself has become a problem. Old age is still assumed to be a period of prolonged illness and disability for all, chronic disease is perceived as following an inexorable downward trajectory rather than a variable and sometimes unpredictable course, and the older population is too easily perceived as homogeneous in its neediness, creating crude tools for service planning for older people.

For example, the underlying assumption that all older people have the same health needs was used in the resource allocation formulae for health authorities, so that a population with a large proportion of older people received proportionately more resources than one with a smaller proportion. Yet the reason for the difference in proportions of older people in different local populations was selective migration at retirement of those affluent and well enough to relocate. Small elderly populations in the inner cities may have greater health needs because they are too ill or too poor to move to seaside towns, but a resource reallocation formula based on age alone transfers funds away from the most needy to those with better health (Williams and Scott 1994). A similar distortion can occur with the Jarman index of deprivation, because it is based on GP perception of workload, as proxy for deprivation (Jarman 1983). The score gives high deprivation value to an area if the percentage of those aged 75 and over living alone is high, even though they are not an 'at risk' group compared with those living with others (Iliffe *et al.* 1992).

Attempts to shape the development of the NHS from a public health perspective have not done much for the older population. As we shall see, the imposition of the 75 and over checks on general practice has inhibited experimentation and development of primary care for older people and reduced the health promotion approach to older people to an over simplified checklist, whereas *The Health of the Nation* approach has largely ignored the older population (Department of Health 1991). For example, this emphasized the need to reduce premature mortality, especially by reducing the rate of heart disease and stroke among those under 74, even though heart disease and stroke are the major causes of death over 75. This use of an age cut-off reflects the paucity of research on medical interventions in later life, because older people tend to be excluded from clinical trials even though they have the potential to benefit directly from therapeutic and preventive strategies,

sometimes benefiting proportionately more than their juniors from technological advances (Medical Research Council 1994).

The evidence is mounting that no significant age difference exists in mortality
or morbidity outcomes of a range of interventions, including cardiopulmonary
resuscitation, coronary arteriography and bypass surgery, liver and kidney
transplantation, other forms of surgery, chemotherapy and dialysis (Jecker
and Scheiderman 1992). In other words, physiological age is more important
than chronological age in determining responses to treatment, rendering both
services and health promotion programmes organized around chronological
thresholds less effective than the older public deserves.

If planning approaches, research and service organization are based on
misconceptions about the patterns of health and illness amongst older people,
can health economics be more sensitive and offer better tools for allocating
resources for care of older people? Primary care commissioners will need to
be clear about this question, if only because the costs of services may be the
first item on their agenda. So far the gain has been small. The division of
social care along purchaser–provider lines has resulted in the introduction of
means testing for services, along with reduced access to social care because
of resource limitations. In medicine the introduction of economic analyses
as the basis of service planning, and of outcome measures that serve as a sur-
rogate for profit – 'health gain', in the jargon – have not been of great benefit
to older people (Jones and Higgs 1992). The hazards to older people of ideas
borrowed from the discipline of health economics and used by untutored
professionals as tools for purchasing services are becoming clear after our
experiences of the 'internal market' and fundholding. For example, the transfer of the care of older people to 'informal' carers in the family or among
neighbours may allow money to be diverted elsewhere in medical care, reducing the opportunity costs of the health service, but only if the actual costs
to carers are not measured or valued, including their withdrawal from the
labour market. Community care of an old, frail individual may require younger
people to make significant changes to their work or daily life that will have
costs for them that they may or may not want to bear.

The complexity and heterogeneity of the older population has not been
acknowledged in service development, with the consequence that the innovation in the primary care of older people that developed organically in the
1970s and 1980s did not take root in the way that hospital based geriatric
medicine did, but has been stultified by the imposition of a crude and
inappropriate population approach; the 75 and over checks. This example of
the damage that a simplistic public health perspective can do when applied
mechanically to health care is one that commissioners of services for older
people could usefully study before initiating changes in the way primary care
staff work in their localities.

**The 75 and over checks**

The terms of service for GPs introduced by a unilateral contract change in
1990 require members of primary health care teams to offer annual assessments

of health to patients aged 75 and over (Department of Health 1990) using a number of broad headings to guide the assessment:

- Sensory function
- Mobility
- Mental condition
- Physical condition including continence
- Social environment
- Medication use

This contractual obligation was not described in detail so it was unclear what was intended, but it was widely interpreted by GPs as a requirement to 'screen' the 75 and over age group. Although there has been extensive research into the possible benefits of regular screening of older populations, the introduction of the 75 and over checks provoked extensive debate because of the lack of conclusive evidence that routine screening made such significant differences to the health of the older population that the effort could be justified (Freer 1987; Royal College of General Practitioners 1990; Harris 1992).

Taylor and Buckley's review of assessment of older people (Taylor and Buckley 1987) summarized the state of the art just before the introduction of the 75 and over checks. Early findings of massive un-met need (Anderson and Cowan 1955; Williamson et al. 1964) had not been confirmed by later research, which showed the impact of the NHS, and of the emergence of geriatric medicine as a speciality, on both the use of services and the health of the older population. Older people were no longer avoiding consultations with their family doctors (Williams 1974), most of their medical pathology was either known to the GP or considered unimportant by the patient (Tulloch and Moore 1979), and older non-consulters in general practice were mainly healthy (Ebrahim et al. 1984). Social change, improvements in the population's health and changes in health services had seemed to make screening for hidden disease among older people inappropriate. By the 1990s the hidden health problem of later life was not undiagnosed pathology, but loss of function that was either unrecognized or wrongly attributed to 'normal ageing'. A dramatic example of this is the extensive unrecognized visual loss found in a recent community study in north London (Reidy et al. 1998).

Functional assessment, and the need to evaluate the range of different approaches to assessment that had developed within primary care, was seen as the central issue by the advocates of a systematic approach to the health of older people in the community. This emphasis on functional assessment was echoed in the introduction of the 75 and over checks, but guidance on how to perform the checks was not available because the evaluations of different approaches called for by researchers (Taylor and Buckley 1987) simply did not happen.

Since the introduction of the 75 and over checks, research into this national screening problem has largely focused on implementation of the assessment procedures, showing variable involvement by GPs and no standardization of methods (Brown et al. 1992). The review by the Manchester group revealed a tendency to delegate assessment to nurses, little or no interest in the assessment process in many practices, and a low priority for 75 and over checks among Family Health Services Authority (FHSA) managers. Research into outcomes for older people themselves has been notable for its absence, along with economic evaluation of the screening programme.

Information about the workload implications of the annual assessment package became available to GPs only after its introduction (Iliffe et al. 1991a, 1991b; Brown et al. 1992).

Doubts about the health gain from the 75 and over checks are not the only concern that has undermined this programme's credibility. Morbidity and disability are prevalent well before 75, so that the choice of age for annual assessment is arbitrary and may not be the most appropriate given limited resources (Pathy et al. 1992). The value of screening programmes beginning at 75 has recently been challenged through reanalysis of data from an intervention trial using health visitors (Vetter et al. 1993). Secondary analysis of data from a random sample of patients over the age of 74 involved in a study covering all the elements of the annual assessment of the elderly demonstrates that this age group is not homogeneous, that annual screening may be too often for some and too infrequent for others, and that different assessment methods may be needed at different ages (Iliffe and Drennan, forthcoming). If comprehensive functional assessment is to become the core of medical care for older people, its components need to be introduced before the age of 75 and applied in flexible ways.

Until recently, no trial had demonstrated an improvement in older people's functional ability. A meta-analysis of trials showed that home assessment was associated with reduced longer-term mortality and higher likelihood of staying at home, but had no measurable impact on functional ability (Stuck et al. 1993). This picture is now changing as evidence appears from North America (Stuck et al. 1995) and Europe (Bernabei et al. 1998) that targeted comprehensive assessment can reduce or even reverse disability and functional loss, but the relevance of work done in societies with poor primary care and over developed specialist services to the UK context is unclear. We are now paying the price for failing to evaluate locally sensitive approaches to primary care assessment of older people's health needs.

## An agenda for development

Primary care workers now face a number of problems in research, service development and policy formulation that need to be solved. They can be summarized as a series of contradictions and paradoxes:

- Although descriptive studies show that screening yields significant amounts of un-met 'need', patients and professionals do not necessarily do anything about need identified by screening. The significance of the problem to the patient and to the professional appears to be crucial. For example, dementia symptoms that do not disturb family life or the family economy will be attributed to 'normal ageing', sometimes delaying the revelation of dementia until it is well advanced (Antonelli Incalzi et al. 1992).

- RCTs show that screening and intervention in older populations can reduce mortality, and length of in-patient stay, while increasing referral to all agencies and patient satisfaction. However, there have been no economic analyses of these interventions, and no estimates of their use to older people and their families.
- Risk factors for increased service use, disability and cognitive impairment are established, making a high-risk approach possible, but 'at risk' groups are very hard to identify. Targeted screening is difficult to implement because most of those with any given functional loss appear to be outside rather than inside the apparent 'at risk' groups.
- There is no consistency in approach to primary care assessment and no standardization of assessment techniques, although such consistency and standardization can be achieved where leadership is given by health authorities.
- Where assessment is done it is mostly delegated to practice nurses, who may lack appropriate training. GPs are better placed to do opportunistic screening, given both usable, brief instruments for detection of functional loss, and available services that can take remedial action.

The recent review of assessment of older people in the community commissioned by the NHS Executive (Iliffe *et al.* 1997) has shown that:

- the NHS administration is unable to identify many instances of assessment of older people, suggesting that the 75 and over checks remain a low priority for the local NHS, and that GPs as a whole are not putting great time and effort into them;
- a range of approaches to the assessment of older people in the community is in use, and several different models of good practice with very different features exist, but the range appears to be narrower than before 1990;
- where assessment is undertaken, nurses play important but usually not leading roles, allowing an emphasis on functional assessment to emerge, although strong pressures for 'medical' assessment (the detection of hidden disease) remains.

What development in the 75 and over checks should now occur, to fit into the emergent commissioning structure as both a source of information about health needs and an example of evolving good clinical practice? Two changes since 1990 are relevant here: the emergence of practice nurses as a large workforce within primary care; and the near universal computerization of general practice. Not all practice nurses have a background in community nursing work, with experience of assessing functional ability, but many do. Not all GPs make appropriate use of their IT systems to collect detailed information about their patients, but an increasing number do. In the next decade these two changes could combine to transform the approach to assessment of older people in the community from an unpopular chore of dubious value to a central component of primary care. Considerable effort and resources will be needed to achieve this change, particularly through training of practice nurses, but the commissioning process with its focus on service use, costs, needs assessment and promotion of good practice requires more than just better training and improved data capture. A number of issues need to be resolved, in particular the meaning of assessment in the new environment of primary care.

## Redefining assessment

What should 'assessment' mean for older people in primary care and how could it contribute to the commissioning process? In the debate that took place between the Royal College of General Practitioners and the Royal College of Physicians at the time of the introduction of the 75 and over checks in 1990, Ebrahim (1990) classified the uses of assessment of older people under five headings:

- Preventive screening.
- Measuring severity and monitoring progress.
- Audit of clinical work.
- Creating a database for rational resource allocation.
- Basic research requiring population studies.

At the practice level there are a number of key questions. Should the practice be reviewing its whole population of older people, and if so how? Should staff concentrate on assessments with any particular groups of older patients, and if so which? And does assessment have a deeper meaning for clinical care, adding detail to the understanding that professionals have about specific patients? These questions address population screening, case finding among those already in contact with the service and assessment of patients to aid clinical management.

In a later conference, addressing the same debate, Idris Williams reviewed the ethical issues associated with each use of the term assessment (Williams 1990), and in doing so demonstrated how problematic preventive screening was. To be ethically acceptable preventive screening of elderly people should:

- be acceptable to the people themselves;
- have a validated process with sensitive and specific screening instruments;
- identify remediable problems for which resources exist;
- avoid dangers like the medicalization of old age, over treatment and poor quality assessment;
- preserve confidentiality.

Annual screening of the kind apparently required by the current GP contract does not fulfil these criteria, and logically should not be pursued in its present form. As Idris Williams made clear in 1990 the form of assessment with the fewest ethical objections, most relevant to individuals and closest to usual practice is comprehensive case management, in which different perspectives from different disciplines are combined with the best available knowledge on the effectiveness of treatment to optimize the care of individual patients. This is essentially reactive, but a proactive dimension appears when we consider its prerequisite, case finding, which requires primary care staff to be alert to change in their patients so that they can identify problems early enough to investigate them further.

### The commissioning process

Firm recommendations on the most cost-effective method of assessing await the results of randomized trials, but the literature reviewed here favours more flexible forms of assessment than that required by the new contract for general practitioners. These are summarized in Table 4.1, reproduced from *Health Care for Older People* (Iliffe *et al.* 1998).

The issues that arise for primary care teams and commissioners from this perspective are:

- adopting opportunistic assessment rather than population screening;
- developing the data capture systems that allow opportunistic assessment and the integration of different professional contributions;
- using evidence based approaches to assessment and intervention;
- emphasizing multidisciplinary collaboration and practice;
- and systematized follow-up.

Opportunistic case finding among mobile and relatively well individuals taking few, if any, prescribed medicines seems appropriate for most of the categories of the annual assessment where the low prevalence level of most problems would make screening involving home visiting too costly. The high consultation rate of the older population make opportunistic assessment feasible especially if assessment focuses on the commonly missed problems where some effective remedial action is possible; for example, major depression, urinary incontinence and visual and hearing impairment. Analysis of consultation patterns may help identify those who are becoming disabled and in need of more detailed assessment (Hall and Channing 1990).

The very elderly probably need a more intensive approach, as will some particularly ill or disabled people of younger age. Annual assessment in the over 85 age group may be insufficient for the most disabled, but probably should be the baseline service offered to all, even if they are currently well and managing to their own satisfaction, to anticipate problems and allow forward planning of services. With these groups the use of relatively complex instruments with adequate sensibility and specificity for cognitive impairment (Folstein *et al.* 1977) and depression (Yesavage 1988; Adshead *et al.* 1992) would seem to be justified given the prevalence of mental ill health, and the need to minimize reassessment of 'false positive' cases.

The US model of assessment and reassessment by community based geriatric consultation teams may be applicable here. Such multidisciplinary assessments have been shown to increase functional ability, reduce short-term mortality and to both reduce hospital readmission rates and contacts with doctors in the community for vulnerable elderly people (Thomas *et al.* 1993). Medical effort is focused on those with problems amenable to medical or social intervention, and the quality of care can be audited by case notes review (Royal College of Physicians 1990) or analysis of significant events like hospital admission (Bennet and Walshe 1990), rather than by annual returns of crude process statistics that are currently required. Review of the process appears essential for success.

**Table 4.1**

| | Screening (of whole populations) | Case finding (among those seen) | Assessment (of those judged to be at risk or affected) |
|---|---|---|---|
| Sensory functions | No reliable brief screening test for hearing loss; Snellen chart widely used for visual loss but not reliable; screening for glaucoma not proven to be of benefit | No reliable brief screening test for hearing loss; red reflex test for cataract allows early detection and intervention improves quality of life; Intra-ocular pressure measurement in first degree relatives of glaucoma cases, hypertensives and symptomatic | Referral for audiological testing unless possible in primary care setting; opticians can play an important role in primary assessment of eye disease |
| Mobility | Lachs 5 point scale too insensitive; no validated brief instrument available; little evidence of benefit from population screening | Use of a simple activities of daily living (ADL) scale justified in patients with cardiovascular, respiratory and joint diseases, to establish baseline dataset | ADL scale useful; Barthel appropriate only for most disabled; community nurses, physiotherapists and occupational therapists most experienced at assessment |
| Mental condition | No evidence of changes in professional behaviour and gain to patient as a consequence of population screening | Age related testing for cognitive impairment justified, as is use of a brief depression scale in patients with significant disabilities, insomnia and anxiety symptoms | Clinical suspicion of change in mental state (in absence of acute confusion) justifies use of standard scales. |
| Physical condition | No evidence of gain from comprehensive investigation in whole populations | Case finding for hypertension justified | Endocrine and haematological disorders relatively common, but best identified through response to symptoms |
| Continence | No evidence to support population screening | Urine testing allows symptoms to be elicited | Self-report of symptoms seems sufficient to prompt appropriate examination |

**Table 4.1** (*cont'd*)

|  | Screening (of whole populations) | Case finding (among those seen) | Assessment (of those judged to be at risk or affected) |
|---|---|---|---|
| Social environment | No evidence to support population screening | No evidence yet to support case finding | No reliable measures suitable for primary care settings to capture the complexity of social relationships |
| Medication use | Regular review of prescribing for the whole population of older people is possible with current IT systems | Special attention to all older people receiving repeat prescriptions is appropriate | Inappropriate prescribing appears to be more of a problem than drug interactions |

The electronic medical record can be the basis for the development of a comprehensive profile of the health and functional ability of older people, and can be fed from a number of streams:

- opportunist brief assessments, by GPs;
- in-depth assessments using standardized instruments, by doctors, nurses, social workers and others;
- reviews from hospital specialists, professionals allied to medicine (physiotherapy, speech therapy and occupational therapy) and others.

At present, electronic medical records available to GPs are unlikely to allow data capture with such flexibility, and to the required level of complexity, but a quantum leap in GP software is imminent and development of decision support and database software specifically for these purposes is now needed.

**Support and training**

The NHS has not given priority to the development of assessment programmes for older people since 1990, but this can be remedied by:

- developing professional training programmes, especially but not exclusively designed for practice and community nurses, that will re-orientate practice staff towards flexible approaches to assessment of older people;
- encouraging practices to develop a 'base-up' approach to meeting need among older people, with provision of appropriate resources and documentation of development in practice annual reports;
- promoting joint working between social services, general practices and specialists in medicine for older people at practice or locality level, perhaps using 'one stop shop' models.

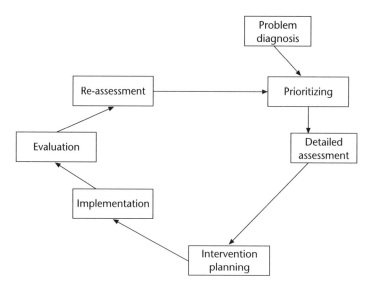

**Figure 4.1**    The community-orientated primary care development cycle

These objectives can be pursued using a community orientated primary care model of service development, of the kind initiated by Camden & Islington Health Authority in 1997–98. This was designed as a practice based approach to needs assessment with older people, utilizing an extended primary care team with public health support and a range of methods of assessing needs and exploring potential service provision (Murray and Graham 1995). A steering group representing the health authority and academic GPs and nurses from the local university department of primary care was established, with a remit to identify and recruit to the project four exemplar practices of different sizes from different parts of the borough. It guided a small academic support group to assist practices to develop new services, without being prescriptive. The steering group disbursed pump-priming funds across the four practices in response to any proposal for a new service that was grounded in evidence and sustainable within existing practice resources after the end of the project, and the academic team linked the innovative practices with other agencies in the locality that provided services for older people.

The model of innovation used in the four practices was derived from the King's Fund's work on community oriented primary care (Freeman *et al.* 1997), and takes the form of a cyclic process, as shown in Figure 4.1.

This cycle allows a continuous process by which primary care is provided to a defined community on the basis of its assessed health needs by the planned integration of public health and primary care practice (King's Fund 1994).

Practices were recruited to the project on the agreement that they would discuss their plans for service development with the academic support group and reach consensus about needs, plans, costs and implementation before initiating new services. The method of beginning the diagnosis and prioritization stage was left to practices to determine, and academic support staff encouraged frequent contact by telephone, letter, face-to-face informal meeting and formal group meetings.

Practice staff were encouraged to acknowledge that:

- a broad interpretation of health needs might result in service developments outside the traditional medical range (Frankel 1991);
- different conceptualizations of need might have different implications for priority setting (Bradshaw 1972);
- a comprehensive approach to the whole older population (however defined) could compromise equity by obscuring the needs of minorities (Hopton and Dlugolecka 1995);
- a range of methods of assessing needs might be necessary (Robinson and Elkan 1996).

Potential innovations were taken by the practices to a full steering committee meeting when they reached the stage where detailed costing was appropriate. Active support was offered at the implementation stage, once the practice innovation had achieved ratification, and an evaluation framework was established using elements common to all practices as well as methods appropriate to each innovation.

The four exemplar practices were able to develop and implement innovative, locally appropriate primary care services for older people, using limited short-term funding, when supported in a non-directive way by an academic department familiar with the nature and problems of general practice and steered by a multi-professional management group including public health professionals from the health authority. Concerns that minority groups in the population will be neglected if unskilled primary care teams undertake public health functions (Pollock and Majeed 1995) do not appear to be substantiated in the exemplar practices, which have not only focused on the needs of older people, but on particularly disadvantaged groups within this population: those with chronic diseases; those less supported by services; those with un-met needs; and those with low incomes and limited resources.

The process of community orientated primary care can be stimulated within a framework of needs assessment and financial sustainability, with active involvement by GPs, who come to take leading roles in the process of change. The rate of innovation may be determined, at least in part, by the size of the group practice and the internal culture of decision making and dissemination. Issues of the impact of innovative care on the health of older people and the long-term sustainability of such innovations remain unclear, but the potential of this 'bottom up' approach appears considerable.

## Conclusion

The failure of the current GP contract to make clear the purpose of annual assessment of the elderly hinders the development of effective, acceptable and appropriate assessment systems. If prevention of a significant disability like loss of mobility becomes possible then mass screening may be justified, but only if intervention of proven benefit can be offered (Hart *et al.* 1990). If, however, improved management of medical and social problems is the main aim then assessment should be focused on the very elderly, whose need is likely to be greater. At the present time the latter seems more appropriate than the former, and it would be sensible to rewrite the GP contract to redefine elderly assessment in this way.

The relationship of disability to age suggests that the contractual obligation to assess elderly patients should be more flexible, with more home visiting of the very elderly and less in the younger elderly. The use of a two-stage process as advocated by Freer (1990), Lachs *et al.* (1990) and Dickinson and Young (1990) with more frequent assessment at later ages may be more appropriate for elderly people, and closer to the problem solving tradition of general practice, than a single assessment package applied to the 75 and over population as if it were homogeneous. Ideally these hypotheses should be tested in randomized controlled trials of focused interventions aimed at reducing the impact of incontinence, reducing vision and hearing impairment, increasing functional ability and treating depression, probably in younger age groups. In the meantime GPs can usefully interpret their contractual obligation to offer assessments to elderly people in creative ways, enabling them to develop appropriate, patient centred and cost effective approaches to case finding and case management.

If commissioning is to succeed and be beneficial to the older population, major changes in both primary care policy and practice will be needed. Such changes are unlikely to be practical in the short timescales favoured by politicians, and are also unlikely to be promoted by having money thrown at them. A long-term strategy for, and commitment to, change are needed; with investment, education, experimentation and development as the key components. This approach may be beyond the capacity of any government, but it is possible for primary care workers and their professional bodies to develop and implement such an agenda. Its essence could be a shift in focus towards systematic case management of older individuals coupled to selective and targeted reviews of some subgroups, particularly the very old. Further development of teamwork will be central to this shift, which will be facilitated by a quantum leap in the functionality of the electronic medical record, as well as in its shared use by different disciplines. The commissioning process requires all these changes to occur if it is to work; we should not miss the opportunities it offers.

### References

Adshead, F., Cody, D. and Pitt, B. (1992) BASDEC: a novel screening instrument for depression in elderly medical inpatients, *British Medical Journal*, 305: 97.

Anderson, W.F. and Cowan, J.R. (1955) A consultative health centre for older people, *Lancet*, 2: 239–40.

Antonelli Incalzi, R., Marra, C., Gemma, A., Capparella, O. and Carbonin, P.U. (1992) Unrecognised dementia: sociodemographic correlates, *Aging* (Milano), 4: 327–32.

Arber, S. (1996) Is living longer a cause for celebration? *Health Service Journal*, 106(5512): 28–31.

Audit Commission (1996) *What the Doctor Ordered: A Study of GP Fund-holding in England & Wales.* London: HMSO.

Baines, D. and Couper, N. (1998) The cultivated commissioner, *Health Service Journal*, 108(5602): 26–7.

Bennet, J. and Walshe, K. (1990) Occurrence screening as a method of audit, *British Medical Journal*, 300: 1248–51.

Bernabei, R., Landi, F., Gambasi, G., *et al.* (1998) Randomized trial of impact of model of integrated care and case management for older people living in the community, *British Medical Journal*, 316: 1348–51.

Bradshaw, J.A. (1972) Taxonomy of social need, in G. Mclachlan (ed.) *Problems and Progress in Medical Care.* Oxford: Oxford University Press.

Brown, K., Williams, E. and Groom, L. (1992) Health checks on patients 75 years and over in Nottinghamshire after the new GP contract, *British Medical Journal*, 305: 619–21.

Department of Health (DoH) (1990) *A New Contract for General Practice.* London: HMSO.

Department of Health (DoH) (1991) *The Health of the Nation.* London: HMSO.

Dickinson, E.J. and Young, A. (1990) Framework for medical assessment of functional performance, *Lancet*, 335: 778–9.

Ebrahim, S. (1990) *Purposes of Assessment in Elderly People.* Presentation to the Royal Conference of Physicians workshop on assessment, March.

Ebrahim, S., Hedley, R. and Sheldon, M. (1984) Low levels of ill health among elderly non-consulters in general practice, *British Medical Journal*, 289: 1273–5.

Folstein, M.F., Folstein, S.E. and McHugh, P.R. (1977) The Mini-Mental State – a practical method for grading the cognitive state of patients for the clinician, *Journal of Psychiatric Research*, 12: 189–98.

Frankel, S. (1991) Health needs, health care requirements and the myth of infinite demand, *Lancet*, 337: 1588–90.

Freeman, R., Gillam, S., Shearin, C. and Pratt, J. (1997) *Community Development and Involvement in Primary Care.* London: King's Fund.

Freer, C.B. (1987) Detecting hidden needs in the elderly: screening or case finding, in R.C. Taylor and E.G. Buckley (eds) *Preventive Care of the Elderly. Occasional Paper 35.* London: Royal College of General Practitioners.

Freer, C.B. (1990) Screening the elderly, *British Medical Journal*, 300: 1447–8.

Fries, J.F. (1980) Ageing, natural death and the compression of morbidity, *New England Journal of Medicine*, 303: 130–5.

Hall, R.P.G. and Channing, D.M. (1990) Age, pattern of consultation and functional disability in elderly patients in one general practice, *British Medical Journal*, 301: 424–8.

Harris, A. (1992) Health checks for the over-75s; the doubt persists, *British Medical Journal*, 305: 599–600.

Hart, D., Bowling, A., Ellis, M. and Silman, A. (1990) Locomotor disability in very elderly people: value of a programme for screening and provision of aids for daily living, *British Medical Journal*, 301: 216–20.

Hopton, J.L. and Dlugolecka, M. (1995) Patients' perceptions of need for primary health care services: useful for priority setting? *British Medical Journal*, 310: 1237–40.

Iliffe, S. and Drennan, V. (forthcoming) *Primary Care for Older People.* Oxford: Oxford University Press.

Iliffe, S., Gallivan, S., Haines, A.P. *et al.* (1991a) Assessment of elderly people in general practice: 1, social circumstances and mental state, *British Journal of General Practice*, 41: 9–12.

Iliffe, S., Gallivan, S., Haines, A.P. *et al.* (1991b) Assessment of elderly people in general practice: 2, functional abilities and medical problems, *British Journal of General Practice*, 41: 13–15.

Iliffe, S., Haines, A., Gallivan, S. *et al.* (1992) Are the elderly alone an at risk group? *British Medical Journal*, 305: 1001–4.

Iliffe, S., Gould, M.M. and Wallace, P. (1997) *The 75 and Over Assessments in General Practice: Report to the NHS Executive.* London: Department of Primary Care & Population Sciences, UCL & Royal Free Hospital Medical Schools.

Iliffe, S., Gould, M.M. and Patterson, L. (1998) *Health Care for Older People.* London: BMJ Books.

Jarman, B. (1983) Identification of underprivileged areas, *British Medical Journal*, 286: 1785–9.

Jarvis, C., Hancock, R., Askham, J. and Tinker, A. (1996) *Getting Around after 60: A Profile of Britain's Older Population.* London: HMSO.

Jecker, N.S. and Scheiderman, L.J. (1992) Futility and rationing, *American Journal of Medicine*, 92: 191.

Jones, I.R. and Higgs, P.F.D. (1992) Health economists and health care provision for the elderly: implicit assumptions and unstated conclusions, in K. Morgan (ed.) *Gerontology: Responding to an Ageing Society.* London: Jessica Kingsley.

King's Fund (1994) *Community Oriented Primary Care: A Resource for Developers.* London: King's Fund.

Kline, D.W., Kline, T.J.B. and Fozard, J.L. (1992) Vision, ageing and driving: the problems of older drivers, *Journal of Gerontology*, 47: 27–34.

Lachs, M.S., Feinstein, A.R., Cooney, L.M. *et al.* (1990) A simple procedure for geriatric screening for functional disability in elderly patients, *Annals of Internal Medicine*, 112(9): 699–706.

Manton, K.G., Stalland, E. and Corder, L. (1995) Changes in morbidity and chronic disability in the US elderly population; evidence from the 1982, 1984 and 1989 national long-term care survey, *Journal of Gerontology*, 50B: S104–204.

Medical Research Council (1994) *The Health of the UK's Elderly Population.* London: Medical Research Council.

Murray, S.A. and Graham, L.J. (1995) Practice based needs assessment: use of four methods in a small neighbourhood, *British Medical Journal*, 310: 1443–8.

Pathy, M.S., Bayer, A., Harding, K. and Dibble, A. (1992) Randomised trial of case finding and surveillance of elderly people at home, *Lancet*, 340: 890–3.

Pollock, A. and Majeed, F.A. (1995) Community oriented primary care, *British Medical Journal*, 310: 481–2.

Reidy, A., Minassian, D.C., Vafadis, G. *et al.* (1998) Prevalence of serious eye disease and visual impairment in a north London population: population based, cross sectional study, *British Medical Journal*, 316: 1643–6.

Robine, J.M. and Ritchie, K. (1991) Healthy life expectancy: an evaluation of global indicators of change in population health, *British Medical Journal*, 302: 457–60.

Robinson, J. and Elkan, J. (1996) *Health Needs Assessment: Theory and Practice.* London: Churchill Livingstone.

Royal College of General Practitioners (1990) *Care of Old People: A Framework for Progress.* London: Royal College of General Practitioners.

Royal College of Physicians (1990) *Medical Audit (1990) – A First Report: What, Why and How?* London: Royal College of Physicians.

Secretariat for Future Studies (1984) *Time to Care.* Oxford: Pergamon Press.

Stuck, A.E., Siu, A.L., Wieland, G.D., Adams, J. and Rubenstein, L.Z. (1993) Comprehensive geriatric assessment: a meta-analysis of controlled trials, *Lancet*, 342: 1032–6.

Stuck, A.E., Aronow, H.U., Steiner, A. *et al.* (1995) A trial of annual in-home comprehensive geriatric assessment for elderly people living in the community, *New England Journal of Medicine*, 333: 1184–9.

Tallis, R. (1992) Rehabilitation of the elderly in the 21st century, *Journal of the Royal College of Physicians*, 26(4): 413–22.

Taylor, R.C. and Buckley, E.G. (eds) (1987) *Preventive Care of the Elderly, Occasional Paper 35*. London: Royal College of General Practitioners.

Thomas, D.R., Braham, R. and Haywood, B.P. (1993) Inpatient community-based geriatric assessment reduces subsequent morbidity, *Journal of American Geriatric Society*, 41: 101–4.

Timaeus, I. (1986) Family households of the elderly population; prospects for those approaching old age, *Ageing & Society*, 6: 27–36.

Tulloch, A.J. and Moore, V.L. (1979) A randomised controlled trial of geriatric screening and surveillance in general practice, *Journal of Royal College of General Practitioners*, 29: 733–42.

Vetter, N.J., Lewis, P.A. and Llewellyn, L. (1993) Is there a right age for case finding in elderly people?, *Age & Ageing*, 22: 121–4.

Waller, J.A. (1991) Health status and motor vehicle crashes, *New England Journal of Medicine*, 324: 54–5.

Warnes, A.M. (1989) Elderly people in Great Britain: variable projections and characteristics, *Care of the Elderly*, 1(1): 7–10.

Wilkinson, J.R. and Murray, S.C. (1998) Assessment in primary care: practical issues and possible approaches, *British Medical Journal*, 316: 1524–8.

Williams, E.S. and Scott, C.M. (1994) Health needs vary among elderly people, *British Medical Journal*, 309: 198.

Williams, I. (1974) A follow up of geriatric patients after sociomedical assessment, *Journal of Royal College of General Practitioners*, 24: 341–6.

Williams, I. (1990) *Assessment – ethical considerations*. Presentation to the RCGP Conference on Assessment of the Elderly, November.

Williamson, J., Stokoe, I.H., Gray, S. and Fisher, M. (1964) Old people at home: their unreported needs, *Lancet*, 1: 1117–20.

Yesavage, J.A. (1988) The geriatric depression scale, *Psychopharmacology Bulletin*, 24: 709–10.

# 5 Disability: from medical needs to social rights

Geoffrey Mercer and
Colin Barnes

## Introduction

The Royal College of Physicians (RCP) report Physical Disability in 1986 and Beyond acknowledged 'professional and public concern about the care given to disabled people' (Royal College of Physicians 1986: 162). Too many were denied the 'advice, equipment, adaptations and services' that could make a significant difference to the quality of their lives. The report recommended increased medical involvement and resources, including the establishment of a Medical Disability Service, with a 'vital co-ordinating and supportive function' identified for the GP (Royal College of Physicians 1986: 191).

Also in the 1980s, a very different diagnosis of disability was being advanced by a growing number of disabled people. This critique was consolidated into a 'social model of disability' (M. Oliver 1990, 1996). It highlighted the excessive medicalization of service provision and lack of support for disabled people, with claims that the 'medical model of care' was inappropriate for most disabled people (Fielder 1988). Where the medical approach viewed disability in terms of individual functional limitations, the social model directed its attention to the 'disabling' social barriers and attitudes experienced by people with accredited impairments. This suggested that the remedy for disability depended on a rethink of health and social support services and, most crucially, on broader social and policy changes.

This chapter will explore key issues for primary care raised by these debates. The discussion begins by outlining the conventional medical perspective, and the claims of disability theorists who adopt a social model approach. It then concentrates on a review of disabled people's experiences of disabling barriers and stereotypes in the primary care context. It is argued that recent proposals for a 'patient centred' and 'primary care led' NHS do not address demands for forms of service support that recognize disabled people's particular circumstances and priorities.

## The medical (or individual) model of disability

Through the twentieth century, medical knowledge and treatment have dominated approaches to disability. In the past two decades, centre stage has been occupied by the World Health Organization's (1980) *International Classification of impairments, Disabilities and Handicaps* (ICIDH). It was designed to supplement the long-established international classification of diseases (for example, World Health Organization 1976) by focusing on the consequences of disease.

The ICIDH was widely interpreted as confirming a shift in medical thinking about disability and its management. It identified 'impairment', as 'any loss or abnormality of psychological, physiological, or anatomical structure of function' (World Health Organization 1980: 27), and 'disability', as 'any restriction or lack (resulting from an impairment) of ability to perform an activity in the manner or within the range considered normal for a human being' (p. 28). More ambitiously, 'handicap' was defined as: 'a disadvantage for a given individual, resulting from an impairment or a disability, that limits or prevents the fulfilment of a role that is normal (depending on age, sex, and social and cultural factors) for that individual' (WHO 1980: 29). For example, a skeletal impairment can produce a 'disability' or difficulty in walking. However, the level and character of 'handicap', or social disadvantage associated with any loss of physical independence, is mediated, to a degree, by social and cultural circumstances.

In Britain, the ICIDH approach is demonstrated in the Office of Population Censuses and Surveys (OPCS) studies of disability in the 1980s. These equated disability with an individual's functional limitations with respect to bathing, bladder and bowel control, dressing, drinking, eating, toileting and walking (Martin *et al.* 1988). This interpretation is complemented by a battery of curative, rehabilitation and preventive measures offered by an increasing range of allied health professionals. Thus, in the case of deafness, interventions include cochlea implant surgery, counselling, occupational therapy, and the provision of hearing aids (Goodwill *et al.* 1997).

The medicalized approach to disability extends into a wider professional influence on how disabled people are thought to experience impairment. This is illustrated by the general embrace of a psychological focus on adjustment and coping. It has been characterized by a 'grieving' sequence of reactions to 'losses' as diverse as blindness and surgical amputation of body parts (Fitzgerald and Parkes 1998). What is typically outlined is a series of four stages of emotional responses exhibited by people coming to terms with their 'complex of losses'. The immediate sense of *shock* and horror is followed by *denial* that the effects are permanent, leading to *anger* either at others or themselves, and finally to *depression* and lowered self-esteem. The last is regarded as a necessary preliminary to coming to terms with their diminished circumstances. Hence, the presumption of a fifth stage, termed 'acceptance' or 'adjustment', which may not be reached until one or two years later. Equally significant, those who stray from this prescribed script – by not being depressed and/or in a state of denial – run the risk of being pathologized (Oliver 1995).

The organizing feature of the conventional approach is its view of 'disability' as an individual health problem or 'personal tragedy', with 'solutions' to disabled people's functional limitations sought through medical and allied health professional measures.

### Enter the social model of disability

The social model of disability is based on a very different distinction between 'impairment' and 'disability'. While the definition of impairment stays close to the ICIDH formulation, it rejects the view that disability is an individual health or medical issue. This revision was first articulated by the Union of the Physically Impaired against Segregation (UPIAS) (1976: 14). It defined 'disability' as: 'the disadvantage or restriction of activity caused by a contemporary social organisation which takes no or little account of people who have . . . impairments and thus excludes them from participation in the mainstream of social activities' (ibid.: 14).

From this standpoint, disability theorists underline three main criticisms of the individual, medicalized approach. Firstly, 'it is society which disables physically impaired people' (UPIAS 1976: 14). The 'causal' link in the ICIDH between impairment and disability/handicap is rejected in favour of an emphasis on material and social barriers as the bases for the social exclusion of people with accredited impairments: 'it is not the inability to walk which disables someone but the steps into the building' (Morris 1991: 10). These barriers are created and sustained by the activities of architects, planners, social workers, teachers, doctors and others (Barnes 1991; Barton and Oliver 1997).

Disability is thus identified as a social status, and the outcome of interaction between an impairment and the social responses to it. While not being able to see rates as a visual impairment, the lack of information in Braille or on tape comprises a disability (or social barrier) in so far as those with such impairments are thereby excluded from such social activity. Conversely, wheelchair users are 'enabled' by an adapted car, an accessible built environment and personal assistance. Hence removing the social barriers overturns the disability (although the impairment remains).

> A Disabled Person is an individual in their own right, placed in a disabling situation, brought about by environmental, economic and social barriers that the person, because of their impairment(s), cannot overcome in the same way as other citizens. These barriers are all too often reinforced by the marginalizing attitudes of society. It is up to society to eliminate, reduce or compensate for these barriers in order to enable each individual to enjoy full citizenship, respecting the rights and duties of each individual.
>
> (Disabled People's International 1994)

Secondly, the emphasis on 'normality' as a fixed or objectively determined state is rejected on the grounds that what is 'normal', or the 'normal' way of performing daily activities, is socially and culturally defined. The social model criticizes the use of medical knowledge to validate bodily or intellectual 'difference' as 'abnormal' or 'inferior' (Abberley 1987). What is perceived as 'difference' and the level and character of disability vary across impairments and social groups. Moreover, disability interacts with other forms of social discrimination in complex ways. Thus, disabled women may feel particularly oppressed because they do not conform to prevailing stereotypes about the female role and femininity. Similarly, the contemporary cultural emphasis on 'healthy minds and healthy bodies' has potential negative consequences for disabled people (Barnes and Mercer 1996).

To argue that disability is a social construction is not to deny that impairment is sometimes a source of illness, physical pain and intellectual discomfort (Morris 1991). Similarly, not all functional limitations can be explained in terms of social barriers: for example, visual impairment inhibits the ability to recognize other people or pick up non-verbal cues (French 1993). This remains a contentious issue among disability theorists, but what the social model attempts to separate out are the impairment and illness related concerns that require medical treatment from social constraints on basic citizenship rights, which are most appropriately the targets for collective action.

Thirdly, the medical approach concentrates on a set of discrete functional limitations requiring technical intervention and individual adjustment, with too little weight given to the meaning of such activities or their social context to the individual disabled person. It both dehumanizes the disabled person and depoliticizes disability (G. Williams 1996). Thus, medicalization has spawned a veritable 'disability business' (Albrecht 1992), involving many different health and social care professionals, pursuing in part their own self-interest, which: 'designates a social problem to be addressed, establishes a set of needs, stimulates a demand, defines who is eligible for services, and often dictates the type of goods and services appropriate for persons with disabilities' (ibid.: 67). This professional 'take-over' of disabled people's lives is vividly documented in Robert Scott's *The Making of Blind Men* (1969). Professional agencies transmit the disabled identity of a 'blind person', through their control of diagnosis, treatment and rehabilitation. They determine what is 'best' for disabled people, but in so doing often confirm negative stereotypes about their 'capabilities', and also reinforce their passivity and dependency on others.

A central illustration of this professional management of disabled people is demonstrated in the continuing influence of psychological theories and interventions. Despite their lack of empirical confirmation (Wortman and Silver 1989), psychological theories of 'grieving' for the 'loss' that impairment is presumed to represent are the basis for individual adjustment or coping strategies widely used in rehabilitation counselling. These emulate the fascination of social researchers with the defensive manoeuvrings of those with the 'stigma' of bodily difference or a 'spoiled identity', without considering the wider social and economic consequences, or the contrasting cultural meanings attached to impairment (Bury 1997).

In contrast, advocates of the social model emphasize the importance of constructing a positive self-identity in the midst of others' denials of their 'normality', which has led to their 'low self-esteem, low self-confidence and a feeling of worthlessness' (Oliver 1995: 275). However, any counselling support should be set within a social barriers perspective rather than a functional limitations one (McKenzie 1992) so that it is properly sensitive to the individual's experience of disability: 'Our dissatisfaction with our lives is not a personality defect but a sane response to the oppression which we experience' (Morris 1991: 9). The possibility that it is quite rational to deny one's impairment, in a world that regards disabled people as 'lesser' human beings, has been given too little credence by professionals (French 1993).

In summary, the objectives of the social model comprise barrier removal at the 'personal level (to enable the individual to set their own goals) and at the social level (where public facilities are available to disabled and non-disabled people alike)' (Finkelstein 1993: 41). Disability theory has stimulated calls to replace the hierarchical encounter dominated by health professionals, so that disabled people make a greater contribution to the assessment of their needs and priorities for service support. It has supplied a significant boost to a more positive disabled identity, and for 'empowering' support services.

### Disabled people's experiences of primary care

The development of a social model approach presents a broad based challenge to those concerned with the organization and delivery of primary care. The specific issues raised here span disabling stereotypes within professional–patient encounters, the gatekeeper role of GPs, and moves towards a 'patient-centred' NHS. The problems of access to buildings where disabled people consult primary care practitioners are not explored. What evidence is available suggests similar access questions in GP surgeries and health centres to other buildings. Criticism comes predominantly from those people with mobility impairments who have difficulty in negotiating the steps and stairs, or who are penalized in obtaining and exchanging information because no allowance is made for their visual, hearing or communication impairments (Begum 1996a).

*Disabling barriers*

The negative stereotypes of disabled people held by health and social welfare professionals have been widely reported (Lonsdale 1990). Services may be delivered in ways that 'stigmatize' rather than 'enable' the person with the impairment. In her survey of disabled women, Nasa Begum (1996a, 1996b) argues that the individual's impairment too easily dominates the exchange, particularly if a relatively 'rare' condition, where it becomes the subject of considerable, but unwelcome, 'professional' interest. However, exaggerated 'praise' may be perceived as condescending: 'I have been viewed as rather a freak. I was made to feel as if I was irresponsible and a cause for concern or that I was wonderful and an inspiration. I did not welcome either label' (Begum 1996a: 188–9).

It is particularly demeaning if practitioners openly express lay prejudices about the 'stigma' attached to some conditions, as when it was suggested to one patient that she should obtain her incontinence supplies 'out of town', to 'avoid bringing shame' on to the family (Begum 1996a: 182). More often, attitudes and practices are less overtly hostile, but are nevertheless based on widely held assumptions about disabled people's 'incapacities' and 'dependency'. In a recent survey organized by Scope of over 1,500 disabled people, a significant minority (29 per cent) felt that doctors did not really listen to them, or when with another person talked to their 'companion': 'The greatest problem I have is getting doctors to take me seriously' (Lamb and Layzell 1994: 33). The respondents agreed strongly that 'people jump to conclusions about what I can and can't do without establishing the facts'. Lack of respect is hurtful, but patronizing and pitying attitudes are also resented (ibid.: 8).

It is a sign of the strength of the common sense view that disabled people are ill, that they are presumed to be routinely obsessed with medical matters. While some impairments are indeed associated with greater levels of sickness, most disabled people, such as those with a visual or hearing impairment, enjoy the same health status as 'non-disabled' people. Indeed, according to the Scope survey of disabled people, health care was well down their list of priorities (Lamb and Layzell 1994). When asked to name their three most pressing concerns, respondents pinpointed shortfalls in social support, resources and relationships: 'Don't have as active a social life as I would like' (50 per cent), 'Not having enough money to make ends meet' (39 per cent), 'Having difficulty finding out about the services which would benefit me' (28 per cent), with only 15 per cent of the sample specifying, 'Have difficulty getting the medical treatment I need' (ibid.: 16).

Nevertheless, many disabled people go to great lengths to not 'give in' to illness exactly because they feel this will confirm the beliefs of 'non-disabled' people (Begum 1996b). Their concerns are reinforced when practitioners do not differentiate the presenting symptoms from their impairment. Stereotypes of disabled people further influence the character of the professional–patient encounter. Information exchange may be inhibited because of low expectations of what a disabled patient is thought capable of understanding, or capable of conveying. Conversely, negative attitudes can trigger patient resistance to professional advice (French 1994). They may also translate into difficulties in access, or registering with a GP, because the disabled person is perceived as more demanding in terms of time and resources, or fits the category of the 'difficult patient' (Cavet 1998). Thus, the health needs of people with learning difficulties, for example, are accorded a low priority (Department of Health 1998).

A particularly instructive analysis of disabling barriers is provided in Carol Thomas's (1997) study of the perceived health risks surrounding motherhood in a group of disabled women. Three main themes emerged: 'first, engagement with the "risk" discourse; second, the pressure felt by disabled women to demonstrate that they are, or could be, "good enough mothers"; and third, the experience of receiving "help" from health and social care workers' (ibid.: 624).

'Taking risks' is an issue for all prospective mothers, but if the woman already has an impairment this raises concerns that her condition might be passed on, or her health affected, or that medical intervention might threaten the foetus. Equally, the 'cost' to the woman of coming off medication versus the potential harm to the foetus must be weighed very carefully. And if the outcome is a child born with an hereditary condition, this often generates strong feelings of guilt.

Yet what underpins this consideration of risks is the social presumption 'about the quality of life and intrinsic value of children and adults with impairments' (Thomas 1997: 632). It is that their lives are 'not worth living'. 'Abnormality' is associated with greater ill health and emotional trauma, and greater demands generally on the family. It is very difficult for a disabled woman to reject this social pressure as 'disabling' and have the child (Morris 1991). However, this is becoming a more contested area replete with very difficult moral issues for health professionals and lay public alike. A growing number of disabled people and their organizations are campaigning against abortion of a 'disabled foetus'. A similar opposition is being advanced to the growth of genetic counselling and 'normalizing' technologies. Certainly many disabled women resent the lack of information or support from primary care staff. 'GP refused to refer me to gynaecologist when I wanted to marry. Refused to prescribe the pill – advised me to obtain sterilisation privately – which I did – reluctantly' (Begum 1996a: 189).

A second theme is the evaluation of the disabled woman's capacity as a mother. The existence of external surveillance and regulation is something to which disabled women, along with other 'socially deviant' groups, are particularly vulnerable. The fear is that health and social welfare professionals might think them not 'up to the job'. Such labelling is hurtful, and at worst, can result in the removal of their child. Disabled women feel pressured to 'present' themselves as well able to 'cope', perhaps at considerable emotional and physical cost. It may also inhibit them from seeking advice or support.

Third, the effectiveness of the 'help' or 'support services' provided to disabled women is questioned. Although professional intervention is usually seen as well motivated, it sometimes demonstrates ignorance of the woman's impairment, or fails to draw on her personal experience as a disabled person. It is routinely presumed that the practitioner knows what is best for the patient. This can prove counterproductive, because where help is 'unwanted but forced upon disabled mothers, or is inappropriate in its form, it can be experienced as . . . intrusive and disempowering' (Thomas 1997: 639–40).

Over all, disabled people identify a range of concerns where services can be characterized as inappropriate and de-humanizing. This accords with a tendency to define the patient as the problem and the professional as the solution (Barton and Oliver 1997). In the specific case of occupational therapy, which formally claims to have embraced a social model approach, Paul Abberely (1995) demonstrates how its practitioners continue to act as both judge and jury of service provision. Their emphasis on an holistic and voluntaristic approach stresses individual responsibility for continuing functional limitations. Professional ideology itself then becomes a disabling barrier, as 'failures' are attributed to patient shortcomings or the lack of resources.

*GPs as gatekeepers*

The 'gatekeeping' role of GPs with respect to disabled people comprises their validation of claims to a wide range of non-medical resources, activities and benefits, plus information on service provision. It offers a highly visible demonstration of disabled people's dependency on professionals, and is an important constraint on challenging the perception of 'disability' as an individual health problem.

Most significantly, approval from a medical practitioner is required before disabled people can access selected aids and adaptations, jobs, leisure facilities, holidays and further education. Disabled people have widely criticized this requirement for professional control over such a broad expanse of their lives, while some may be put off because of the charge for obtaining a GP's signature. Lamb and Layzell (1994) report that 66 per cent of their sample found the welfare benefit tests humiliating and designed to confirm their incapacity. Moreover, appeals are discouraged because the GP acts as the first and often final port of call in determining 'incapacity' entitlement.

> I find difficult the extent to which my doctor is given control over my life. In the last year she has had to confirm that I can travel abroad, need the adaptations in my house, can have alcoholic drinks and give a full medical for a second mortgage . . . I have to pay for these services. She did not design the system and would like it to be different, nevertheless it does affect our relationship.
>
> (Begum 1996b: 164)

Those working in primary care are also regarded as one of the key sources of information on entitlement to services and other support. Yet Lamb and Layzell (1994) report that inadequate advice was a concern for 45 per cent of the respondents. The sources currently used showed friends on top (45 per cent), followed by charities/voluntary organizations (38 per cent), social service departments (37 per cent), and GPs (36 per cent), well ahead of Citizens' Advice Bureaux (16 per cent). Informal 'carers' experienced similar problems in accessing information, and relied on much the same sources (Lamb and Layzell 1995).

Some disabled people report feeling let down by the lack of information and advice, with older people expressing dismay at the reluctance of health personnel to prepare them for the relationship between ageing and impairment, or make them aware of the availability of support services and their eligibility for welfare benefits (Zarb and Oliver 1993). Research suggests that GPs demonstrate considerable variation in their familiarity with, or interest in advising on, welfare benefits and support to which they can refer clients, or the issues associated with living with an impairment and of disabling social barriers generally (Begum 1996b). Their lack of knowledge about services organized by disabled people's groups is particularly marked. However, health practitioners are suspicious of some user groups, either because they are deemed too 'political', or not sufficiently under medical/professional control (Gething and Fethney 1997). Professionals must also set disabled people's needs against existing demands and resource constraints.

*Patient centred practice?*

In the past decade, the education and training of medical and other health professionals has encouraged a more 'patient centred' philosophy (Royal College of General Practitioners 1995). The early initiatives were guided by concerns for better patient management and compliance with prescribed treatment regimens. Subsequently, the emphasis shifted to a 'listening and learning' approach, bolstered by an attempt to understand the patient's presenting symptoms by locating them within a broader backcloth of individual and social circumstances. Most recently, NHS reforms in the 1990s have promoted a more overt form of consumerism in which patient evaluation of service provision has become a key element (Rogers and Popay 1996).

In practice, primary care is judged against a diverse range of criteria, that vary across different contexts. Most disabled people follow the majority of the population in valuing practitioners with good interpersonal and communicative skills, and prefer accessible and conveniently situated premises (Lewis 1994). Research also suggests a number of areas of tension in the practitioner–patient encounter. There are regular complaints that people receive too little information on their impairment, what offers the most effective and appropriate treatment, and their preferred support services (Bury 1997). The way in which disclosure of impairment is handled illustrates a clash between the patient's demand for information and professional judgement (Leonard 1994). There has been criticism of the general rigidity and limited range of rehabilitation programmes (Johnson 1993; Nolan and Nolan 1998). Another widely expressed view is that not enough significance is attached to helping disabled people explore and express their feelings, in the context of disability (Morris 1989; Carpenter 1994). As a result, many disabled people are emotionally overwhelmed, and socially isolated in what is often an unsupportive community (Oliver *et al.* 1988). This links with a general argument that there is too little professional awareness of the social impact of treatment regimes, or support for a patient's active response to disabling attitudes and practices (Barnes and Mercer 1996).

A 'patient centred' health service should recognize and respect experiential lay knowledge and priorities, even though this may conflict with professionally defined 'clinical need' (B. Williams 1998). Yet professionals are not generally committed to involving disabled people in the determination of service needs and priorities. This presents difficulties for many practitioners, whether it is the notion of sharing 'expertise' with disabled patients, recognizing the accumulated experience of those with an impairment, or allowing a lay ranking of clinical priorities (Lonsdale 1990; B. Williams 1998). Nevertheless, some disabled patients complain that GPs are not sufficiently knowledgeable about their impairment (Oliver *et al.* 1988; Jessop 1996). This is aggravated where disabled people argue for service support that generates greater autonomy rather than health 'care', or advance contrary opinions on their condition or treatment. Nasa Begum reports a complaint from a woman with learning difficulties: 'I had to stand up and advocate my ability to participate in student holidays, jobs and travel abroad. My GP was going to take my rights away from me because of his assumptions of people with learning difficulties' (1996a: 178). This risks raising professional hackles, but for the individual striving to establish greater feelings of self-worth, such 'assertiveness' may be very important.

Conversely, where the GP adopts an enabling role, this is much appreciated: 'On the positive side he has been interested in my purchase of a powered wheelchair seeing it (rightly) as an extension of my freedom and independence rather than as a symbol of having given up (the reaction of some of my friends)' (Begum 1996b: 171). A similar positive response attaches to professional commitment to joint working: 'He has never hesitated to ask my opinions or feelings with regard to the type of treatment or drugs (and their effects) with which he has attempted to treat my problems . . . We usually work as a team to try and find the best alternatives' (Begum 1996a: 184).

Disabled patients are not all anticipating a 'magic bullet' cure, but are looking to primary care practitioners for greater help in enhancing the quality of their lives: 'I'm not asking for cure . . . I'm asking for support in managing my situation. This might mean acknowledging it's tough, helping me access resources, helping me plan health management and learn relevant skills' (Begum 1996a: 191). Those with an impairment since birth or early childhood, who have accumulated often considerable expertise in their condition, are more likely to accentuate their 'abilities' rather than 'limitations'. As a consequence, they are likely to express more disenchantment with the medical approach, and report lower levels of satisfaction with health practitioners, compared to those who acquired an impairment later in life. More generally, although most disabled patients commend practitioners' responses to their health needs, there is rather less appreciation of the interest displayed in generating wider service support (Begum 1996a). Indeed, professional groups in primary care have been noticeably slower than some others, such as social workers, to recognize the importance of disability equality training and innovative equal opportunities policies; both to change current professional practice and to encourage the recruitment and retention of more disabled health and welfare professionals (French 1994, 1996).

This brief overview of the experiences of disabled people in primary care settings illustrates several dimensions of the 'disabling barriers and attitudes' approach to disability. It is not suggested that all disabled people are speaking with the same critical voice, or articulate a social barriers approach, but there is abundant research evidence that an increasing number of disabled people are questioning inappropriate direction of their lives; for example, in the growing demand for self-directed 'care' or personal assistance packages.

## Organizing services for disabled people

The rhetoric of primary care policy proposals over the past decade has shifted towards recognition of some of the concerns expressed by disabled people, without embracing a social model agenda. Yet whatever the intentions of the NHS and Community Care Act 1990, primary care has remained largely medicalized. Moreover, the division of responsibilities between the primary and secondary services, as well as between health and other social support sectors remains a source of bewilderment. The lack of co-ordination noted in the 1980s remains a feature of provision in the late 1990s. As a result, disabled people are often required to liaise with many different practitioners and agencies, which does little to facilitate a coherent pattern of service support.

Intra-NHS, and intersectoral collaboration is complicated in a climate of cost containment because the system of funding provides an incentive to different parts of the system to off-load service responsibilities on to others. The consequences of directing disabled users elsewhere range from inconvenience to the denial of desired service support (Glendinning 1996). This replicates the experience of disabled people who were moved out of long-stay institutions. Hence recent initiatives to redesign the primary/secondary care interface, and to give more emphasis to local level provision have produced unease that access to the range of services will be inhibited. This has also resurrected the issue of who should coordinate service provision for disabled people. There remains little evidence that GPs are sufficiently well prepared or motivated to play a central coordinating role. However, there has been no agreement on whether other professionals, such as nurses or health visitors, should take on this long-term management role.

In arguing for more effective, appropriate and accessible services, disabled people and their organizations have begun a debate about their content and underlying philosophy. This has led to the identification of 'key principles' on which more 'enabling' services should be based. An illustration of what might be involved was advanced by The Prince of Wales Advisory Group on Disability in the mid-1980s:

- *choice* about options for more independent living;
- *consultation* with disabled people about services;
- *information* that is easily accessible;
- *participation* in the 'mainstream' of local and national communities;
- *recognition* of the shortcomings of the medical model;
- *autonomy* in personal decision making (Fielder 1988: 7).

Principles such as these have informed radical alternatives to current practice developed by disabled people themselves. These have been spearheaded by Centres for Independent (or Integrated) Living (CILs) that are controlled by disabled people. The formal consensus underpinning user-involvement hides very different approaches to its implementation (Beresford and Croft 1993). Not all envisage that user involvement should be 'integral to decision making processes'. For this to be achieved, structural changes will have to take place within and between organizations to better accommodate users' needs. It is also necessary to prepare professionals thoroughly (to share control) and disabled people (to maximize their involvement) if joint working is to be a success (Barnes 1997: 98). Indeed, one way of demonstrating the commitment to the de-medicalization of disability would be to extend the role of CILs (Finkelstein 1993).

Disabled people's determination to redesign services has been formulated into a comprehensive strategy by the Derbyshire Coalition of Disabled People, which is based on seven needs and priorities (Davis and Mullender 1993):

information, which has led to the setting up of a nation-wide Disablement Information and Advice Line (DIAL); personal assistance, where statutory provision replaces the reliance on unpaid, informal 'carers'; technical aids and equipment, where serious gaps in provision are widely acknowledged; counselling, which offers a peer-provided services; an accessible environment; housing; and transport. In recent years, the issue of 'personal assistance' has highlighted disabled people's concerns and ambitions. They have argued for a system of 'direct payments' that would enable them to employ their own personal assistant; something that has only recently been legalized. This cuts across traditional professional domination of service provision, although worries remain about whether sufficient funding will be maintained, or how user-led services might be developed for the many older disabled people (M. Oliver 1996).

## Review

This chapter has explored the implications of a social model perspective on disability with reference to the organization and delivery of services in primary care. In contrast to an individual, medicalized approach, it focuses on the significance of social barriers in the exclusion of people with accredited impairments from the mainstream of social life. Research studies have underlined disabling practices and the lack of disability awareness in primary care. Professional–disabled patient encounters are thus constrained by, for example, low expectations, presumptions of dependency and less valued lives, and an inaccessible built environment. In turn, these influence how services are provided and what they are. The social model challenges professional experts to reconsider their approach to disabled people and better differentiate the matters that relate to impairment from those that are disability related.

In addition, there are significant structural and funding constraints on service provision and particularly the division of responsibilities between primary and secondary services, and between health and other sectors. These have had a greater impact on disabled people than most other groups because their needs are so diverse and straddle different levels and sectors. More attention must be paid to who is best placed to provide and coordinate material or other practical support, information and advice. For increasing numbers of disabled people, equal opportunities to lead more independent and integrated lives depend on much enhanced social support and associated social and environmental changes rather than increased medical intervention. This suggests a higher profile for CILs.

The campaigns mounted by disabled people have sought more control over their lives and influence over what services are available to meet their needs and priorities. Professional regulation and surveillance is particularly significant for groups such as people with learning difficulties and those individuals with intellectual impairments. Overall, disabled people have argued for a radical shift in professional–lay relationships that supports 'patient centred' practice, or the much vaunted 'meeting between experts', while expressing considerable reservations about a 'primary-care led' NHS which does not show greater appreciation of the range of barriers confronting disabled people.

## References

Abberley, P. (1987) The concept of oppression and the development of a social theory of disability, *Disability, Handicap and Society*, 2(1): 5–19.

Abberley, P. (1995) Disabling ideology in health and welfare – the case of occupational therapy, *Disability and Society*, 10(2): 221–32.

Albrecht, G. (1992) *The Disability Business*. London: Sage.

Barnes, C. (1991) *Disabled People in Britain and Discrimination*. London: Hurst and Co.

Barnes, C. and Mercer, G. (eds) (1996) *Exploring the Divide: Illness and Disability*. Leeds: The Disability Press.

Barnes, M. (1997) *Care, Communities and Citizens*. Harlow: Addison Wesley Longman.

Barton, L. and Oliver, M. (eds) (1997) *Disability Studies: Past, Present and Future*. Leeds: The Disability Press.

Begum, N. (1996a) Doctor, doctor . . . disabled women's experience of general practitioners, in J. Morris (ed.) *Encounters with Strangers: Feminism and Disability*. London: The Women's Press.

Begum, N. (1996b) General practitioners role in shaping disabled women's lives, in C. Barnes and G. Mercer (eds) *Exploring the Divide*. Leeds: The Disability Press.

Beresford, P. and Croft, S. (1993) *Citizen Involvement: A Practical Guide for Change*. Basingstoke: Macmillan.

Bury, M. (1997) *Health and Illness in a Changing Society*. London: Routledge.

Carpenter, C. (1994) The experience of spinal cord injury – the individual's perspective – implications for the rehabilitation process, *Physical Therapy*, 74(7): 614–27.

Cavet, J. (1998) *Findings: Children, Young People and their Families Living with a Hidden Disability*. York: Joseph Rowntree Foundation.

Davis, K. and Mullender, D. (1993) *Ten Turbulent Years. A Review of the Work of the Derbyshire Coalition of Disabled People*. Nottingham: University of Nottingham Centre for Social Action.

Department of Health (DoH) (1998) *Moving into the Mainstream: Inspection of Services for Adults with Learning Difficulties*. London: Department of Health.

Disabled People's International (1994) *Agreed Statement*, at Human Rights Plenary Meeting in Support of European Day of Disabled Persons, Brussels, 17–18 October. London: Disabled People's International.

Fielder, B. (1988) *Living Options Lottery: Housing and Support Services for People with Severe Physical Disabilities*. London: Prince of Wales Advisory Group on Disability.

Finkelstein, V. (1993) Disability: a social challenge or an administrative responsibility, in J. Swain, V. Finkelstein, S. French and M. Oliver (eds) *Disabling Barriers – Enabling Environments*. London: Sage, in association with The Open University.

Fitzgerald, R.G. and Parkes, C.M. (1998) Blindness and loss of other sensory and cognitive functions, *British Medical Journal*, 316: 1160–3.

French, S. (1993) Disability, impairment or something in-between, in J. Swain, V. Finkelstein, S. French and M. Oliver (eds) *Disabling Barriers – Enabling Environments*. London: Sage, in association with The Open University.

French, S. (1994) Disabled people and professional practice, in S. French (ed.) *On Equal Terms: Working with Disabled People*. Oxford: Butterworth-Heinemann.

French, S. (1996) The attitudes of health professionals towards disabled people, in G. Hales (ed.) *Beyond Disability: Towards an Enabling Society*. London: Sage, in association with The Open University.

Gething, L. and Fethney, J. (1997) The need for disability awareness training among rurally based Australian general medical practitioners, *Disability and Rehabilitation*, 19(6): 249–59.

Glendinning, C. (1996) The changing interface between primary care and social care, in National Primary Care Research and Development Centre, *What is the Future for a Primary Care-led NHS?* Oxford: Radcliffe Medical Press.

Goodwill, C.J., Chamberlain, M.A. and Evans, C. (1997) *Rehabilitation of the Physically Disabled Adult*, 2nd edn. Cheltenham: Stanley Thornes.

Jessop, E. (1996) Managing chronic diseases, in G. Meads (ed.) *A Primary Care-Led NHS*. Edinburgh: Churchill Livingstone.

Johnson, R. (1993) Attitudes don't just hang in the air: disabled people's perceptions of physiotherapists, *Physiotherapy*, 79(9): 619–26.

Lamb, B. and Layzell, S. (1994) *Disabled in Britain: A World Apart*. London: Scope.

Lamb, B. and Layzell, S. (1995) *Disabled in Britain: Behind Closed Doors. The Carers' Experience*. London: Scope.

Leonard, A. (1994) *Right from the Start. Looking at Diagnosis and Disclosure*. London: Scope.

Lewis, J. (1994) Patients' views on quality care in general practice, *Social Science and Medicine*, 39(5): 655–71.

Lonsdale, S. (1990) *Women and Disability*. London: Macmillan.

McKenzie, A. (1992) Counselling for people disabled through injury, *Social Care Research Findings*, No. 19. York: Joseph Rowntree Foundation.

Martin, J., Meltzer, H. and Elliot, D. (1988) *OPCS Surveys of Disability in Great Britain: Report 1 – The Prevalence of Disability among Adults*. London: HMSO.

Morris, J. (1989) *Able Lives*. London: The Women's Press.

Morris, J. (1991) *Pride Against Prejudice*. London: The Women's Press.

Nolan, M. and Nolan, J. (1998) Rehabilitation following spinal injury: the nursing response, *British Journal of Nursing*, 7(2): 97–104.

Oliver, J. (1995) Counselling disabled people: a counsellor's perspective, *Disability and Society*, 10(3): 261–79.

Oliver, M. (1990) *The Politics of Disablement*. Basingstoke: Macmillan and St.Martin's Press.

Oliver, M. (1996) *Understanding Disability: From Theory to Practice*. Basingstoke: Macmillan and St. Martin's Press.

Oliver, M., Zarb, G., Silver, J., Moore, M. and Salisbury, V. (1988) *Walking into Darkness: The Experience of Spinal Cord Injury*. Basingstoke: Macmillan.

Rogers, A. and Popay, J. (1996) User involvement in primary care, in National Primary Care Research and Development Centre, *What is the Future for a Primary Care-led NHS?* Oxford: Radcliffe Medical Press.

Royal College of General Practitioners (1995) *The Nature of General Medical Practice. Report from General Practice. No. 27*. London: Royal College of General Practitioners.

Royal College of Physicians (1986) Physical disability in 1986 and beyond, *Journal of the Royal College of Physicians of London*, 20(3): 160–94.

Scott, R.A. (1969) *The Making of Blind Men*. London: Sage.

Thomas, C. (1997) The baby and the bathwater: disabled women and motherhood in social context, *Sociology of Health and Illness*, 19(3): 622–43.

UPIAS (1976) *Fundamental Principles of Disability*. London: Union of the Physically Impaired Against Segregation.

Williams, B. (1998) Defining 'people-centredness': making the implicit explicit, *Health and Social Care in the Community*, 6(2): 84–94.

Williams, G. (1996) Representing disability: some questions of phenomenology and politics, in C. Barnes and G. Mercer (eds) *Exploring the Divide: Illness and Disability*. Leeds: The Disability Press.

World Health Organization (1976) *International Statistical Classification of Diseases, Injuries and Causes of Death.* Geneva: World Health Organization.

World Health Organization (1980) *International Classification of Impairments, Disabilities and Handicaps.* Geneva: World Health Organization.

Wortman, C. and Silver, R. (1989) The myths of coping with loss, *Journal of Consulting and Clinical Psychology*, 57(3): 349–57.

Zarb, G. and Oliver, M. (1993) *Ageing with a Disability.* Greenwich: University of Greenwich.

## 6 The new genetics and general practice: revolution or continuity?

Satinder Kumar

### Introduction

Since 1990, general practice has emerged as the most contested discipline in the NHS. This is evident in the continuing attempts of agencies both within general practice (for example The Royal College of General Practitioners) and outside (for example governments, patients' groups, secondary care) to influence and control its future development. Through their power as executive, and not through persuasion or considered debate, governments have been particularly successful in their attempts at influence. For example, the imposition of the 1990 contract in tandem with a shift to market forces arose from government legislation. The aims were to increase efficiency, effectiveness, choice, quality, and accountability (Lewis 1997), while the measures to achieve these aims were legitimated through a rhetoric of progress and modernization. However, the interpretation of imposed change as *progress and modernization* is not upheld by many GPs. Instead, dissenting practitioners find resonance with a view of the 1990 contract as an instrument of control that, ironically if predictably, created instability by reducing practitioner autonomy and threatening the very 'nature' of general practice (Stott 1994; Fugeli and Heath 1996; Little *et al.* 1999).

In light of the continued reorganization, attempts to define 'the nature of general practice' and its 'core values' have themselves become contentious (Heath 1995; Olsen 1996; Roland 1996; Kendrick and Hilton 1997; Pringle and Heath 1997; Royal College of General Practitioners 1998). On the one hand, there is resistance to relinquishing the ideal of GPs as autonomous providers of personal, holistic and generalist medical care; while on the other there is a desire to develop the more recent role as contracted providers of increasingly specialized care, with the focus shifted from the individual to the practice population. While some GPs see the changing landscape as an opportunity for developing and extending specialist skills within general practice and forging links with other providers of primary and secondary care services (Kendrick and Hilton 1997), others have expressed concern that this will erode the traditional core skills of general practice (Heath 1995; Olsen and McMichael 1998). Debates surrounding the role of general practice in implementing the 'new genetics' can be seen in the context of these existing controversies. Indeed, the new genetics speaks to these issues with unexpected directness.

General practice has been identified by health policy makers, the RCGP and clinical geneticists as occupying a pivotal position for the future successful application of genetic advances to society (Beecham 1995; Harris and Harris 1995; House of Commons, Science and Technology Committee 1995; Royal College of General Practitioners 1998). As the point of first contact, general practice will be the site where most enquiries about genetics occur. This has been taken to indicate that GPs will need to extend their existing services to include providing information, advice and genetic risk assessment based on the new genetics and refer appropriately to scarce secondary genetic services (Austoker 1994; Royal College of General Practitioners 1998). This delegation to general practice comes at a time when GPs perceive they are being asked to take on more and more with the consequent marginalization of *'the real substance of their work'* (Heath 1995). However, I shall argue that it is this 'real substance', specifically patient advocacy and patient centredness, that makes GPs suitable for managing some of the psychosocial and ethical aspects of the new genetics (see Figures 6.1 and 6.2).

General practice occupies a unique position within medicine because it requires its practitioners to make diagnoses in the context of the patient's physical, psychological and social state (Royal College of General Practitioners 1998). Postgraduate general practice training schemes are organized to ensure that GPs possess a diverse range of consultation skills drawn from clinical medicine, sociology and psychology; as well as an understanding of ethical and legal implications of diagnoses. Furthermore, the RCGP advocates that GPs should also consider the broader implications of a consultation, balancing their role of patient advocacy with the needs and attitudes of society, the scientific community and specialist clinicians (Royal College of General Practitioners 1998). Figure 6.1 illustrates the boundaries managed by general practitioners.

Debates on how the new genetics will impact on general practice, have tended to focus on the tasks it will generate for practitioners (Austoker 1994; Kinmonth *et al.* 1998; Royal College of General Practitioners 1998). Some of the skills, information and knowledge that it is predicted GPs will require are:

- an awareness of the genetic dimension to common diseases such as cancers;
- the dimensions of family history that are needed to assess genetic risk, such as age of onset of the condition in the relative, the degree of relatedness, and so on;
- the scope of genetic testing for common diseases, such as its benefits, limitations and risks;
- issues surrounding pre- and post-test counselling and continuing support for those at high risk;

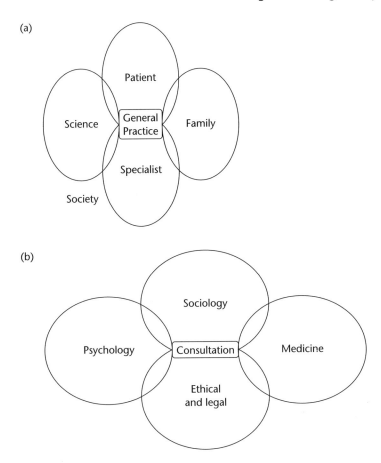

**Figure 6.1**  The unique position of the general practitioner

- issues around recording sensitive information in notes/ownership of genetic information;
- implications for insurance, employment and the family;
- where to refer and from whom to seek further expert advice;
- how to counsel those who do not require referral.

In this context, the new genetics is seen to raise issues of new skills, knowledge and training. Presented in this light, and in the context of changes already underway, it is not surprising that many GPs see the new genetics as another agency of change; one that seeks control of the clinical space of the consultation. GPs voice concern that existing pressures to record physical parameters and collect lifestyle and behavioural information will be compounded by the demands of the new genetics – specifically the collection of family history and assessment of risk (Kumar and Gantley 1998) – echoing Heath's (1995) and Olsen's (1996) perception that little space will remain for

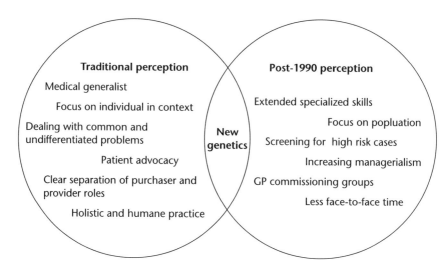

**Figure 6.2** The new genetics and its relation to the traditional and post-1990 perception of the general practitioner

the patient's or the GP's agenda during the consultation; a situation that may lead to a loss of consultation skills.

My aim in writing this chapter is not to focus on the biology of disease susceptibility genes or their epidemiological implications but to highlight the issues the new genetics raises for our identity as GPs. I argue that the presentation of the new genetics in terms of a revolution generating 'new tasks' for general practice detracts attention from its potential to preserve the traditional skills perceived to be under threat (Figure 6.2). The rhetoric of 'revolution' inherent in the epithet 'new genetics' obscures the extent to which the implementation of genetic research in general practice will need to draw on both traditional and new skills.

## The new genetics

The term 'new genetics' was coined by David Comings, Editor of the *American Journal of Human Genetics* (Weatherall 1991), to describe recent approaches in DNA analysis. It specifically referred to novel techniques such as the polymerase chain reaction, the development of recombinant DNA technology, gene cloning and DNA sequencing, which have made initiatives such as the Human Genome Project feasible. The Human Genome Project was launched in 1990. It aims to map all of the 50,000 to 100,000 human genes; to construct a physical map of the entire human genome; and to determine the nucleotide sequence of the 24 human chromosomes.

At the time of writing, it is anticipated that by the end of the century all genes responsible for single gene disorders will have been mapped (Yates 1996). Perhaps more importantly, because of the immense potential benefit to public health, most of the genetic loci responsible for common diseases such as common cancers will have been identified. As applied to clinical medicine it is predicted that the new genetics will have four main consequences. Firstly, it will provide a clarification of the genetic contribution to the development of common diseases, such as common cancers, heart disease, diabetes and depression. Secondly, by identifying and cloning disease susceptibility genes it will be possible to identify gene products and to examine their function, which may lead to a clearer understanding of the underlying molecular and biochemical patho-physiology in disease and health. Thirdly, it will lead to the development of predictive genetic tests to detect carriers of genes conferring increased susceptibility to disease. For example before BRCA 1 (which accounts for 2 per cent of breast cancer and 3 per cent of ovarian cancer diagnosed before the age of 70 years) was cloned, predictive genetic testing was only possible by linkage analysis, which required multiple samples from extended families so the test was limited to a small number of families. The cloning of BRCA 1 has made it feasible for more individuals to be tested because confirmation of the mutation requires a smaller number of affected family members (one or two) than linkage analysis (Eeles 1996). Fourthly, it will lead to the development of new drug based knowledge of genetic variation, which, in turn, may allow specific drugs to be targeted to individuals/populations to improve drug efficacy (Bell 1998).

As Bell asserts, most diseases are currently described in terms of their phenotype. For example, type II diabetes is defined as an elevated blood sugar without any specific understanding of the underlying mechanisms (Bell 1997). In this context knowledge of genetic loci associated with elevated blood sugar may help reveal underlying biological mechanisms. Such knowledge may show why our current system of disease classification may be too simplistic, for the phenotype, for example raised blood sugar, may signify not one but several diseases distinct at the molecular level. This in part may explain the difficulty epidemiologists have had in identifying coexisting environmental factors, as they have been dealing with a heterogeneous group of phenotypically defined disorders. From this it is apparent that the new genetics promises a level of diagnostic and therapeutic refinement and precision previously unavailable to medicine. Some clinicians herald this as a 'revolution' which in turn will lead to a 'paradigm shift' in health care (Baird 1990; Sweeney 1997; Royal College of General Practitioners 1998).

**Revolution or continuity?**

Rhetorics of 'revolution' and 'paradigm shift' require reflection. Although such rhetoric may be important in capturing public imagination and perhaps appeals to funding bodies, it must be regarded with a degree of suspicion. Specifically, one needs to bear in mind the level at which revolution is implied. For example, if one takes an epistemological stance then the new genetics does not herald a revolution but remains constant to the dominant force within Western biomedicine for the past 400 years: reductionism. As a medical explanatory model reductionism can be traced back to, and extends, a Cartesian concept of the body as machine. As part of this conception, the human body is explained, diagnosed and treated in terms of constituent units. In the context of health and disease this is evident in our attempts to understand the body by analysing progressively smaller fragments; the history of medicine involves a series of ever greater anatomical reductions, from the study of anatomy by dissection, to the dissection of organs, of tissues, of cells, of organelles and now DNA. Can we assume, in this light, that DNA will prove to be a final level of reduction, or might still more specific sites of biological process be identified? Admittedly, in the past 400 years, advancements in the treatment of disease have been firmly linked to the reductionist enterprise. Vaccines, blood groups and blood transfusions, immunology, transplant surgery and molecular pharmaco-therapeutics are the successes of this approach. However, reductionism has been linked to the professionalization of knowledge and thus to a communication problem between patients and doctors, as well as between medical specialists and generalists (Bunton 1997). The new genetics exacerbates this problematic with the additional complication that GPs are not themselves informed or knowledgeable about new genetic knowledge. Additionally, GPs share with specialists an uncertainty over how, precisely, such knowledge should be deployed and managed within specialist and generalist contexts. Only in the extent to which the new genetics currently destabilizes the premises of knowledge/power upon which the distinctions 'specialist', 'GP' and 'patient' are based can it be said to deserve its revolutionary epithet.

This destabilization of a professional knowledge/power base is ironic given the close links between the new genetics and the Conservative politics of right-wing health policy. Clarke (1995) has described the increasing reliance on genetic variation to explain differences between individuals as the 'geneticization' of society. At its extreme this may allow governments to evade their responsibility for creating environmental, social and economic policies that acknowledge the association of factors such as poverty, poor housing and unemployment with illness and disease. Rose *et al.* (1990) have mapped the growing primacy of the new genetics over the past two decades with the implementation of health policies in which individual responsibility for health was presented as a moral and at base economic obligation. One might add here the Conservative promotion of private health care as an extension of this fundamentally economic rhetoric. By individual responsibility was meant a patient's commitment to securing their own health through the adoption of medically approved lifestyle and behaviour, for example, by giving up smoking, taking up exercise or reducing saturated fat intake. In particular, the 1990 general practice contract attempted to define the relationship between patients and GPs as one aimed at transferring responsibility for sustaining health to the individual's decisions about lifestyle and behaviour. Genetic research has similarly directed focus upon the individual; indeed it is the culmination of a discourse of personal responsibility.

Paradoxically, however, individual responsibility evaporates at the genetic level. This is so because, within the discourses of biological determinism, an individual is seen to have no direct control over the fate of their health. The scientific validity of such a view is of course dubious, given the established links between environment, behaviour and phenotype.

There is clear evidence supporting the role of behavioural, lifestyle and environmental factors in determining disease aetiology as amassed by epidemiological research during the second half of the twentieth century. This evidence, together with evidence of the genetic contribution to disease, converges at the interface between gene and environment, thus renewing debate about the boundary between nature and nurture and the relative importance of each in disease causation. The exact details of how gene expression may be altered by specific behavioural and life style choices remains largely unclear in the context of common diseases. For example, within a BRCA 1 family there is variation in the age at which females develop breast or ovarian cancer. Furthermore, 15 per cent of women with BRCA 1 do not develop cancer. The reasons for this are unclear. The presence of protective or modifying genes, lifestyle or environmental factors may be significant. Their elucidation and the rate at which women with a particular BRCA 1 mutation develop cancer requires longitudinal studies. While this gap in knowledge remains doctors will be unable to provide tailored statistical estimates of genetic risk even for hereditary breast cancer. This gap underlines the need to develop a model of risk assessment that takes into account individuals' specific gene mutations, lifestyles and social, economic and environmental conditions.

For GPs practising holistic medicine, in accordance with the Royal College discussion paper (Stott *et al.* 1996), it is precisely such established links that will need to be considered. The new genetics intensifies the dilemma of how to accommodate knowledge produced in a determinist framework with the social and economic factors that are known to influence health at many levels, including the genetic. As far as the role of the GP is concerned, the danger of the new genetics is that it potentially promotes a biological determinism that threatens our collective consideration of social, political and economic determinants of (ill) health. As for patients themselves, the new genetics is potentially disempowering, and encourages fatalistic acceptance of behavioural and environmental risk factors (Marteau and Richard 1996; Nelkon and Lindee 1995; Emery *et al.* 1998). Another paradox is at work here. By over estimating an individual's predisposition to disease, the biologically determinist model risks under estimating the individual's capacity to influence their medical history.

In marking the internal contradictions in discourses of individual responsibility, as they culminate in the new genetics, I do not mean simply to challenge the authority and credibility of such rhetoric. Instead, I wish to use this critique as a basis upon which to (re)articulate general practice's sense of its own commitments. In the final section of this paper I thus offer some provisional proposals for the implementation of the new genetics in general practice.

## A role for general practice

Why should GPs play a part in the new genetics? One answer lies in resources. As the numbers of people presenting to GPs with concerns about the inheritance of disease increases, existing genetic services will not be able to cope with the demand from the public for referral. There are only one or two consultant geneticists per million of the population, whereas there is one general practitioner for approximately every 2000 people (Kinmonth *et al.* 1998). Given the numerical argument alone it is apparent why we need GPs to manage most patient enquiries. Another answer is based on our current knowledge of the extent of the population with genetic susceptibility to common diseases. Most of the population are currently thought to be at low risk and so inappropriate for referral to specialist genetic services. Thus informed reassurance at primary care level forms the most appropriate management strategy. None the less, even this strategy presupposes informed GPs, and there has as yet been little research focused upon how this will be achieved. My own research is aimed at raising these issues within general practice. In a qualitative study of 50 GPs and their concerns over providing counselling and referral for patients with a family history of common cancers, it has emerged that there are both conceptual and practical issues to be addressed. Among the conceptual problems are GPs' attitudes to disease prevention, diagnosis and management. Currently, GPs expect to provide information about genetic risk primarily during consultation on reproduction and in child health surveillance clinics. I have termed this existing expectation about the time and place when GPs offer genetic advice the 'genetic window'. In my opinion, this window also offers a way of beginning to address GPs' management of diseases newly defined as genetic. This in turn leads to the second conceptual issue.

The terms 'familial' and 'hereditary' disease are increasingly confusing to GPs. Remarkably, in the case of breast cancer, the concept of shared genes as a cause of the cancer was not immediately recognized. Instead, GPs tended to stress shared environmental factors, such as exposure to a shared carcinogen. That is, GPs currently locate cancers towards nurture rather than nature. This belief, coupled with limited knowledge about advances in genetics, led to heredity being given a low priority during risk assessment. Even in reading family history, GPs tended to focus on such history as an indication of a patient's likely psychological and emotional state, rather than as an indicator of genetic risk. In these ways, GPs are well equipped to mediate between biological determinism and holism. However, if they are to perform effectively, formal education and training programmes need to be developed at several levels to encourage a conceptual shift in the way GPs use family history to assess multifactorial diseases such as cancer (Kumar and Gantley 1997).

How might this process of education proceed? Information and education alone might not be sufficient to close the gap between knowledge and clinical practice. Since GPs currently in practice typically received little training in genetics, there may be a need to couple practical and theoretical education with exploration of the issues, in the same manner that knowledge of other aspects of practice are acquired. During their GP registrar year, GPs could be required to attend specialist genetic clinics to experience first hand both calculation of genetic risk, consultation/counselling, and patient–specialist dialogue. In general practice itself, a nurse facilitator, working with a group of practices, could act both to inform GPs and consult with patients who perceive themselves to be at risk. Since it is unlikely that patients will possess a complete and exact family history of disease over several generations, a nurse facilitator may advise and guide patients on collecting potentially sensitive information from family members. Patients will need to know which facts are needed in order to assess their risk; for example the site(s) of the primary cancer(s) and not the sites of metastatic spread. Given that genetic knowledge is likely to be constantly updated and changed, computer software would be a suitable medium for supporting genetic risk assessment. This is currently a focus of research at Oxford University (Emery 1998).

The application of genetic technologies to human populations has a powerful historical context. The practice of eugenics in the first half of this century, along with continued ethnic cleansing on the world-historical stage, highlights potential dangers attending the abuse of 'neutral' biomedical research. Genetic research will inevitably inform social policy; exactly how it does should be the concern of us all. Some of these issues have been articulated through the emerging discourse of concern (MacIntyre 1997):

- The geneticisation of society: a process by which differences between individuals are reduced to their DNA codes, with most disorders, behaviours and psychological variations defined, at least in part, as genetic origin. The emphasis is on genetic determination.
- Underestimation of the role of environmental factors in disease. Clarke (1995) has expressed the fear that commercial pressures for susceptibility testing for common disorders 'will promote the notion that genetic endowment and chosen lifestyle together determine future health, while the importance of future health, and the importance of material circumstances (especially poverty) in creating ill health will be glossed over'.
- Discrimination in the workplace, in insurance and by the family. Billings *et al.* (1992) have highlighted that a new category of the 'asymptomatic ill' may be created as people are required to undergo genetic testing for reasons of employment or insurance cover. Healthy people may be stigmatized by the various institutions of our society and treated as if they were chronically disabled.
- Commodification of babies. There is concern that babies may be seen as objects to which adults have a right, and furthermore a right to have a perfect version.
- Diversion of care, treatment and resources away from disabled people or people with genetic abnormalities.
- Screening for conditions for which there is no effective treatment as is the case for most common cancers.
- Uncertainty about whether lifestyle changes would occur as a result of screening, and about whether they would be effective.

Not all the issues raised here are new and most are evident in relation to other screening and testing services. However it is not possible to predict how individuals, families and service providers, such as GPs, will respond to the potential of the new genetics. What may be certain is that the benefits and the hazards of the new genetics will be experienced differentially by different groups in society. GPs, again, are well situated to manage the concerns listed by drawing on skills and experiences acquired through their clinical experience and through implementing existing screening programmes in general practice.

## Conclusion

I have attempted to diverge from representation of the new genetics as simply another agency of change for general practice and GPs. Issues raised by genetic advances reach beyond the biomedical. The broader philosophical, social, psychological, ethical, political and legal implications for the individual/family and society are areas that GPs have successfully managed in other contexts. In doing so they have developed a range of specific skills and patient centred values that mark them as a unique breed within medicine. Among the challenges implicit within genetic advances is the need to maintain and reinvest in the traditions and values that define our holistic approach. Although scientists and geneticists emphasize the rhetorics of 'revolution' and 'paradigm shifts', in the context of general practice the new genetics can be seen to reveal more than opportunities for change. For general practice it provides strong reasons why we need to preserve and develop those traditional and core values considered to be under threat.

## References

Austoker, J. (1994) Cancer prevention in primary care. Current trends and some prospects for the future-II, *British Medical Journal*, 309: 517–20.

Baird, P. (1990) Genetics and health care, *Perspectives in Biological Medicine*, 33: 203–13.

Beecham, L. (1995) Medico-political digest: GPs need to keep abreast of genetics, *British Medical Journal*, 311: 579–80.

Bell, J. (1997) Genetics of common disease: implications for therapy, screening and redefinition of disease, *Philosophical Transactions of the Royal Society, London*, 352: 1051–55.

Bell, J. (1998) The new genetics in clinical practice, *British Medical Journal*, 316: 618–20.

Billings, P., Kohn, M.A. and De Cuevcas, D. (1992) Discrimination as a consequence of genetic testing, *American Journal of Human Genetics*, 50: 476–82.

Bunton, R. (1997) Popular health, advanced liberalism and good house keeping magazine, in R. Peterson and R. Bunton (eds) *Foucault Health and Medicine*. London: Routledge.

Clarke, A. (1995) Population screening for genetic susceptibility to disease, *British Medical Journal*, 311: 35–8.

Eeles, R. (1996) Testing for the breast cancer predisposition gene, BRCA 1, *British Medical Journal*, 313: 572–3.

Emery, J. (1998) Computer support for recording and interpreting family histories of breast and ovarian cancer in primary care (RAGS). Qualitative evaluation with simulated patients, *British Medical Journal*, 319: 32–6.

Emery, J., Kumar, S. and Smith, H. (1998) Patient understanding of genetic principles and their expectations of genetic service within the NHS; A qualitative study, *Community Genetics*, 2: 78–83.

Fugeli, P. and Heath, I. (1996) The nature of general practice, *British Medical Journal*, 312: 456–7.

Harris, R. and Harris, H. (1995) Primary care for patients at genetic risk, *British Medical Journal*, 311: 579–80.

Heath, I. (1995) *The Mystery of General Practice*. London: The Nuffield Provincial Hospital Trust.

House of Commons, Science and Technology Committee (1995) *Human Genetics: The Science and its Consequences*. London: HMSO.

Kendrick, T. and Hilton, S. (1997) Broader team work in primary care, *British Medical Journal*, 314: 672–5.

Kinmonth, A-L., Reinhard, J., Bobrow, M. and Pauker, S. (1998) The new genetics: implications for clinical services in Britain and the United States, *British Medical Journal*, 316: 767–70.

Kumar, S. and Gantley, M. (1997) The conceptual challenge of the new genetics: A qualitative study of GPs. Conference Paper, British Medical Association Scientific Meeting, San Francisco 12 October.

Kumar, S. and Gantley, M. (1998) A qualitative study of GP concerns in providing genetic counselling for patients with a family history of common cancer. Paper presented to the International Qualitative Health Research Conference, University of British Colombia, Vancouver, 20 February.

Lewis, J. (1997) The changing meaning of the GP contract, *British Medical Journal*, 314: 895–6.

Little, P., Kumar, S. and Gantley, M. (1999) A qualitative study of GPs' views of health promotion and reimbursement for health promotion: Jumping through hoops or embedded in the consultation? *British Medical Journal*.

MacIntyre, S. (1997) Social and psychological issues associated with the new genetics, *Philosophical Transactions of The Royal Society, London*, 352: 1051–2.

Marteau, T. and Richard, M. (1996) *The Troubled Helix*. Cambridge: Cambridge University Press.

Nelkon, D. and Lindee, M.S. (1995) *The DNA Mystique. The Gene as a Cultural Icon*. New York: W.H. Freeman and Company.

Olsen, N.D.L. (1996) Sustaining general practice, *British Medical Journal*, 312: 525–6.

Olsen, J. and McMichael, M. (1998) Europe's health research: Getting the right balance, *British Medical Journal*, 316: 795.

Pringle, M. and Heath, I. (1997) Primary care opportunities and threats, *British Medical Journal*, 314: 595–9.

Roland, M. (1996) Defining core general practitioner services, *British Medical Journal*, 313: 704.

Rose, S., Lewontin, R.C. and Kamin, L.J. (1990) *Not In Our Genes*. Harmondsworth: Penguin.

Royal College of General Practitioners (1998) *Genetics in Primary Care. Royal College of General Practitioners Occasional Paper 77*, North West England Faculty Genetics Group. London: Royal College of General Practitioners.

Stott, N. (1994) The new general practitioner? *Journal of the Royal College of General Practitioners*, 44: 5–8.

Stott, N., Boland, M., Hayden, J. *et al.* (1996) *Report from General Practice 27.The Nature of General Practice*. London: Royal College of General Practitioners.

Sweeney, B. (1997) Genetic advances: great promise tempered with concern, *Journal of the Royal College of General Practitioners*, 47: 544–5.

Weatherall, D.J. (1991) *The New Genetics and Clinical Practice*. Oxford: Oxford University Press.

Yates, J.R.W. (1996) Medical genetics, *British Medical Journal*, 312: 1021–4.

## 7 Socio-economic inequality: beyond the inverse care law

Lorna Arblaster and
Adrian Hastings

### Introduction

In 1971 Julian Tudor Hart used the term 'inverse care law' to describe the poorer provision of medical services in deprived areas, where mortality and morbidity were greatest (Tudor Hart 1971: 412). He said then that 'the availability of good medical care tends to vary inversely with the need for it in the population served'. Current problems of recruiting GPs to work in deprived areas confirms one aspect of this continuing situation. In the late 1990s the UK government has set up Health Action Zones in England to improve health and health care for 13 million people living in the most deprived areas (Department of Health 1998a). Primary care groups are expected to promote the health of the local population (Department of Health 1997).

There is a strong case to argue that 'the primary determinants of disease are mainly economic and social, and therefore its remedies must also be economic and social' (Rose 1992: 129). Without epidemiological *and socioeconomic analysis*, PHC staff in deprived areas may not fully appreciate the extent to which their workload is socio-economically patterned.

This chapter proposes that, to promote the health of the local population, the socio-economic context of PHC needs to be considered, both to facilitate provision of good PHC in deprived areas and to make sure that the work of PHC in deprived areas is supported by socio-economic conditions that promote the health of the people living there. It explores the socio-economic context of PHC by considering social disadvantage and health, trends in socio-economic factors in the UK and issues relating to PHC provision and practice in deprived areas. It then provides a response from a GP for improving PHC in deprived areas and looks at other responses to poverty and deprivation aimed at improving health, as well as at more general measures for promoting health.

## Social disadvantage and health

Throughout this century in the UK levels of health have steadily improved (Department of Health 1998b). However, improvement in health has been greater for people who are more affluent (Townsend *et al.* 1992). Even after the introduction of the NHS, inequalities in health persisted, with poorer people experiencing poorer health. In the 1990s poor people live shorter lives than affluent people (five years less for men – 70 years compared with 75 years; and three years less for women – 77 years compared with 80 years (Office of National Statistics 1997). Of particular concern is the fact that the difference in death rates between rich and poor men has increased in the past 20 years (Drever *et al.* 1996).

Poverty affects people's health (Townsend *et al.* 1992), their access to medical services (Ben-Shlomo and Chaturvedi 1995), and the work of PHC staff (Balarajan *et al.* 1992). Social disadvantage is associated with increased ill health (Eachus *et al.* 1996), higher rates of utilization of medical services (Ebrahim 1995), inequitable access to medical services (Azeem Majeed *et al.* 1994; Payne and Saul 1997) and inequitable provision of medical care. For example inequities exist in the provision of coronary artery bypass grafts for men living in poorer areas (Ben-Shlomo and Chaturvedi 1995), although the need there for such treatment may be greater than in more prosperous areas (Payne and Saul 1997). Housing tenure and car ownership predict the workload of GPs (Balarajan *et al.* 1992). Unemployment is as useful a proxy for morbidity as the Jarman score (Payne *et al.* 1993), and unemployment rates powerfully indicate serious mental illness that will need treatment in hospital in under 65-year-olds (Kammerling and O'Connor 1993).

In deprived areas consultation rates are higher and consultation times shorter (Balarajan *et al.* 1992). A disproportionate amount of out of hours workload falls on deprived inner city practices, however high general practice and accident and emergency activity are found in the same areas rather than one service substituting for the other (Carlisle *et al.* 1998). Patients living in deprived areas of Glasgow have emergency medical admission rates twice as high as those from affluent areas of the city (Blatchford and Capewell 1998).

Money and class contribute to the quality of life in the year before death (Cartwright 1992), and data suggest that hospital as the place of death for patients with cancer is strongly associated with deprivation (Higginson *et al.* 1994), despite more than half of patients expressing a desire to remain, and be cared for, at home.

In deprived areas patients and PHC staff have different priorities and attitudes in relation to health (Stilwell and Stilwell 1995). In deprived areas people may have more pressing problems than their health; women in a deprived area were found to be more worried about money, relationships, housing, coping with children and their children's health, than about their own health (James *et al.* 1992).

## Trends in socio-economic factors in the UK

Poverty is widespread in inner city areas, urban estates and rural areas. Recently there have been changes in people's socio-economic circumstances that have implications for PHC. In the past 20 years poverty has increased. Definitions of poverty are: *low income families* – families living on, below or up to 140 per cent of supplementary benefit/income support; and *households below average income* – those living on 50 per cent of average income after housing costs. The number of people living in poverty increased from 5 million (9 per cent) in 1979 to 13.4 million (25 per cent) in 1994–95 (MacDermott 1998a). The number of children living in poverty increased from 1 in 10 in 1979 to 1 in 3 in 1994–95 (4.3 million children) (Oppenheim and Harker 1996). Groups most at risk of poverty are lone parent families and single pensioners. Lone mothers, who have worse health than couple mothers, increased from 12 per cent of all mothers in 1979–84 to 21 per cent by 1992–95.

Inequality of income has also increased. Although the average person's income increased by 37 per cent between 1979 and 1992–93 the poorest experienced an 18 per cent reduction in real income (after paying housing costs). The gap between rich and poor widened rapidly. Unemployment was one million in 1979, and reached almost 3 million before falling to two million in 1996, widening the financial gap between workers and non-workers.

Since 1971 tax burdens have shifted from affluent to middle and poorer groups of people; cuts in direct tax being paid for by cuts in welfare benefits (Hills 1990), and with stricter tests of eligibility.

Since the early 1980s welfare benefits have fallen behind earnings. Previously benefits were increased in line with wages or prices, whichever were higher. Since the 1980s benefits increased in line with prices only, whereas earnings rose at a higher rate than inflation (Oppenheim and Harker 1996). In Oxford the number of people claiming income support increased by 30 per cent between 1991 and mid-1993 (Noble and Smith 1994).

Many poor people have deductions made from their income support benefit to pay bills. In August 1992, 1.28 million income support claimants had some deductions made, meaning that they were living on less than the government believed was the minimum amount needed to survive, that is full income support (Slade *et al.* 1995). Following the introduction of the Incapacity Benefit in 1995 many people lost benefit entitlement. Helping those affected to appeal increases the workload of GPs and Citizens' Advice Bureau (CAB) advice workers. Nationally over 45 per cent of incapacity benefit appeals are successful, but with supporting medical evidence, this increases to 67 per cent (Coard and Maguire undated).

Government spending on public services fell significantly as a share of gross domestic product from 38.3 per cent in 1978–79, to 36.2 per cent in 1996–97, to 34.7 per cent in 1997–98 (MacDermott 1998b). Expenditure by government on housing fell from £13 billion in 1979 to £4.7 billion in 1995 (Wilcox 1996). This was the greatest reduction in any public service expenditure in that period, as housing policies emphasized owner occupation. Housing affects health, and it provides shelter, security and employment (Burridge and Ormandy 1993; Ineichen 1993).

Without investment in housing the amount of social housing (local authority and housing association housing) fell from 7 million units in 1979 to 4.5 million in 1995 (Wilcox 1996). Poor people, and thus those with the greatest health needs, were concentrated in social housing in particular geographical areas; a process described as residualization. In Great Britain the number of homeless households, usually households with children, went up from 70,000 in 1979 to 178,000 in 1991 and was 134,000 in 1995 (Wilcox 1996). GPs on the Isle of Dogs in east London felt that the shortage of social housing contributed to increased racism there (Roberts 1993). Jobs in the building industry were lost and thousands of homes were repossessed by building societies. Without investment both local authority and private housing stock has deteriorated. Almost 1.7 million homes in the UK are unfit for habitation, most of them in the private sector (Department of the Environment 1993). Rented housing is also very energy inefficient (McSmith and Tickell 1996), making it difficult for people on low incomes to keep warm in winter (Boardman 1994).

The idea that the UK has an exceptionally generous welfare system or that the welfare system has grown to economically unaffordable levels is untrue (MacDermott 1998b). By 1997 the UK had the lowest share of tax to gross domestic product of any European Union (EU) country except Ireland. Also, in comparison to other EU countries, UK social welfare payments are low; accounting for a lower share of national income (13 per cent in the UK; 20 per cent in Germany; 25 per cent in the Netherlands) than any other EU country except Ireland at 13 per cent (MacDermott 1998b).

## Issues relating to PHC provision and practice in deprived areas

A number of issues relate to the provision of good PHC in deprived areas. These include: the availability of, and access to, PHC (equity of delivery); recruitment of PHC staff, staff morale and the organization of PHC for delivery of services in deprived areas; the quality of PHC, variations in care and referral rates; resource allocation (equity of funding) and incentives to PHC to deal with health appropriately; socio-economic cultural differences (in addition to cultural differences of ethnic diversity); addressing determinants of health such as poverty; and the roles and training of PHC staff for work in deprived areas. Many of these issues are the subject of ongoing research (National Primary Care Research and Development Centre 1998).

### Availability of, and access to, PHC

Equity of access to health care is important and is discussed by Goddard and Smith (1998). Geographic distribution of GPs is one aspect of equity of access. Considerable regional variation exists between the need for and distribution of GPs. Some reduction in the inequality of GP distribution occurred between 1974 and 1980, but the downward trend has not continued (Gravelle and Sutton 1998). There may have been an increase in inequality of GP distribution after 1985. In the early 1990s Cornwall and the Isles of Scilly had an excess of almost a fifth whereas Rotherham had a shortfall of more than a third (Benzeval and Judge 1996). Inequalities in the distribution of GPs are reinforced by inequalities in other primary care resources (Gravelle and Sutton 1998). Inequitable geographical distribution of GPs in 1995 was less than that for practice nurses, practice staff, opticians and dentists (Gravelle and Sutton 1998; Hirst *et al.* 1998). Bloor and Maynard propose that expenditure in the south-west needs to decline by up to 16 per cent to achieve greater geographical parity in PHC (Bloor and Maynard 1995); and Gravelle and Sutton estimate that it would be necessary to transfer 2308 GPs (8.1 per cent of the total) from areas with above average provision to those areas with below average provision in order to achieve equal provision. This would lead to a loss of 187 GPs for the area losing the most GPs (Hampshire) and a gain of 190 for the area gaining the most (Mid Glamorgan) (Gravelle and Sutton 1998).

### Recruitment of PHC staff to deprived areas

The number of GPs entering PHC fell from 1565 in 1990 to 1400 in 1994. Currently, recruitment of GPs is a widespread problem; one that is most difficult in areas with the greatest health needs (Carlisle and Johnstone 1996). Salaried status, skill-mix and repayment of student loans, are some proposed solutions.

### PHC staff morale

Concern exists about low moral among GPs. Among Leeds's GPs, half were found to have a high level of psychological symptoms (Appleton *et al.* 1998). In deprived areas, PHC work can be made difficult by crime, violence and arson. However, GP well being was not associated with area deprivation in London (Grieve 1997).

### Quality of PHC

Practices providing poor quality care and an inadequate range of services need to be brought up to acceptable standards. In 1992 the Tomlinson Report acknowledged that 46 per cent of London GP premises failed to meet minimum standards. Some suggest that PHC in deprived areas is inadequate, citing the lack of availability of GPs out of hours, the higher proportion of GPs who are single-handed or over 65 years of age, and the poor quality of practice premises (Boyle and Smaje 1993). Linking these factors with the level of deprivation, Baker suggests that these factors are closely associated with the standard and development of PHC services (R. Baker 1992).

However, general practice in inner city areas of Manchester was considered to be no poorer than that in other parts of the city (Wilkin *et al.* 1984); and patients from an affluent area of Glasgow, and those from a deprived area, were equally satisfied with PHC services (Wyke *et al.* 1992).

*Variations in care*

Differences exist in treatment and patient referral rates between GPs and between practices. Better understanding of this is needed. Educational and service development programmes to reduce these variations are suggested if they are not clinically justified (Azeem Majeed 1998); however those variations due to ill health relating to deprivation need to be taken into account when doing this.

*Effectiveness of PHC in deprived areas*

Evaluation of the effectiveness of PHC therapeutic interventions is important. When evaluating effectiveness of care for people living in deprived areas, the additional effects of deprivation on health need to be taken into consideration.

*Equity and use of resources*

Resource use in PHC is a complex issue. One factor is the increased cost of providing care to patients in deprived areas (Worrall *et al.* 1997). Another factor is that of the lower incomes of GPs who work there compared to the incomes of GPs working in more prosperous areas (Slingsby 1998).

Workload and costs of drugs increase with decreasing socio-economic status of the patients (Worrall *et al.* 1997); the difference in cost for patients in social classes IV and V combined compared with those in classes I and II combined was about £150 per person year at risk, over the four and a half year period ending July 1994 (£47 for workload and £103 for drugs). Deprivation payments for patients met only half this extra workload cost. Introduced in 1990, deprivation payments are made to doctors working in deprived areas. Numerous problems relate to deprivation payments. Needs adjusted formulae are to be introduced for certain PHC budgets – capitation, GMS, prescribing – with adjustments for socio-economic factors.

Issues of equitable resource allocation arise locally as PCGs are expected to use resources to best benefit patients, including patients in deprived areas. One issue is the use of the savings made by GPs who practise 'efficiently'. How, and by whom, will these savings be used? What incentive will there be for GPs to be efficient when their savings may be used by other GPs, including those practising in deprived areas? Matching policy and incentives to improve health in deprived areas is a challenge.

Secondary care needs to be available to support PHC staff working in deprived areas, in proportion to the health and care needs of the patients there.

*Socio-economic cultural differences*

Socio-economic cultural differences (in addition to ethnic cultural differences) need to be understood by PHC staff providing medical care and health promotion. Patients in deprived areas are often reluctant to take part in screening and preventive health activities. Differences exist in attitudes towards health issues between health professionals and local people, and this can inhibit people's access to services (Stilwell and Stilwell 1995).

Smoking is a health hazard linked to social and economic disadvantage. Working-class mothers who smoke heavily care for more children, for children in poorer health, and are more likely to be caring alone; they carry extra responsibilities for family members. A higher proportion of smokers are dependent on benefit level incomes, and are caring on less than they need to meet the basic necessities of their families (Graham 1994). It is suggested that women use cigarette smoking to cope with the pressures of relentless child care in the context of strained financial resources (Romans *et al.* 1993). Unexpectedly a New Zealand study showed a higher rate of recovery from psychiatric ill health among women smokers than among non-smokers (Romans *et al.* 1993). Health promotion in socially disadvantaged areas needs to be sensitive to sociocultural factors.

*Addressing determinants of health*

Some PHC practices consider that addressing determinants of health, such as poverty, by, for example promoting access to welfare benefits advice is part of their responsibility (Little 1995). In certain practices funding to provide benefits advice in the practice premises is a practice expense; in others the health authority or local authority funds it.

*Multisectoral working*

Problems of recruiting PHC staff to work in deprived areas have led to innovative ways of providing care to prevent loss of services, such as skill mix and team-working. These have yet to be evaluated. Organizational structures and management are important factors for facilitating or inhibiting skill mix and team-work, and require time and resources.

*Professional roles and training of PHC staff to work in deprived areas*

PHC responsibility has expanded to include: care formerly provided by secondary care services; budgets encompassing a larger proportion of total expenditure than formerly; and the commissioning and planning services, taking into account local health and health care needs. In doing this, performance indicators proposed by government, local targets, equitable access, efficiency and health outcomes are to be considered. Roles implicit in these tasks – provider of PHC services, budgeting, management (including change management) and that of 'public health physician' – raise questions about the training of PHC staff. Is current training adequate or should a new approach be instigated enabling PHC staff to meet the challenges better?

**Improving PHC in deprived areas – the primary care response**

People working in PHC services in urban deprived areas (UDAs) know that deprivation damages the health of their patients. They were frustrated that the problem was described in detail by sociologists and epidemiologists while a Conservative government denied the link between poverty and ill health.

The stated commitment of the Labour government to tackle health inequality is welcome but it would be a mistake for PHC workers to volunteer to be the shock troops in a new war on poverty. A vision for the future requires us to concentrate on what we know and to test new ideas when opportunities arise. These are the pre-conditions to create PHC services in UDAs to rival the best in Britain:

- provide adequate resources, using formulae sensitive to the complex needs of deprived areas;
- focus on medical and nursing interventions of proven benefit;
- improve the networking practice of PHC workers;
- defend the concept of the personal doctor against increasing threats;
- recognize that recruitment and retention of staff in general practice is a greater problem in deprived areas.

These are considered in turn.

*Match resources to needs*

In 1990 the government recognized the need to provide extra resources to practices in deprived areas. The distribution formula chosen, the Underprivileged Area Score, had been designed for a very different purpose; measuring the correlation between census variables associated with poverty and GP workload (Jarman 1983). The payments are unconditional and it is unclear whether they should provide extra staff and facilities for patients or financial compensation to doctors for working in UDAs. Many modifications to the system were proposed but none were adopted in England (Crayford *et al.* 1995). The Departments of Health in Scotland and Wales modified the formula because of anomalies, which classified ex-mining communities in Wales and Scotland as being less deprived than suburbs in affluent English towns. AGUDA (Association of General Practice in Urban Deprived Areas) maintained a consistent policy on deprivation payments:

- deprivation payments should be calculated for the smallest possible population unit (enumeration districts) to target payment on those in most need;
- payment should allow GPs working in UDAs to have similar incomes to those working in more prosperous areas while maintaining smaller lists.

The complex physical, social and emotional problems of people living in UDAs result in a heavier workload for PHC. Crude consultation rates are high necessitating a higher doctor:patient ratio (Myers 1987). Longer consultation times are needed to provide health care opportunistically because 'health promotion clinics' are ill suited to these areas (Wilson *et al.* 1992). The prevalence of most major diseases is highest in the most deprived areas, including the common chronic diseases that form so much of the workload of primary care: vascular disease, including heart disease, hypertension and stroke; asthma and chronic obstructive airways disease; and mental illness. Equitable resource allocation means that staff, prescribing and referral budgets for UDAs will exceed those of more prosperous areas. GP fundholding perversely rewarded practices with the highest historical costs unrelated to health care needs, because these were best placed to make savings. The abolition of fund-holding in 1998, and the introduction of methods of resource allocation that take account of deprivation, should result in a more equitable distribution, with redistribution of funds for hospital and community services towards UDAs (Smith *et al.* 1994). A similar process for general practice funding would have the same effect (Brennan and Carr-Hill 1996).

The subdivision of resources to practices within PCGs is the outstanding problem of resource allocation. PCGs include practices whose patients have widely different health care needs. Practices serving similar communities often have different prescribing and referral patterns due to differences in doctor behaviour rather than objective health needs (Fleming *et al.* 1991). Weighted capitation formulae can guide the allocation of prescribing budgets between practices but do not take into account differential rates of ascertainment for chronic disease. Practices that actively screen for hypertension and asthma will discover more cases, and may introduce new treatments of proven benefit – for example using lipid-lowering drugs for the prevention of heart disease – earlier than other practices. Both factors will increase the prescribing costs of the innovative practice over those of a less effective one.

Health visiting provision will test the ability of PCGs to make equitable allocation of resources. Of community health services, health visiting is most sensitive to the effects of deprivation on workload (Audit Commission 1994). Despite this health visitors are usually allocated to practices using an under-fives capitation formula. The justification for equal allocation becomes increasingly tenuous as evidence based reviews of child health surveillance do not support universal screening (Hall 1996).

Abolition of fund holding presents PCGs with a difficult problem of intro-ducing equity (Bevan 1998). They will be given a single, unified cash-limited budget for primary and secondary care provision. Practices with high and low drug and referral costs can be identified. Are high cost practices provid-ing a quality service with high rates of ascertainment of disease and its effective treatment, or are they profligate prescribers of expensive, brand name drugs of no greater benefit than generic alternatives? Are patients referred to hospital who could be cared for at home? Moves to produce financial equity between practices, even allowing for deprivation, will not produce clinical equity. To achieve this detailed epidemiological surveillance of variations in care between practices needs to be linked to evidence based practice. The Department of Health should acknowledge the increased man-agement costs and political consequences of transferring resources from prac-tices in prosperous areas to UDAs.

*Focus on interventions of proven benefit*

Patients are ill served by health workers giving unrealistic promises of help while failing simultaneously to provide effective essential care. Between 1980 and 1991 numbers of courses of antibiotics prescribed in general practice increased by 45.8 per cent (Davey *et al.* 1996). Evidence exists that antibiotics rarely influence the conditions for which they are commonly prescribed

(Belongia and Schwartz 1998). The effect is malignant. Patients believe that minor illness can only be cured by doctors, resources are wasted, life saving drugs are rendered useless and those with health needs amenable to treatment are pushed out of the system. Antibiotic prescribing rates are sensitive indicators of GP behaviour, being rarely driven by hospital recommendation. They are prescribed for common conditions and the indications for their use are well established, thus variations in use reflect differences in attitude and behaviour of doctors. High prescribing rates are associated with short consultations with less information given to patients and lower levels of satisfaction (Howie et al. 1997). Patients given inappropriate prescriptions rather than careful explanations are more likely to re-consult with similar symptoms (Little et al. 1997). This cycle of dependence wastes patients' time in unnecessary visits to doctors who are thereby less able to devote time to more useful activities.

The core activity of primary care – the consultation between patient and doctor – is the only service most patients experience each year. Without relevant skills, and the time to exercise them, GPs fail their patients. Social and psychological distress often presents in the form of physical symptoms. Underlying problems can be recognized when consultations are unhurried, but time pressured or less skilled doctors are likely to resort to physical diagnosis with costly investigation and unnecessary treatment. Also patients are confirmed in belief in a physical cause for their problem and opportunities to help mobilize their own coping strategies are lost.

Chronic disease management assumes increasing importance for PHC as the population ages, the care of uncomplicated chronic disease is transferred from hospitals and new treatments become available. These trends particularly affect UDAs because of the high prevalence of disease there. Effective treatment requires efficient administration with the skills of doctors and nurses supported by good computer systems. Continued audit of their work is essential to raise and maintain standards. Dr Hart's team produced significant health gains, although the time required to show benefit was long (Tudor Hart et al. 1991). Most practices are too small for outcomes to be measured in the short term. However, if the process of care is good, better outcomes can be expected (Davies and Crombie 1995). To deliver this care resources must be matched to needs, and time and training provided to put effective processes in place.

Although the 1990 contract for GPs emphasized health promotion clinics, subsequent research found that health gain was marginal (Coulter et al. 1995). Incentive payments to provide clinics were withdrawn in 1994 and replaced by payments to manage asthma and diabetes. Alternative means of health promotion need to be identified and implemented. A community based project reduced smoking and increased low fat milk consumption at modest cost (Baxter et al. 1997).

The key messages for PHC in focusing its activity effectively are to:

- develop skills in accurately diagnosing illness, including the recognition of psychological and social distress presenting as physical symptoms;
- avoid 'medical' treatments of minor self-limiting illness, which induces dependence on professional advice;
- provide well organized, audited care of chronic diseases.

*Improve the networking practice of primary care workers*

PHC workers in UDAs are often asked to help with the housing, school and welfare benefit problems of patients. They become aware of the importance of domestic violence, fear of crime and road safety for health. These problems rarely have 'medical' solutions. Listening and empathizing can provide support but people need effective solutions. PHC cannot compensate for inadequate education and social services, particularly if health workers' own responsibilities are not fulfilled. Nevertheless PHC workers need to help their patients. Recognition of the importance of social problems in determining health and the need to use the knowledge and skills of people in different agencies to tackle them resulted in the multi-agency project in Leicester. The project aims to provide the relevant skills needed by people promptly. It operates from a building housing most of the agencies involved, which facilitates communication and management. Generalizing the concept to other areas may be limited if existing agencies operate from different centres. The project shows that it is important to:

- create an area forum to represent local residents with real influence over the agencies operating on the estate;
- train team managers in the process of change;
- improve the ability of people working in health and social care and education to listen to and understand people living in the area;
- use local residents to provide education and research un-met needs, both as paid and as voluntary workers (A. Lennox, pers. comm.).

If formal evaluation of such projects confirms the benefits of effective networking between agencies research into how to implement similar changes in areas without the aid of special facilities will be needed, although it is probable that additional funding will always be required.

*Defend the concept of the personal doctor against increasing threats*

Continuity of care with a doctor known to a patient is the most valued attribute of practice organization, and only a doctor's listening and problem solving skills are regarded as more important by patients (Haigh-Smith and Armstrong 1989). Patients of small practices consistently express greater satisfaction (Baker and Streatfield 1995). Department of Health policy has encouraged group practice because single-handed practices are believed to offer a poorer range of patient services, fewer facilities and their doctors are professionally isolated. How can acceptable levels of continuity be ensured, while recognizing the need of doctors and other PHC staff, to prevent 'burnout' by spending time on alternative professional work or increased leisure? PHC services are often the only universally accessible and socially acceptable source of help in deprived areas. People whose lives can be a chaotic struggle to meet basic needs value the stability that a relationship with a familiar GP or health visitor (HV) can provide. Many innovations in general medical services since 1990 have affected UDAs disproportionately. The expansion of deputizing services, the increasing number of GPs choosing to working part time and the growth of academic appointments for teaching and research are all examples. These may improve morale of GPs and combat the recruitment crisis but have problems of their own. Practices with several part-time staff, or salaried doctors on short-term contracts, and where out of hours care is delivered by an unknown doctor will need to consider continuity issues.

Freeman and Hjortdahl suggest ways to do this by adopting continuity as a key goal, examining organizational factors that work against continuity, educating patients about continuity and ensuring good communication between PHC team members (Freeman and Hjortdahl 1997). A doctor who knows and understands a community is more effective than one who doesn't. Every community has a culture subtly different from others. Most PHC staff have a different cultural background than their patients. Time, experience and willingness to learn are the only means of acquiring this knowledge (Heath 1995). If working in UDAs is regarded as a short-term option for staff starting their careers, PHC services could be permanently damaged (R. Baker 1997). Health authorities should encourage staff to remain in a practice long enough to gain this experience.

*Improve morale among primary care staff*

Morale among GPs is lower than it was 10 years ago. No direct evidence exists about whether this is worse in deprived areas but studies have reported greater difficulty in both recruitment and retention of GPs (Carlisle and Johnstone 1996; Taylor and Leese 1998). Similar difficulties exist in attracting experienced health visitors to inner city areas (Hughes *et al.* 1979). The Medical Practitioners Committee may allow smaller average lists in UDAs recognizing the impact of deprivation on workload (Medical Practitioners Committee 1997). This will help a serious cause of stress; lack of time to do a good job. However, it can only be implemented if measures are taken to reduce recruitment where the workload is less. This will require political decisions to restrict the expansion of consultant posts or to increase list sizes in suburban and rural areas. Even if the government accepts that the UK requires 1000 additional medical graduates per year, none will be available to work as GPs until 2007.

The difficulties some practices have experienced in their development has led to the introduction of salaried GPs (Liverpool) or the provision of female doctors in practices with only male doctors (Leicester). These pilot studies aim to develop services in practices that are seen to be under performing. There has been interest recently in proposals to introduce a salaried option for GPs in place of independent contractor status. Others have suggested that all GPs should be salaried. Whether changing the basis of doctors' remuneration will ensure the provision of high quality primary care in UDAs is uncertain. Unless other causes of low morale are identified and addressed it will be difficult to provide sufficient health workers for the demand, let alone attract the best motivated and skilled staff to meet the challenge of expanding PHC in UDAs.

Other suggestions have been proposed to improve PHC in deprived areas (Lorentzon *et al.* 1994; Heath 1997; Pringle 1997).

## Responses to poverty and deprivation, aimed at improving health

Interventions exist to address the determinants of ill-health, such as poverty, with the aim of improving health. These may have been instituted by PHC practices, health authorities, local authorities or voluntary agencies, working either alone or collaboratively. Also, to address un-met health needs, additional medical services have been provided for certain groups of disadvantaged people. Some of these interventions have the support of the Department of Health; for example services for people with mental health problems living in the inner city.

In Birmingham, CAB staff provided welfare benefits advice to patients in PHC; those with mental ill-health were significantly more likely to be eligible for unclaimed benefits (Paris and Player 1993). In Rochdale, housing advisers work in a GP's surgery, providing a service to patients, many of whom are from the Indian subcontinent.

Examples of 'one stop shops' exist similar to the one described earlier in Leicester (Elston 1996). In Leeds, a community based multi-agency facility provides PHC, welfare benefits advice, housing, social services, pharmacy, community mental health services and health promotion (South Seacroft One Stop Services 1996). The facility developed from collaboration between the local authority, PHC, the health authority and other agencies. The former Enfield and Haringey Family Health Services Authority established a rent deposit scheme of £25,000 to underwrite 65 lettings in the private rented sector, enabling homeless people, who frequently have difficulty registering with a GP, to register more easily from a permanent address and to access health services other than those provided under temporary medical registration.

Birmingham's SNUG and Healthy Homes projects aim to reduce admission of patients to hospital. Regional and local health authority funding provided small grants (£1500–£2500) for building work on the homes of people nominated by PHC staff (Williams 1997). Cornwall Health Authority gave £50,000 each to six Cornish District Councils in 1994–95 to install central heating and insulation in 120 damp houses, where children suffering from asthma lived (I.F. MacKenzie, pers. comm.).

Arrangements exist to address the un-met medical needs of people in particular deprived circumstances, for example families living in 'bed and breakfast' type accommodation, including the appointment of GPs, HVs, and mental health workers. A project in Bristol, funded by the Department of Health (£100,000 a year for three years) serves nine general practices and is addressing the higher levels of psychiatric illness in an urban deprived area (Carmichael *et al.* 1996). In Glasgow the provision of a free and readily available patient transport service to out of hours PHC centres may be contributing to equity of access to out of hours primary care for patients from different socio-economic groups (O'Donnell *et al.* 1998).

These innovative approaches to promoting health often involve commitment and the courage of personal convictions. Collaboration between agencies may be difficult, involving time and resources, although it is encouraged by the government.

Like many therapeutic interventions, most of the above interventions have not been evaluated for their contribution to promoting health. This may be because of lack of funds for evaluation, or because evaluation is methodologically challenging, or because to do so might restrict professional clinical freedom. However, evaluation is important to determine effectiveness. Only then can resources be used efficiently, and, health outcomes compared with other, including more traditional, forms of therapy.

*Reducing inequalities in health*

Ways of reducing health inequalities in PHC have been described (Marsh and Channing 1988). A systematic review of interventions aimed at reducing inequalities in health, which the health service, either alone or in collaboration with other agencies, could use to reduce inequalities in health to promote the health of people who are deprived, has been carried out (Arblaster *et al.* 1996). An agenda for action in tackling inequalities in health has also been proposed (Benzeval *et al.* 1995).

## General measures to improve health

Are there general measures that could be taken to support the work of PHC staff in deprived areas that might be expected to improve the health of the local population? What research issues do such measures raise?

*General measures*

Cross nationally, higher levels of both social expenditure and taxation, as a proportion of gross domestic product, are associated with longer life expectancy, lower maternal mortality and a smaller proportion of low birthweight deliveries (Gough and Thomas 1994). Davey Smith considers the argument against redistributive social policies; namely that they hinder economic growth (Davey Smith 1996). That view supposes that greater rewards offered to the entrepreneurially successful make them even more successful and in turn drives economic growth, which through the 'trickle down' effect, benefits the poor. However, international comparisons show the reverse: if anything, countries with greater income inequalities have lower levels of economic growth (Glyn and Miliband 1994).

Evaluated interventions exist that address social disadvantage to promote health. If effective such interventions could be expected to support the work of PHC staff. The Income Maintenance Experiment in Gary, Indiana, USA, guaranteed a minimum income to pregnant women in low income families by using a negative income tax. This significantly increased birthweight. A high level of family benefits has been found to be associated with low infant mortality rates (Wennemo 1993). These support the argument for income support for at risk families. Evaluations exist of nutrition support programmes such as free school milk (I.A. Baker *et al.* 1980), iron (James *et al.* 1992), and other nutritional supplementation (Rush *et al.* 1988), confirming that welfare support can significantly improve infant and child health (Avruch and Cackly 1995). Early and comprehensive programmes such as Head Start and the Infant Health and Development Programme in the USA may effectively promote the health and nutritional status of disadvantaged children (Schweinhart and Weikart 1993).

*Research issues*

Economic evaluation of health producing measures in the UK have concentrated on health care treatments and technologies. Assessing health promoting measures of other sectors, such as education, safety programmes, income maintenance and improvements to the physical environment is challenging. Drummond and Stoddart examined the principles of assessing health promoting measures across different sectors and the methodological issues involved (Drummond and Stoddart 1995). They propose:

- more attempts at intersectoral analysis along lines already undertaken;
- pilot studies in intersectoral evaluation;
- ministries and agencies required to provide a minimum data set to justify spending plans (numbers in the target group, expected benefits, cost, evidence of effectiveness);
- institutional changes to foster intersectoral evaluation;
- incentives for intersectoral collaboration.

## Conclusions

Before the introduction of the NHS the UK health system was inequitable, inefficient and near to financial collapse. Introduced over fifty years ago the NHS went some way towards improving the health of people living in deprived circumstances through free access to health care and by attempts to ensure a more equitable distribution of health services. Universal access to health care free at the point of delivery is important. In the USA reducing financial barriers to accessing health care improved the health of people living in deprived areas (Keeler *et al.* 1985) but of itself is not sufficient (Short and Lefkowitz 1992).

In the UK inequalities in health and inequalities in access to health care persist and have been increasing. By targeting effective PHC to people living in deprived areas, delivered in ways sensitive to socio-economic cultural differences, as well as to differences of ethnic diversity, poor levels of health might be expected to improve. Such interventions need to be evaluated using rigorous study designs and cannot be assumed to be effective simply because they are 'progressive'.

Health care interventions alone when targeted at people who are poor leave intact the system that generates the inequalities. Therefore other strategies to tackle poor health, including social and economic policies aimed at addressing the more fundamental inequalities in society, for example income distribution, need to be considered. Research is required to assess the relative effectiveness and efficiency of these different approaches to promoting the health of people who are deprived. Only then will governments be able to estimate the proportion of poor health that could be reduced by these different approaches. It is likely that non-health service factors would contribute substantially to promoting the health of people living in the most deprived circumstances.

PHC staff continue to manage patients with health problems associated with deprivation. The government expects PHC staff to be involved in promoting the health of the local population. As PHC staff address issues at the practice level they should be supported in this by general measures, including social and economic policies aimed at addressing the more fundamental inequalities in society, in order to go beyond the inverse care law.

# References

Appleton, K., House, A. and Dowell, A. (1998) A survey of job satisfaction, sources of stress and psychological symptoms among general practitioners in Leeds, *British Journal of General Practice*, 48: 1059–63.

Arblaster, L., Lambert, M., Entwistle, V. *et al.* (1996) A systematic review of the effectiveness of health service interventions aimed at reducing inequalities in health, *Journal of Health Services Research and Policy*, 1(2): 93–103.

Audit Commission (1994) *Seen But Not Heard: Co-ordinating Community Child Health and Social Services for Children in Need*. London: HMSO.

Avruch, S. and Cackly, A.P. (1995) Savings achieved by giving WIC benefits to women prenatally, *Public Health Reports*, 110: 27–34.

Azeem Majeed, A. (1998) Commentary: Equity in the allocation of resources to general practices will be difficult to achieve, *British Medical Journal*, 316: 43.

Azeem Majeed, F.A., Chaturvedi, N., Reading, R. and Ben-Shlomo, Y. (1994) Monitoring and promoting equity in primary and secondary care, *British Medical Journal*, 308: 1426–9.

Baker, I.A., Elwood, P.C., Hughes, J. *et al.* (1980) A randomised controlled trial of the effect of the provision of free school milk on the growth of children, *Journal of Epidemiology and Community Health*, 34: 31–4.

Baker, R. (1992) General practice in Gloucestershire, Avon and Somerset: explaining the variations in standards, *British Journal of General Practice*, 42: 415–18.

Baker, R. (1997) Will the future GP remain a personal doctor? *British Journal of General Practice*, 47: 831–4.

Baker, R. and Streatfield, J. (1995) What type of general practice do patients prefer? Exploration of practice characteristics influencing patient satisfaction, *British Journal of General Practice*, 45: 654–9.

Balarajan, R., Yuen, P. and Machin, D. (1992) Deprivation and general practitioner workload, *British Medical Journal*, 304: 529–34.

Baxter, T., Milner, P. and Leaf, M. (1997) A cost effective, community based heart health promotion project in England: prospective comparative study, *British Medical Journal*, 315: 582–3.

Belongia, E. and Schwartz, B. (1998) Strategies for promoting judicious use of antibiotics by doctors and patients, *British Medical Journal*, 317: 668–71.

Ben-Shlomo, Y. and Chaturvedi, N. (1995) Assessing equity in access to health care provision in the UK: does where you live affect your chances of getting a coronary artery bypass graft? *Journal of Epidemiology and Community Health*, 49: 200–4.

Benzeval, M. and Judge, K. (1996) Access to health care in England: continuing inequalities in the distribution of GPs, *Journal of Public Health Medicine*, 18: 33–40.

Benzeval, M., Judge, K. and Whitehead, M. (eds) (1995) *Tackling Inequalities in Health: An Agenda for Action*. London: King's Fund.

Bevan, G. (1998) Taking equity seriously: a dilemma for government from allocating resources to primary care groups, *British Medical Journal*, 316: 39–42.

Blatchford, O. and Capewell, S. (1998) Emergency medical admission rates: general practices vary despite adjustment for age, sex, and deprivation. Paper presented at the Society for Social Medicine 42nd Annual Scientific Meeting, Cardiff.

Bloor, K. and Maynard, A. (1995) *Equity in Primary Care*. York: Centre for Health Economics, University of York.

Boardman, B. (1994) Energy efficiency measures and social inequality, in M. Bhatti, J. Brooke and M. Gibson (eds) *Housing and the Environment: A New Agenda*. London: Chartered Institute of Housing.

Boyle, S. and Smaje, C. (1993) *Primary Health Care in London: Quantifying the Challenge*. London: King's Fund.

Brennan, M. and Carr-Hill, R. (1996) *No Need to Weight Community Health Programmes for Resource Allocation?* York: Centre for Health Economics, University of York.

Burridge, R. and Ormandy, D. (eds) (1993) *Unhealthy Housing: Research, Remedies and Reform*. London: E. & F. N. Spon.

Carlisle, R. and Johnstone, S. (1996) Factors influencing the response to advertisements for general practice vacancies, *British Medical Journal*, 313: 468–71.

Carlisle, R., Groom, L.M., Avery, A.J., Boot, D. and Earwicker, S. (1998) Relation of out of hours activity by general practice and accident and emergency services with deprivation in Nottingham: longitudinal survey, *British Medical Journal*, 316: 520–3.

Carmichael, C., Ford, J. and Williamson, C. (1996) Inner-city blues, *Health Service Journal*, 14 November: 30–31.

Cartwright, A. (1992) Social class differences in health and care in the year before death, *Journal of Epidemiology and Community Health*, 46: 54–7.

Coard, C. and Maguire, C. (undated) Untitled. Leeds: Leeds Citizens' Advice Bureau.

Coulter, A., Fowler, G. and Fuller, A. (1995) Effectiveness of health checks conducted by nurses in primary care: final results of the OXCHECK study, *British Medical Journal*, 310: 1099–1104.

Crayford, T., Shanks, J., Bajekal, M. and Langford, S. (1995) Analysis from inner London of deprivation payments based on enumeration districts rather than wards, *British Medical Journal*, 311: 787–8.

Davey, P.G., Bax, R.P., Newey, J. *et al.* (1996) Growth in the use of antibiotics in the community in England and Scotland in 1980–1993, *British Medical Journal*, 312: 613.

Davey Smith, G. (1996) Income inequality and mortality: why are they related? *British Medical Journal*, 312: 987–8.

Davies, H.T.O. and Crombie, I.K. (1995) Assessing the quality of care, *British Medical Journal*, 311: 766.

Department of the Environment (DoE) (1993) *English House Condition Survey: 1991. Preliminary Report on Unfit Dwellings*. London: Department of the Environment.

Department of Health (1997) *The New NHS: Modern – Dependable*. London: The Stationery Office.

Department of Health (DoH) (1998a) *Fifteen New Health Action Zones to Tackle Health Inequalities*. Press release 98/329. London: Department of Health.

Department of Health (DoH) (1998b) *On the State of the Public Health: The Annual Report of the Chief Medical Officer of the Department of Health for the Year 1997*. London: The Stationery Office.

Drever, F., Whitehead, M. and Roden, M. (1996) Current patterns and trends in male mortality by social class (based on occupation), *Population Trends*, 86: 15–20.

Drummond, M. and Stoddart, G. (1995) Assessment of health producing measures across different sectors, *Health Policy*, 33: 219–31.

Eachus, J., Williams, M., Chan, P. *et al.* (1996) Deprivation and cause specific morbidity: evidence from the Somerset and Avon survey of health, *British Medical Journal*, 312: 287–92.

Ebrahim, S. (1995) Changing patterns of consultation in general practice: fourth national morbidity study, 1991–92, *British Journal of General Practice*, 45: 283–4.

Elston, G. (1996) Better by design, *Doctor*, 16 May: 75–7.

Fleming, D., Crombie, D. and Cross, K. (1991) An examination of practice referral rates in relation to practice structure, patient demography and case mix, *Health Trends*, 232: 100–4.

Freeman, G. and Hjortdahl, P. (1997) What future for continuity of care in general practice? *British Medical Journal*, 314: 1870–3.

Glyn, A. and Miliband, D. (1994) *Paying for Inequality: The Economic Cost of Social Injustice*. London: Oram Press.

Goddard, M. and Smith, P. (1998) *Equity of Access to Health Care*. York: Centre for Health Economics, University of York.

Gough, I. and Thomas, T. (1994) Why do levels of human welfare vary among nations? *International Journal of Health Services*, 24: 715–48.

Graham, H. (1994) Gender and class as dimensions of smoking behaviour in Britain: insights from a survey of mothers, *Social Science and Medicine*, 38(5): 691–8.

Gravelle, H. and Sutton, M. (1998) *Inequalities in the Geographical Distribution of GPs in England and Wales 1974–1995*. York: Centre for Health Economics, University of York.

Grieve, S. (1997) Measuring morale – does practice area deprivation affect doctors' well-being?, *British Journal of General Practice*, 47: 547–52.

Haigh-Smith, C. and Armstrong, D. (1989) Comparison of criteria derived by governments and patients for evaluating general practitioner services, *British Medical Journal*, 299: 494–6.

Hall, D.B.M. (1996) *Health For All Children*. Oxford: Oxford University Press.

Heath, I. (1995) *The Mystery of General Practice*. Oxford: The Nuffield Provincial Hospitals Trust.

Heath, I. (1997) Distributing primary care fairly: threat to social justice, *British Medical Journal*, 314: 598–9.

Higginson, I., Webb, D. and Lessof, L. (1994) Reducing hospital beds for patients with advanced cancer (letter), *Lancet*, 344: 409.

Hills, J. (1990) Untitled. London: Child Poverty Action Group.

Hirst, M., Lunt, N. and Atkin, K. (1998) Were practice nurses distributed equitably across England and Wales, 1988–1995? *Journal of Health Services Research and Policy*, 3(1): 31–8.

Howie, J., Heaney, D. and Maxwell, M. (1997) *Measuring Quality in General Practice*. London: Royal College of General Practitioners.

Hughes, J., Stockton, P., Roberts, J.A. and Logan, R.F.L. (1979) Nurses in the community: a manpower study, *Journal of Epidemiology and Community Health*, 33: 262–9.

Ineichen, B. (1993) *Homes and Health*. London: E. & F. N. Spon.

James, J., Brown, J., Douglas, M., Cox, J. and Stocker, S. (1992) Improving the diet of under fives in a deprived inner city practice, *Health Trends*, 24: 161–4.

Jarman, B. (1983) Identification of underprivileged areas, *British Medical Journal*, 286: 1705–9.

Kammerling, R.M. and O'Connor, S. (1993) Unemployment as a predictor of rate of psychiatric admission, *British Medical Journal*, 307: 1536–9.

Keeler, E.B., Brook, R.H. and Goldberg, G.A. (1985) How free care reduced hypertension in the health insurance experiment, *Journal of the American Medical Association*, 254: 1926–31.

Little, P., Williamson, I., Warner, G. *et al.* (1997) Open randomised trial of prescribing strategies in managing sore throat, *British Medical Journal*, 314: 722–7.

Little, S. (1995) Practice gives patients fund of welfare advice, *Fund-holding*, 6 December: 25–6.

Lorentzon, M., Jarman, B. and Bajekal, M. (1994) *Report of the Inner City Task Force of the Royal College of General Practitioners*. London: Royal College of General Practitioners.

MacDermott, T. (1998a) *Key Poverty Statistics: Households Below Average Income 1994–95*. London: Child Poverty Action Group.

MacDermott, T. (1998b) *Fact Sheet 13: Government Spending*. London: Child Poverty Action Group.

McSmith, A. and Tickell, O. (1996) Rented homes keep poorest in the cold. *Observer*: 29 January.

Marsh, G.N. and Channing, D.M. (1988) Narrowing the health gap between a deprived and an endowed community, *British Medical Journal*, 296: 173–6.

Medical Practitioners Committee (1997) *Newsletter*.

Myers, P.C. (1987) Factors influencing consultation rates in a suburban general practice, *Practitioner*, 231: 231–7.

National Primary Care Research and Development Centre (1998) *Summary of Past Work 1995–1998 and Future Plans*. Manchester: University of Manchester.

Noble, M. and Smith, G. (1994) *Changing Patterns of Income and Wealth in Oxford and Oldham*. York: Joseph Rowntree Foundation.

O'Donnell, C.A., McConnachie, A., Moffat, K. *et al.* (1998) Social variation in out of hours primary care. Paper presented at the Society of Social Medicine 42nd Annual Scientific Meeting, Cardiff.

Office of National Statistics (1997) *Health Inequalities – Decennial Supplement*. London: The Stationery Office.

Oppenheim, C. and Harker, L. (1996) *Poverty: The Facts*. London: Child Poverty Action Group.

Paris, J.A.G. and Player, D. (1993) Citizens' advice in general practice, *British Medical Journal*, 306: 1518–20.

Payne, J.N., Coy, J., Milner, P.C. and Patterson, S. (1993) Are deprivation indicators a proxy for morbidity? A comparison of the prevalence of arthritis, depression, dyspepsia, obesity and respiratory symptoms with unemployment rates and Jarman scores, *Journal of Public Health Medicine*, 15: 161–70.

Payne, N. and Saul, C. (1997) Variations in use of cardiology services in a health authority: comparison of coronary artery revascularisation rates with prevalence of angina and coronary mortality, *British Medical Journal*, 314: 257–61.

Pringle, M. (1997) Distributing primary care fairly: an opportunity to improve primary care, *British Medical Journal*, 314: 595–7.

Roberts, J. (1993) How GPs cope amid rising racial tension, *Pulse*, 16 October: 50.

Romans, S.E., McNoe, B.M., Herbison, G.P., Walton, V.A. and Mullen, P.E. (1993) Cigarette smoking and psychiatric morbidity in women, *Australian and New Zealand Journal of Psychiatry*, 27: 399–404.

Rose, G. (1992) *The Strategy of Preventive Medicine*. Oxford: Oxford Medical Publications.

Rush, D., Alvir, J., Kenny, D., Johnson, S. and Horwitz, D. (1988) The national WIC evaluation: evaluation of the special supplemental food programme for women, infants and children. III historical study of pregnancy outcomes, *American Journal of Clinical Nutrition*, 48: 412–28.

Schweinhart, L.J. and Weikart, D.P. (1993) Success by empowerment – the high scope perry pre-school study through age 27, *Young Children*, 49: 54–8.

Short, P.F. and Lefkowitz, D.C. (1992) Encouraging preventive services for low-income children. The effect of expanding Medicaid, *Medical Care*, 30: 766–80.

Slade, M., McCrone, P. and Thornicroft, G. (1995) Uptake of welfare benefits by psychiatric patients, *Psychiatric Bulletin*, 19: 411–13.

Slingsby, C. (1998) The winners and the losers in GPs pay pool system, *Medeconomics*, 19: 46–8.

Smith, P., Sheldon, T.A., Carr-Hill, R.A. *et al.* (1994) Allocating resources to health authorities: results and policy implications of small areas analysis of use of inpatient services, *British Medical Journal*, 309: 1050–4.

South Seacroft One Stop Services (1996) *Information Leaflet.* Leeds: Leeds City Council, Leeds Health Authority and the Seacroft One Stop Services.

Stilwell, P. and Stilwell, J. (1995) A locality focus on health for Wolverhampton, *Health and Social Care in the Community*, 3: 181–90.

Taylor, D. and Leese, B. (1998) General practitioner turnover and migration in England 1990–1994, *British Journal of General Practice*, 48: 1070–2.

Townsend, P., Whitehead, M. and Davidson, N. (eds) (1992) *Inequalities in Health: The Black Report and the Health Divide.* London: Penguin Books.

Tudor Hart, J. (1971) The inverse care law, *Lancet*, 1: 405–12.

Tudor Hart, T.J., Thomas, C., Gibbons, B. *et al.* (1991) Twenty-five years of case finding and audit in a socially deprived community, *British Medical Journal*, 302: 1509–13.

Wennemo, I. (1993) Infant mortality, public policy and inequality – a comparison of 18 industrialised countries 1950–85, *Sociology of Health and Illness*, 15(4): 429–46.

Wilcox, S. (1996) *Housing Review 1996/97.* York: Joseph Rowntree Foundation.

Wilkin, D., Metcalfe, D.H.M. and Hallam, L. (1984) Area variations in the process of care in urban general practice, *British Medical Journal*, 289: 229–32.

Williams, H. (1997) *SNUG and Healthy Homes: A Progress Report.* Birmingham: Birmingham City Council.

Wilson, A., McDonald, P., Hayes, L. and Cooney, L. (1992) Health promotion in the general practice consultation: a minute makes a difference, *British Medical Journal*, 304: 227–30.

Worrall, A., Rea, J.N. and Ben-Shlomo, Y. (1997) Counting the cost of social disadvantage in primary care: retrospective analysis of patient data, *British Medical Journal*, 314: 38–42.

Wyke, S., Campbell, G. and MacIver, S. (1992) Provision of, and patient satisfaction with, primary care services in a relatively affluent area and a relatively deprived area of Glasgow, *British Journal of General Practice*, 42: 271–5.

Part III

# Challenges of research

# 8 Locality planning and research evidence: using primary care data

Joanne Jordan

## Introduction

Since the beginning of the 1990s primary care has undergone fundamental changes in both organization and delivery, which have brought it increasingly centre-stage in the provision of health care services within the wider NHS. This chapter examines a number of key issues facing this new primary care led NHS, particularly in light of the growing emphasis on responding to *local* health needs. Such emphasis holds clear implications for a developing public health/primary care partnership, as it suggests the need for detailed *local-level* morbidity and health needs data as a key component in effective targeting of *population* health care services and appropriate use of health resources.

Against the backdrop of structural changes, increasing recognition has been made of primary care as a potentially rich source of morbidity and related data (Westcott and Jones 1987; Pringle and Hobbs 1991; Watkins 1994; Murray and Graham 1995; Shanks and Kheraji 1995). However, while much has been made of the likely value of this information, less attention has been paid to two major questions that impact upon both its delivery and use. Firstly, how is the information held within primary care to be accessed? Here, the increasing use of computer systems to record all aspects of primary care work would appear, on the face of it at least, to enhance the accessibility of relevant information and, therefore, to improve significantly the opportunities for individual or joint initiatives that involve its utilization. Secondly, not only is the issue of *access* salient but the more fundamental issue of whether, and to what extent, primary care data is *useful* in the context of local health care planning and management needs to be addressed.

What follows uses the experiences of two independent projects, each with a combined research and service development orientation and each involving collaboration between primary care and public health, to begin to answer these questions. It does so through a detailed focus on project organization and process, using both differences and similarities to highlight issues pertinent to the effective development and use of primary care data in the new world of locality based commissioning.

## The impetus behind primary care/public health partnership in care

Since the late 1980s successive government initiatives have elevated the role of primary care in the delivery of health care. Under the previous administration this process reached its culmination in 1994 with the introduction of primary care led purchasing (National Health Service Management Executive 1994), which, more than any previous initiative, made general practice central to the provisioning of services and allocation of resources within the NHS. However, a fundamental weakness in the scheme, based on differential involvement between fundholding and non-fundholding general practices, meant that GP involvement in purchasing and commissioning remained piecemeal. Further, authority remained exclusively with GPs, with other members of the primary care team given no formal role in decision making.

This divisive and fragmentary arrangement looks set to disappear with the creation of the new primary care groups (Department of Health 1997a). Indeed, this White Paper may be seen as strengthening the role of primary care in commissioning as the new model requires GPs to combine with other health care professionals locally to plan and develop health services for all patients in a defined area. Thus, the inequity that existed under the previous system is diminished as all general practice gains representation and, moreover, responsibility for commissioning decision making is extended to other members of the primary care team.

Meanwhile, again beginning in the late 1980s, the role of public health in the planning and provisioning of health care has been expanding. Under the previous system, in which health authorities and primary care were administered separately, departments of public health held responsibility for advising health authorities on how to promote health as well as commission effective care. This responsibility was formally extended to primary care with the formation of the Health Commissions in 1996. Most recently, the Labour Party's focus on 'a contract for health' (Department of Health 1997b) has served to yet further enhance the status of public health, clearly symbolized by the appointment, for the first time ever in England, of a Minister of Public Health.

This evolving process has given, step by step, increasing priority to local level health care planning and commissioning and the central involvement of primary care in this. Further, the role of public health in supporting and facilitating the commissioning activity of both primary care and local health authorities has been given formal emphasis. For those working within primary care, responsibility for locality based health care carries with it an obvious requirement to look beyond the needs of individual patients to consider those of the local community. For public health professionals, the need to adopt a 'bottom-up' approach, that is, to focus on the needs of relatively small populations, necessarily involves being sensitive to local particularities, often not reflected in the aggregate data with which they typically work.

The gradual convergence of primary care and public health responsibilities in locality commissioning means that both now need access to accurate, up-to-date and locally sensitive aggregate person based health information. This can provide a baseline to support decision making regarding service provision and resource allocation, as well as for monitoring and evaluating outcomes. Clearly, primary care has the potential to deliver relevant information. It makes obvious sense that its exploitation occurs, to a greater or lesser degree, on a joint basis.

Over the past few years examples of where this has been happening have been on the rise. Exactly what forms future collaboration take will materialize over the short to medium term. In the meantime, given that the focus on primary care as a provider of local level data looks set to increase, it is perhaps judicious to look back at the experiences of previous initiatives that have sought to use such data as a preliminary means of identifying issues salient to its effective development and (shared) use. This initial, and by necessity, brief review is subsequently carried forward into a more detailed analysis of two independent projects.

## Evidence from previous initiatives involving primary care information collection and use

What do the experiences of previous initiatives that have sought to exploit primary care data reveal about the possibilities of using this data for the purposes of locality planning? First of all, it should be said that such initiatives are few in number and those that have taken place have done so only relatively recently. Thus, up until the mid to late 1980s there had been little in the way of research and/or service development projects specifically investigating the potential of primary care data.

One of the earliest studies, The Oxford Community Health Project (Mant and Tulloch 1987; Coulter et al. 1989), included an investigation of the level of chronic disease recording in general practice. Significant inconsistencies were found, leaving researchers to conclude that general practice could not be relied upon to provide accurate estimates of disease prevalence. Since then a survey conducted in 1993 found that approximately 80 per cent of practices were operating with a computer (National Health Service Management Executive 1993) and it is likely that this figure will have increased in the intervening years, especially in light of the NHS information and technology strategy (National Health Service Management Executive 1992). Has the increase in use been reflected in an improvement in the quality of data recorded? Findings are conflicting, with particular doubt being cast on morbidity that is managed solely within primary care (Jick et al. 1991; Johnson et al. 1991).

One of the most recent studies, Scobie et al. (1995), was based on an intensive investigation of general practice data quality in a number of inner

London practices. Of particular significance is the finding, similar to earlier studies, that relatively few chronic problems were being coded. Given that much chronic ill health is managed exclusively within primary care this leaves open to question the possibility of deriving *detailed* information on chronic disease, currently unavailable from any other source. On a more positive note, the authors found recording of information to be more complete and consistent when of obvious practical use to practices, for example, when computer protocols were being used for regular patient reviews. In general terms, they identified a number of confounding factors to be undermining the capacity of recorded clinical information to generate reliable prevalence data. These factors included inconsistent coding, use of preliminary diagnoses or symptom codes, difficulties in data extraction and ambiguity surrounding some diagnosis and coding, for example, in relation to mental health.

What about the projects that have involved joint working between primary care and public health? Predictably, the development of policy creating a climate of need for closer working relationships has been accompanied by the emergence of a broad range of collaborative projects on the ground. There has been a proliferation of independent projects that have seen, typically, general practice being invited by the local health authority to participate in an investigation and/or development of the potential of computer held data for a wide range of purposes. All, in some way or another, have addressed the information priorities of both primary care and the local health authority. Individual projects have differed in terms of who collects the information, what information gets collected, how it gets collected and, subsequently, how it is used. It is perhaps not surprising, then, that these collaborative initiatives have produced variable findings. The conclusions reached by two of the more extensive studies will serve to demonstrate this variability.

The study conducted by Pearson *et al.* (1996) involved 11 general practices collaborating with the local department of public health in the production of data relating to disease presenting in primary care. The aim was to use this data to inform service provision. Because of this, project facilitators went to strenuous lengths to ensure that participating practices were representative of the local health authority population for both general practice and population characteristics; this involved the use of a computerized model designed specifically for the purpose. However, despite the fact that representativeness was achieved, this could not be done on a purely random basis. Rather, only those practices using Read codes and computer software compatible with the project's data extraction software, and that were also representative, could be involved.

Practices were asked to supply morbidity data by recording Read and episode type codes for each face to face contact between patients and practice medical and nursing staff. Data quality was maximized through a range of measures, including: training of relevant practice staff; periodic data validation checks; computer generated edit checks for incorrect data entry and/or misappropriate Read coding; and regular general practice user group meetings to allow discussion around data feedback and interpractice comparison.

These meetings also allowed agreement to be reached on the common use of Read codes where this was considered appropriate. The project was able to put together a data set on a range of morbidity, elements of which were used subsequently to inform service provision.

Although clearly a thorough and, in turn, successful study in that it fulfilled its objective of supplying complete and representative data that aided the commissioning of local services, it can be argued that this success is circumscribed in a number of important ways. Firstly, practices were asked to supply data that they were, in essence, already collecting. The ability and willingness of general practice to collect data not immediately relevant to its own requirements was, therefore, not addressed. On this point, although standardization of Read codes was probably not necessary, given the limited nature of data being provided, such standardization may well be appropriate where a more complex data set is being developed. Secondly, and related, although the project secured a breadth of morbidity information, a concomitant depth was missing. For example, data relating to severity as well as to service use was not collected. The usefulness of such 'isolated' morbidity data, particularly for locality planning and service provision, is questionable.

These two points come together when we consider that if primary care is to deliver the complexity of information needed to inform locality planning *fully* then it is inevitable that some degree of disruption to normal collection procedures will be required. On this note, the authors' claim that their approach offers a 'practical, *non-disruptive* method of gathering data [author's emphasis]' (Pearson *et al*. 1996: 1519) may not be as appealing as first appears.

While Pearson *et al*. (1996) found the collection of morbidity data from primary care to be relatively unproblematic, Wilson *et al*. (1995) encountered significant difficulties, particularly in relation to the dual (primary care and health authority) use of data. This study brought together 14 practices with the local health authority with the aim of developing a computerized primary care information gathering network capable of producing routine and reliable data on risk factors and specific morbidities. Participating practices were not representative of the wider health authority population; rather, their inclusion was based on willingness to collect data. Consequently, practices exhibited a broad range of computer expertise and data 'sophistication'.

The outcomes achieved by the project were hampered by the fact that eight different GP computing systems were in use as well as, initially, four different clinical coding structures. This diversity meant that the data could not be relied upon as either accurate or consistent, in that the potential range of codes on which to search was vast (increasing the likelihood of data loss) and practices were using the same or similar codes differentially. Moreover, the variability in the reporting capacity of GP computing systems meant that data could not be reported in standard formats. As a result of these and other confounding factors, including the incomplete recording of many of the practices as well as their inability to supply requested information within agreed deadlines, the data produced by project activity could not be taken as a reliable summary of local morbidity and other health related behaviour.

This said, the project was one of the earliest initiatives focusing on the potential of primary care information. Consequently, it 'suffered' from the relative lack of (primary care) motivation in developing the collection and use of computer data. Since then, the policy developments outlined in the previous section have served to boost awareness of the centrality of primary care data and the role of computers in securing access to them. In the process, improvements in commercial GP computer systems, technological advances in data extraction and a growing acknowledgement on the part of primary care practitioners of the need for consistency in data recording, have all contributed to improvements in data quality as well as their accessibility.

Given that subsequent projects, such as the Pearson *et al.* (1996) study reported above, have concentrated on relatively data 'sophisticated' practices, this project was particularly valuable in exposing the problems that arise when practices that are less skilled in the collection and use of information are involved. Such problems include: lack of/differential computer skills and motivation among practice staff; limited appreciation of the potential of computer held information; and lack of coordination or agreement between staff members on what information to record and when to record it. If primary care data is to be used to generate locally representative data, it is inevitable that, at some point, these and similar problems are going to be confronted.

The collective evidence from these studies would seem to suggest that there has been limited improvement only in the quality of primary care data *overall* since the earlier days of the Oxford Community Health Project. Certainly, that is the clear message from both the Scobie *et al.* (1995) and Wilson *et al.* (1995) studies. While Pearson *et al.* (1996) are more optimistic, and with good reason, it should be remembered that their study concentrated on aspects of data collection with which primary care practitioners were more likely to feel at ease. When Wilson *et al.* (1995) asked primary care practitioners to supply data beyond the 'routine', for example, risk factors as well as social characteristics such as ethnicity, significant motivational problems arose.

Despite the problems and pitfalls outlined above, the number of projects that seek to exploit primary care data are on the increase. So what is it about primary care data that is so seductive?

## Why collect/use primary care data?

The appeal of primary care data stems both from inherent properties as well as external context. In terms of the character of primary care data itself, three main attributes are clear: the range/coverage of information collected in the course of routine practice work; the patient based detail of that information; and the fact that, in aggregate form, it pertains to specified local populations. Consequently, primary care practitioners are capable of providing a vast wealth of information including that relating to health, illness and social circumstance as well as health and social care provision. Moreover, this data can be manipulated in a whole host of ways, to assemble patient based as well as local population profiles. However manipulated, the data are always locally sensitive, a quality that makes them particularly valuable in the context of locality based commissioning.

In terms of external context, and setting aside the drive for locality commissioning already discussed, two further factors, in particular, are encouraging the use of primary care data. Firstly, the growth of the use of computers to collect and store a wide range of individual patient clinical data, typically by Read coding (Chisholm 1990) the summary details from patients' written medical records. Such technological advances vastly improve the accessibility of the data held within primary care over that previously available from written records. Secondly, the fact that there exists a lack of routinely available, up to date and accurate information on the prevalence and incidence of ill health and disease managed in the community. National sources of morbidity data, for example, the national morbidity studies, are often unrepresentative of smaller localities or populations and can quickly become out of date as they are undertaken decennially (Pearson *et al.* 1996). Moreover, the morbidity and health event data held in primary care covers the actual morbidity people experience, unlike proxies such as death data, census data or hospital in-patient data.

So far, the theoretical potential of primary care data has been established. In addition, there has been some consideration of the issues germane to the practical realization of this potential. The discussion is now developed along the following lines. An initial and relatively brief account of the design and content of two separate projects in which I was involved as an independent evaluator (for the funding organization) is presented as the backdrop to a subsequent analysis of two inter-related issues: the complexities inherent in gathering and using primary care data; and the conditions that therefore need to be in place for the successful development of primary care data.

## Project 1: An investigation of the quality of primary care data

The first project brought together a group of eight general practices with public health medicine in a programme of activity extending over a 15-month period. Project activity was based on the formal aim to determine the availability, comparability and uses of routinely collected general practice morbidity information. This aim was devised by the health authority as a framework for guiding project activity. Within that framework the following objectives existed:

- prevalence and incidence data for selected morbidities were to be collected, extracted, analysed and fed back to practices;
- practice computer based data were to be compared with other sources of aggregate information and selected practice data were to be compared with same practice written records;
- practices were to be assisted in the use of information collected for operational, audit and purchasing purposes.

Project activity centred on the collection of incidence data (all new cases reported) for the year 1994 on three morbidities: ischaemic heart disease, cerebrovascular disease and peptic ulcer. Parameters for collection were set in terms of Read codes and related to data extraction rather than to data input since prescriptive definitions were not considered feasible. A working group, consisting of several of the participating GPs, was asked to consider the possibility of using standardized diagnostic and coding protocols. Their recommendation was that these should not be imposed because of the difficulties in reaching consensus as well as the impracticability of applying strict definitions and coding procedures.

Given that the project set itself up as essentially non-interventionist in nature, that is as an investigation of the possibilities for existing data use, it was decided that only those practices already using a computer to record patient data on a routine basis would be invited to participate. Thus, only established training practices were approached on the grounds that they would be both motivated and skilled in information retrieval and use. This said, the health authority did originally aim to put together a group of practices demographically representative of the district population. However, by the time the selection process was completed, the criterion of 'representativeness' had been abandoned, given the comparatively few practices with adequately developed information systems.

In this regard, the atypical position of participating practices is highlighted by the fact that three out of the eight had employed individuals specifically to input retrospective patient data with the aim of bringing all records up to date. In one practice this meant a total of ten months' employment for one individual inputting 12,000 records, typically working from 7.30am through to 3.30pm. In another, two members of staff were employed for a fixed period to create and transfer written summaries into the computer; in total the cost of this employment amounted to over £10,000.

From the outset of the project the underlying perspective informing the health authority's approach to using not only the data collected as part of project activity but, seemingly, to using data *per se*, may be summarized as follows: that the proposed use of data is a main determinant of required data quality. The clear implication here is that acceptable quality varies depending upon the context in which data are to be used. Thus, in terms of project aims and objectives, the focus on primary care use of data directed the nature of, and extent to which, data reliability was investigated. For example, a cross-check of practice myocardial infarction (MI) data against hospital in-patient records was conducted in order to establish the degree to which practices were coding MIs recorded in hospital discharge letters. Discrepancies were investigated via consultation of written patient notes. Again, the computer records of some practices were compared with manual records, with the latter being used as a baseline against which completeness could be assessed.

Project activity continued for approximately 12 months. During that period, and despite the strenuous attempts made to advance to a stage of primary care use of information, this had not happened. Rather, activity had concentrated on the investigation of the quality of information recorded, that investigation being limited to the quality related to use within individual practices. Consequently, the focus was on data completeness, with no attention paid to other aspects of data quality, relevant to its use at interpractice as well as health authority level.

In terms of short-term benefit, practice participants were clear that the project had been of particular benefit to them, facilitating data collection (typically, the computer summarization of retrospective patient data) and providing detailed quality checks on that data. In addition, the data collection exercise stimulated considerable thinking about the potential of data actually or potentially accessible by computer. Thus, some practice representatives had, by their own admission, rather fixed ideas on how to use computer based data prior to becoming involved in the project. Participation enabled them to appreciate more fully how data might best be collected as well as applied, stimulated by discussion with both primary care and public health colleagues. There was universal acknowledgement that the health authority had not materially benefited from project activity. Nevertheless, from the latter's perspective, the project had contributed to the development of an effective database for health care monitoring and planning.

A promotional meeting held in March 1996 brought the project to a formal close. The meeting was devoted to a review of project activity and outcomes over the previous 15 months as well as a discussion of possible future collaborative work. Significantly, this discussion was dominated by suggestions primarily relating to individual practice objectives including, for example, various audits and management reviews.

## Project 2: An investigation of the potential of primary care data

The second project brought together 11 general practices with the local public health department in a programme of activity that began in early 1995 and remains ongoing. The discussion conducted here focuses on the first wave of activity, during which time efforts were concentrated on putting together a diabetic dataset that satisfied both primary care and health authority information requirements.

From the outset, the project's guiding aim, to supply information to commission health care relevant to the needs of local populations, established the drive for tangible outcomes in terms of the delivery of data that could be used, *inter alia*, for local population health care planning and provisioning. Underpinning this aim was the health authority's acknowledgement of the need to develop some means of ensuring the collective reliability of the data produced. To this end, initial project activity centred on reaching consensus regarding a standard method for data collection. This was achieved through an extended period of negotiation during which time a Read coded dataset, initially devised by the department of public health, was subsequently refined via discussion with participating GPs.

A standard recording procedure was considered crucial to the achievement of consistency and, thereby, to the reliability of the data collected. Ironically, an early obstacle to such consistency proved to be the very mechanism originally envisaged as its principal facilitator, the Read code system. The range of different codes under which the same information could be recorded meant participating practices were recording data in a range of ways.

As this increased the potential for information loss, decisions had to be taken on which Read codes to use to ensure that all relevant information was captured. This took considerable time, effort and concession but agreement was reached on a standard dataset with which all participants felt comfortable.

Significantly, the more fundamental question of exactly what information was to be supplied by practices was not as fervently debated as might first be anticipated. However, its resolution did require some compromise between the information requirements of the health authority and what general practice was willing and able to deliver. The following examples provide some idea of the nature and extent of compromise necessary.

Health authority representatives considered it essential that they gained information regarding the monitoring of diabetic patients. Concerns were raised by GPs regarding their ability to provide such information, given that it depended on a flow of information from secondary care. For example, where a patient was being seen by the local podiatry service, examination of lower limbs was, typically, not conducted by the practice. Therefore, for monitoring data to be recorded at practice level required regular feedback from the podiatrist regarding screening results. Participating GPs complained that such feedback was frequently absent from both podiatry and ophthalmology clinics. In an effort to improve the local situation, the lead public health doctor undertook to contact relevant services requesting that procedures for feedback be developed. In turn, GPs agreed to provide the relevant information.

The health authority also required information regarding site of care. The fact that, for the purposes of individual patient management, GPs did not need to record who was providing care at what site, meant the prospect of extra work with no tangible benefit to themselves. However, it was eventually agreed that practices would supply relevant information but in a very succinct way, condensing all possible detail into two codes. Thus, if the GP did the annual review then site of care would be coded as 'GP only' and if the hospital did the annual check then site of care would be coded as 'hospital only'. The code 'shared care' was rejected as being too vague.

Data reliability was also thought to depend on consistency in the way recorded data were extracted from computer systems. The project sought to standardize data extraction through the use of a computer interrogation software package, MIQUEST (MIQUEST Project Board 1994), designed to overcome problems associated with having to locate the same information stored at different places in different computer systems. However, considerable difficulties arose because project activity required complex data trawls not previously attempted using the package. Consequently, purely operational difficulties, whereby MIQUEST repeatedly failed to capture relevant data, caused considerable frustration and demotivation among participants. A total of five data trawls were required before problems were resolved to the satisfaction of all. In the process much time, effort and goodwill was expended on the very mechanism originally employed to ease the burden of project involvement (in that practices would not have to write their own queries).

As a result of the course of activity followed by the project, including the not inconsiderable difficulties encountered, it took just over one full year before participants reached the stage at which they felt comfortable with, and confident of, the data generated. At that point, however, all were able to claim confidence in the diabetic dataset as a true record of morbidity and related health event data, and one on which future health care provisioning and planning could be based.

In turn, project activity generated tangible outcomes at both general practice and health authority level. At a basic level, practice data recording procedures were reviewed to become more systematic. As the dataset contained items relating to prevalence, risk factors, monitoring tests, site of care and outcomes it could be, and was, used by practices to refine clinical care, as well as identify necessary staff skill mix and training needs. In addition, fundholding practices were able to set new contracts for support services. Similar to the first project, participation informed thinking about the possible uses of computer held data, both in general terms as well as in relation to specific practice clinical or management initiatives.

The health authority also used the data in a number of important ways. It aided the development of a local diabetic register for the first time ever as well as the production of health indices for the local population, published in the Annual Health Report. The data were used in a review of local physical rehabilitation services, where no other data were available, highlighting the higher prevalence of diabetes and complications than expected. The diabetic dataset was subsequently agreed locally as the standard dataset for diabetes across three trusts and primary health care on a district wide basis. This was achieved through the efforts of the public health doctor heading up the project, who ensured that the dataset was disseminated across the district for other practices to use, creating a roll-on effect by which the data collection protocols were taken up by others, thereby encouraging standardization on a district wide basis.

### Organization, process and outcome in primary care data development: what do project experiences reveal?

Clearly there were significant differences between, as well as some similarities in, the two projects in terms of organization, process and, consequently, outcomes achieved. This section will use a detailed examination of some of these characteristics as a means of highlighting the complexities inherent in the development and (shared) use of primary care data.

*Project organization: achieving representative data*

Perhaps the most telling area of correspondence between the two projects is that relating to the nature of the practices involved. Given the otherwise considerable distance between them, this throws into stark relief the current difficulties in achieving representative data from primary care.

As already indicated, the first project involved recognized training practices on the grounds that these were more likely to be recording and using data than non-training practices. Although, initially, the health authority also sought to include a representative cross-section of practices, capable of producing data reflecting the demographic and geographical make-up of the wider population, this aim was subsequently abandoned as it became clear that the two criteria, that is, data 'sophistication' and representativeness, could not both be secured. As the project was primarily concerned with an investigation of the potential, as opposed to the practicalities, of using primary care data, priority was placed on involving practices most likely to have a track record in data use.

Given the aims of the second project, greater emphasis was placed on achieving some degree of representativeness. Therefore, the health authority initially approached 20 practices as being representative of the wider district population in terms of age, sex and geographical location. However, using MIQUEST immediately restricted possible participants to those using Meditel System 5, EMIS and Genisyst (all either already compatible, or being adapted for use, with MIQUEST). This meant that 11 of the original practices were lost. In the event, two practices not using MIQUEST compatible systems were included as the health authority attempted to increase data representativeness. This reduced the loss to nine. Given that the 11 practices eventually remaining were capable of producing data that could be taken as 'reasonably' representative of the wider district, the health authority concluded that the project remained a potentially valuable exercise.

*Project process: data coverage*

The first project was limited to the collection of data on incidence/counts of specific morbidities. Consequently, practices were asked to supply, in essential respects, information that they were already routinely recording on the computer. The second project cast its information net considerably further, seeking data not only on 'counts of' but also 'types of' care, monitoring tests/outcomes, complications, referrals and co-morbidity. As has already been indicated, the complexity of the dataset meant practices needed to collect information normally not coded on the computer. The process by which agreement on data collection procedures was reached involved considerable negotiation and compromise on the part of both parties, but a resolution was reached. Notwithstanding the reservation expressed by some practices concerning their long-term ability to provide the full range of data requested, they continued to make strenuous efforts to comply with the health authority dataset requirements. From the point of view of the latter, unless aggregate data on a broad range of local health features was forthcoming, primary care could not improve upon the quality of (typically, proxy) information available from other sources.

*Project process: data interrogation*

Throughout the course of the first project, practices provided data generated by their own query systems. Participants suggested that it was the relative simplicity of the information requested that enabled them to write the necessary queries (with support from the project information analyst); they considered that requests for more complex information would have to be accompanied by greater support from the health authority. In the second project, precisely because practices were being asked to supply quite complex data, queries were run using MIQUEST, which, in theory, should have greatly eased the process of data extraction. Although initially unreliable, MIQUEST did become a valuable aid to the production of reliable data. As has been made clear throughout the course of this discussion, the health authority considered depth, breadth and reliability of data as essential to effective locality planning. Such high quality data could not be expected from primary care practitioners without the development of a comprehensive 'support' infrastructure; MIQUEST was (eventually) an essential component of this.

### Project process: investigation of data quality

The first project used interpractice comparison as the framework for subsequent data quality checks, with results being fed back to practices in an anonymized fashion. However, validation of data completeness was conducted on an essentially intrapractice basis by comparing computer notes with manual records as well as with hospital records. There was no independent assessment of the quality of information being recorded in manual notes. Consequently, the confidence invested in them as a comparative measure may have been misplaced. As Scobie *et al.* (1995) discovered, quality of manual records varies considerably so it cannot be assumed that they can be used for comparative purposes.

Although the approach of marginalizing the issue of *aggregate* data consistency was adopted, the health authority continued to be aware of its bearing on data reliability. This awareness was manifested at various stages in the course of data collection and review, including the commentary accompanying the results of the 'first cut' of data, which highlighted a number of factors potentially confounding apparent interpractice variation including, for example, disparities in individual practice data collection methods and irregularities in computer query systems. However, the imperative was always to move to a situation in which data were available. Once secured, their further investigation, including in terms of consistency and reliability, was considered a more realistic pursuit. However, no such investigation ever took place, with the result that the question of *why* interpractice variation was occurring was never fully addressed.

In the second project, the investigation of data quality was pursued in a number of ways, including interpractice comparison as well as cross-checking against national and other local statistics. However, such cross-checking was considered a first step in, rather than an end to, the investigation of the quality of the data being recorded. Thus, the investigation did not stop at the identification of variation but sought to determine *why* such variation occurred. Where comparison revealed gaps and discrepancies, lengthy and detailed discussions paid close attention to the detail of data collection, including diagnosis and coding protocols. Only after consistency across the diabetic dataset had been achieved was the latter considered a valid basis of health care decision making.

*Project outcomes: use of data*

Clearly, the first project was very much oriented towards investigating and, where appropriate, improving the quality of primary care data. Data use was confined to exposing gaps in the collection and recording procedures of some of the participating practices, with the result that these procedures, and consequently data completeness, were improved. Although there was a stated interest in exploring primary care use of *aggregate* data, in the end, collected data were only ever used in the context of individual practice clinical and/or management. Why was this the case? And, in particular, why was this the case given the project's emphatic focus on use of data within primary care? It is my contention that this failure was directly related to practice confidence in the data as an accurate measure of *interpractice variation* in morbidity. This is discussed in more detail in the next section.

In stark contrast, the second project made many and diverse uses of the diabetic dataset at individual practice, group practice and health authority level. Significantly, participants were agreed that such extensive usage was possible only because data quality had been so thoroughly investigated, meaning that it could be relied upon as an accurate indicator of health and health care status.

## Discussion: what do project experiences suggest to be the prerequisites of successful primary care data development and use?

*Commonality in project experiences*

The common experiences of both projects exposed a number of deeply rooted problems associated with the development of primary care information. Three of these are discussed below.

*Achieving representative data*

To differing degrees the data produced by both projects were unrepresentative of the local populations served by the two health authorities. In this regard, their usefulness for locality health care planning becomes questionable. From their experiences it would appear that although health authorities may design information projects in the hope of achieving representativeness, such is the rudimentary state of GP information systems that it is likely, at least in the short to medium term, that they will have to continue to accept available, as distinct from preferred, practices. Meanwhile, a body of data from practices currently not recording patient morbidity and related data, or doing so in a limited fashion only, is missing from the various local 'pictures' of health and health care needs currently being built up across the UK.

Consequently, the necessity to target provision of appropriate support to practices with less highly developed computerized information systems would appear crucial. It is perhaps significant that by the close of the first project a clear line of division in opinion had emerged between participating GPs and health authority representatives. While most of the former were convinced of the absolute necessity to involve less well resourced practices with under developed information systems, the latter suggested that these practices should be encouraged, not dragooned, into participation.

*Variability in GP computer systems*
A variety of computer systems continue to be used in primary care. This situation creates considerable problems in relation to the extraction of data where this is being attempted on a collective basis. This is due to the fact that each of the systems organizes and stores information in different ways, making its uniform extraction particularly difficult. As the experiences of the second project amply demonstrate, consistency in data extraction is not only extremely difficult but, at present, seems possible only at the cost of data representativeness.

It is clear that, at present, the variability built into commercial GP computer systems hinders opportunities for the extraction of data on anything approaching a locality basis. However, this rather pessimistic state of affairs looks set to change over the medium to long term. The recently launched Collection of Health Data from General Practice (CHDGP) (National Health Service Executive 1997a) has opted to use MIQUEST to obtain data from all contributing practices and, in the process, has developed a new version of the MIQUEST query (HQL) editor as well as made improvements to the integration software. Not only will this improve the operational quality of the software but its uptake at national level has already encouraged GP system suppliers to make their products suitable for use with MIQUEST. In the process, the ability to derive consistent, comparable and, eventually, representative, data from primary care should improve.

*Other practical issues*
The common experiences of both projects revealed a number of other practical issues to be adversely affecting the possibilities for deriving reliable data from primary care. Pressure of space prevents anything more than a simple listing: variability in diagnoses and clinical definitions; ambiguity caused by the hierarchical nature/flexibility of the Read code system; practice (in) consistency in data collection and recording; vulnerability of data collection to pressures of routine work; generality of primary care work; and, finally, the ambiguity inherent in much primary care diagnosis.

The final two points will be illustrated as a way of fleshing out the rather abbreviated summary presented above. In relation to the generality of practice work, on occasions, practice representatives mentioned home visits as a 'crisis' point in the collection of data, given the impossibility of coding information directly on to a computer and the fact that follow-up recording did not always take place. In relation to the ambiguity inherent in much primary care work, it has been estimated that it may be possible to make a firm diagnosis in only 30 per cent of cases (Morrel 1991); much of what is initially presented in primary care requires further investigation before a diagnosis can be confirmed. These two facets of primary care work alone mean that at any one point in time a considerable body of relevant data may be unavoidably missing from practice computer records.

*Diversity in project experiences*

As has already become clear, the most conspicuous difference in project experiences centred on collaborative use of data; that is, use of aggregate data at interpractice and/or health authority level. Given that such an approach to planning is fundamental to the new arrangements for locality commissioning, the reason(s) for, and implications of, this difference are now discussed in considerable detail.

*Reaching the stage of collaborative information use*
Although the first project was essentially an exploration of the contemporary state of general practice computer morbidity data, the idea of promoting the use of such data underpinned activity throughout. However, as has been seen, there was a conspicuous failure to advance to the stage of data use. This is despite the fact that, in the push towards the creation of a tangible body of data, the project intentionally avoided some of the more complex issues associated with variation in practice data, issues comprehensively investigated by the second project.

Perhaps naïvely, it was thought that producing a body of data relatively quickly and without protracted deliberation would prevent frustration, encourage a more focused discussion of interpractice variation and, crucially, increase the likelihood that the data would be put to some form of collective or collaborative use. With regard to the latter, the comments made by one senior health authority representative, that the project had 'broken through' the data quality barrier to produce valuable health information and that a body of data had been produced precisely by leaving this issue 'to one side' are pertinent.

It is obviously the case that a body of data was produced and that its production did indeed occur in the absence of a full investigation of data quality. But how valuable was the resulting data? The following quote is illuminating: 'At present, the variation in incidence rates between practices cannot be ascribed directly to variation in morbidity. This is because other factors – such as varying data collection definitions and completeness – may be the cause of apparent variation in incidence.'[1]

This statement encapsulates the fundamental weakness in the approach adopted by the first project. It began with the aim of investigating the potential uses of primary care data both at intra- and interpractice level. To this end, project administrators acknowledged the need for a broad investigation of data quality. However, once the working party's recommendation that standard coding protocols *not* be imposed was accepted, this investigation was inevitably narrowed to one aspect of data quality only, that of data completeness. Consequently, other aspects of data quality, to do with its comparative reliability, were not addressed. And as the second project so clearly demonstrated, such collective reliability is crucial to the use of data when that use occurs outside individual practices.

Adopting this rather narrow approach to data assessment meant that the comparative data generated did not inform the actual assessment process, rather, they acted merely as a prompt for assessment to be undertaken. Thus, differences in interpractice data were observed, but without a concomitant investigation of how these differences, *between* practices, had come about. For example, the project failed to investigate in any detail the respective information collection systems of participating practices including, the (lack of) systems in place for inputting information into the computer or the Readcodes used to record that information. This meant that the confounding influence of a whole host of factors remained unknown.

For the first project, the upshot of not investigating all possible determinants of data quality is that variation in interpractice *incidence* rates could not be ascribed directly to variation in interpractice *morbidity* rates. Consequently, practice participants could not be confident of the data as a reliable basis of collaborative activity. Its value was, therefore, limited to intrapractice work only. The following two quotes from participating GPs should serve to illustrate my point:

> How accurate we don't know. It's whether the differences are differences because of the population, or whether they are differences because the individual doctors are recording differently, or whether . . . It could even be different in terms of how the different doctors treat things in terms of screening, management or whatever.

> . . . the incidence rate of these diseases that we're looking at is actually fairly similar. We're somewhat disappointed that ours isn't higher because we expected it to be higher but . . . we're not always convinced that we are comparing like with like . . . it is difficult to comment on other people's [data] because we don't know how they practice.[2]

So, despite the comments of some project leaders commending the marginalization of data quality issues, it is my contention that such marginalization acted against one of the project's fundamental aims: promoting interpractice use of data. Such use of data failed to materialize precisely because the range of issues to do with data quality were overlooked in the rush to produce a dataset.

### The immediate future of primary care information development

To date, the collaboration involving public health and primary care has been happening on an *ad hoc* basis across the UK. As such, any correspondence in project design and process has been both coincidental and limited, meaning that the aggregate data produced cannot be relied upon as consistent. However, this state of affairs is slowly beginning to change as the potential of primary care to provide locally accurate morbidity and health care data is given formal acknowledgement. Currently, the NHS is part way through a national feasibility study, the CHDGP (National Health Service Executive 1997a). The project's starting point is the evidence from previous and ongoing local data collection schemes, such as the two projects reviewed in this chapter, aiming to capitalize on their respective experiences.

The national project has recognized that because of the practical difficulties associated with data collection including, for example, diversity in GP computer systems and in-practice procedures for data collection, progress to date has necessarily been slow. It aims to avoid these problems by producing data recording and data quality guidance, providing practical help with training and support, setting up a central analysis service to produce comparative data and working with GP computer system suppliers to provide the necessary software facilities.

It is no coincidence that the second project reviewed here has been held up as an example of good practice regarding the collection and shared use of primary care data. With regard to this, the project has been praised as having 'highlighted the areas where lessons could be learnt' (National Health Service Executive 1997b: 1).

### *The longer-term potential of primary care information*

So far, in discussing barriers to the successful development of primary care information, there has been a concentration on the detail of data collection. However, other obstacles, to do with the context in which primary care operates, exist. These include: disparities in levels of computerization (smaller practices tending to have lower levels), patient turnover, list inflation and the fact that at any one time a proportion of the population will not be registered with a GP. Prevalence rates will thus be subject to inaccuracy. For example, Scobie *et al.* (1995) found that 29 per cent more people were registered with a group of inner London practices than OPCS estimates indicated. While it may be the case that some practices clean their list on becoming computerized, the potential for built-in inaccuracy must be acknowledged.

However, recent developments mean that now, more than at any other time, the potential for the effective development of primary care data is at its greatest. It is no coincidence that the Scobie *et al.* (1995) study found a higher proportion of patient data being recorded on the computer (for example health risk factors, disease registers) compared with previous studies. The authors note that their research took place after the introduction of a number of schemes that provided financial incentives for improving data collection. In the interim, one of these schemes (the health promotion scheme introduced in 1993) has been abandoned. The demise of such a scheme might well be considered a significant disincentive to information collection. In the meantime, however, other developments more than make up for any potential loss.

Thus, while it remains the case that, as of now, GPs remain primarily concerned with the immediate demands of their practice populations (Jordan *et al.* 1995), this should change as the commissioning responsibilities of the new PCGs encourage primary care practitioners to undertake broader assessments of local need in line with their statutory responsibility to plan and commission health care. In light of these recent developments, the imperative must be to bring together primary care commissioning with a broader public health agenda. As Evans argued back in 1994, there is a critical need to 'ensure that the often individualistic approach of GPs is embedded in a strategic vision of the community's health needs and that public health concerns do not fall off the agenda' (Evans 1994: 44).

Significantly, then, the new arrangements eliminate an age-old obstacle to the development of a primary care/public health working relationship. Under the previous system general practice was given no encouragement to look beyond the needs of practice specific populations. Now emphasis will be given to communities, rather than individuals, with a geographical as distinct from a practice base, to health care planning. The emphasis will be on responding to local (as distinct from practice) population need (Jordan and Wright 1997; Ruta *et al.* 1997). Previously, it was left up to local practices to establish this local or neighbourhood dimension. Now it will be built into the system of health care. Further, up to now primary care has been essentially demand driven, with this demand arbitrarily divided into practice specific populations that may, but more often do not, correspond with naturally occurring geographic/demographic localities and populations. Under the new arrangements there is a fundamental shift in official thinking, towards an acknowledgement of the appropriateness of adopting a proactive approach to health care, uncovering, anticipating and planning for health need, as opposed to relying on the more traditional approach of a largely reactive response to presenting need.

There is no doubt that improving the quality of information that is routinely collected in primary care remains a significant challenge. However, the preceding discussion should have demonstrated that the ongoing move towards a primary care led NHS, in all its manifestations, has already made, and in the future will make even more, the collection and use of such information routine. As Scobie *et al.* (1995) suggest, improvements in data quality should follow on from increased use. Given that this use will increasingly occur within an interpractice context, it is inevitable that such improvements will be centred on producing reliable, comparative data.

While the imperative to collect and use information is now apparent, how will this be translated in practice? With regard to this it may, initially at least, be appropriate to use available practice based morbidity data in conjunction with data from other sources (such as demographic data), including that held within the practice (for example test results). However, the degree to which this is possible is limited by the availability of that data, as well as the skills needed to analyse all datasets together. This is an issue for which further work could usefully identify key information areas and ways to make use of, including reconciling, the information coming from disparate sources.

*Does the information buck stop at primary care?*

This chapter has concentrated on the differences in design and activity between two independent projects; in particular, the implications for the potential development of primary care information systems and their use. In one crucial respect, however, both projects were alike in that questions were raised concerning the value of using only available, or existing, information. Essentially, these questions focused on the fact that such information provides only one 'angle' on health status and needs and is therefore limited in what it can reveal. For the 'bigger' picture to emerge, available data need to be complemented by that which is currently unavailable, that is, information relating to un-met or unknown health needs. This presents an even greater challenge to burgeoning PCGs, not least because it raises the spectre of making patients central to the assessment of health care status and need. However, without such patient involvement, the stated imperative to respond to *local* health need will remain hollow rhetoric.

## Notes

1 This quote is taken from an official project document. Further details are available from the author.
2 These quotes are taken from the independent evaluation report. Further details are available from the author.

## References

Chisholm, J. (1990) The Read clinical classification, *British Medical Journal*, 300: 1092.
Coulter, A., Brown, S. and Daniels, A. (1989) Computer held chronic disease registers in general practice: a validation study, *Journal of Epidemiology and Community Health*, 43: 25–8.
Department of Health (DoH) (1997a) *The New NHS: Modern – Dependable*, Cm 3807. London: The Stationery Office.
Department of Health (DoH) (1997b) *Our Healthier Nation: A Contract for Health*, Cm 3852. London: The Stationery Office.
Evans, D. (1994) Setting the agenda: Health Commissions, public health and primary care, *Critical Public Health*, 5: 41–5.
Jick, H., Jick, S. and Derby, L. (1991) Validation of information recorded on general practitioner based computerised data resource in the United Kingdom, *British Medical Journal*, 302: 766–8.
Johnson, N., Mant, D., Jones, L. and Randall, T. (1991) Use of computerised general practice data for population surveillance: comparative study of influenza data, *British Medical Journal*, 302: 763–5.
Jordan, J. and Wright, J. (1997) Making sense of health needs assessment, *British Journal of General Practice*, 48: 695–6.
Jordan, J., Wright, J., Wilkinson, J. and Williams, D.R.R. (1995) *Health Needs Assessment in Primary Care: A Study of Understanding and Experience in Three Districts*. Leeds: Nuffield Institute for Health.
Mant, D. and Tulloch, A. (1987) Completeness of chronic disease registration in general practice, *British Medical Journal*, 294: 223–4.
MIQUEST Project Board (1994) *MIQUEST Project Report Version 3.3*. Northumberland: MIQUEST Project.
Morrel, D. (1991) *The Art of General Practice*. London: Oxford University Press.
Murray, S.A. and Graham, L.J.C. (1995) Practice based health needs assessment: use of four methods in a small neighbourhood, *British Medical Journal*, 310: 1443–8.
National Health Service Executive (NHSE) (1997a) *Collection of Health Data from General Practice: Plans for the Pilot Stage*. Leeds: NHSE, Information Management Group.
National Health Service Executive (NHSE) (1997b) *Collection of Health Data from General Practice: Information*. Leeds: NHSE, Information Management Group.
National Health Service Management Executive (NHSME) (1992) *An Information Management and Technology Strategy for the NHS in England*. London: NHSME.

National Health Service Management Executive (NHSME) (1993) *Computerisation in GP Practices, 1993 Survey.* Leeds: NHSME.

National Health Service Management Executive (NHSME) (1994) *Developing NHS Purchasing and GP Fund-holding.* EL (94) 79. Leeds: NHSME.

Pearson, N., O'Brien, J., Thomas, H. *et al.* (1996) Collecting morbidity data in general practice: the Somerset morbidity project, *British Medical Journal*, 312: 1517–20.

Pringle, M. and Hobbs, R. (1991) Large computer databases in general practice, *British Medical Journal*, 302: 742–3.

Ruta, D.A., Duffy, M.C., Farquharson, A. *et al.* (1997) Determining priorities for change in primary care; the value of practice-based needs assessment, *British Journal of General Practice*, 47: 353–7.

Scobie, S., Basnett, I. and McCartney, P. (1995) Can general practice data be used for needs assessment and health care planning in an inner-London district? *Journal of Public Health Medicine*, 17: 475–83.

Shanks, J. and Kheraji, S. (1995) Better ways of assessing health in primary care, *British Medical Journal*, 310: 480–1.

Watkins, S. (1994) Public Health 2000, *British Medical Journal*, 309: 1147–9.

Westcott, R. and Jones, R.V.H. (1987) *Information Handling in General Practice: Challenges for the Future.* London: Croom Helm.

Wilson, A., Pollock, C., Weeks, T. and Dowell, T. (1995) Can general practice provide useful information? Evaluation of a primary health care information project in northern England, *Journal of Epidemiology and Community Health*, 49: 227–30.

# ⑨ Counselling: researching an evidence base for practice

John Mellor-Clark

## Overview

Counselling is a growing field of mental health care provision developing *ad hoc* in primary care. Evidence suggests that this growth is driven by several factors, which include: policy changes allowing enhanced purchasing flexibility; increased prevalence of emotional distress presenting to primary care; increased demand for 'counselling' services; limited access to NHS therapy service providers; and proactive counselling in primary care development initiatives. In this chapter it is argued that counselling in primary care is an area that is likely to continue to grow, despite a number of constraints, including (as yet) any supportive evidence base as to its effectiveness. This is a position that appears at odds with policy advocating both the promotion of clinical effectiveness (National Health Service Executive 1996) and the drive for quality and efficiency in the new modern and dependable NHS (Department of Health 1997). Although there is research activity in the domain, the argument herein is that the results of current initiatives can only be premature, uninformative and unrepresentative in the absence of a more pluralistic strategic enquiry. In sum, this chapter challenges the sole reliance on data from randomized controlled trials to supply the evidence base for practice development, and coordinates calls from a variety of stakeholders for complementary, standardized, evaluative audit for 'quality' service provision.

## Counselling in primary care: the background

The provision of counselling in primary care (CPC) is becoming increasingly recognized as an area of health and social care developing without any coherent or national strategy (for example Sibbald *et al.* 1993; King 1995; Sedgwick Taylor 1996; Wesley 1996), and in the absence of any evidence base as to its effectiveness (for example Roth and Fonagy 1996).

The employment of counsellors as part of primary care service provision has shown significant growth in recent years despite warnings attempting to stem it (for example Martin 1988; Fahy and Wesley 1993; Roth and Fonagy 1996; Department of Health 1996; Wesley 1996). In 1992, it was reported that of all general practices in England and Wales, 31 per cent had a counsellor, and of those practices without such provision, 80 per cent expressed a wish to provide such a service (Sibbald *et al.* 1993). Two years later, in the wake of the financial restructuring of general practice, a survey by Corney (1994) found 45 per cent of 100 first wave GP fundholders employed a counsellor, compared to 20 per cent of a similar group of non-fundholders. In 1995 the Counselling in Primary Care Trust (CPCT) (a charitable body working for the establishment of a nationwide, competent, professional counselling service in general practice), reported that 25 per cent of all general practices in England and Wales employ a counsellor, including more than 50 per cent of second and third wave fundholding practices (Curtis-Jenkins 1995). Most recent estimates from CPCT (Curtis-Jenkins 1996) suggest 60 per cent of all general practices in England and Wales now employ a counsellor; although this figure remains (as yet) unsubstantiated. Clearly, there is evidence to suggest that we are witnessing what Wesley (1996) describes as an explosion in counselling. In order to understand the background of this new provision, Table 9.1 attempts to present a sequential rationalization by considering some of the driving forces behind the growth, with Table 9.2 considering restraining forces calling for curtailment.

Collectively, the themes identified in Table 9.1 present a potential rationale for the growth of CPC. In summary, the picture is one of GPs having to deal with increasing presentations of minor psychiatric illness, having limited access to statutory mental health resources and an increasingly mobilized but uncoordinated supply of 'counselling' resources ready to assist. However, Table 9.2 questions this growth, suggesting that in the absence of any regulation, coordination or strategy, CPC may be an inappropriate, inefficient, ineffective

**Table 9.1**   Driving forces to the emergence and growth of counselling in primary care

| | |
|---|---|
| **Policy changes allowing GPs greater flexibility in purchasing** | In 1987 the Department of Health publication *Promoting Better Health* increased opportunities for other health professionals to work in general practice, and funding became available for part reimbursement of salaries of attached staff such as counsellors (King 1995).<br><br>   In 1991 the General Practitioners' Fundholding Initiative gave practices control of prescribing and staff resources enabling GPs to purchase specified health and community services. |
| **Increasing prevalence of emotional distress presenting to primary care** | Mental health policy changes have led to a shift in the locus of treatment from specialized mental health institutions and hospitals into the community (Department of Health 1990). |

Table 9.1   (*cont'd*)

|  | In 1966 it was estimated that the annual GP caseload presenting with 'psychiatric symptoms' might be about 14 per cent (Shepherd 1966). In 1980 this figure had risen to 24–29 per cent (Goldberg and Huxley 1980), and by the early 1990s estimates have increased to 30–40 per cent (Dowrick 1992; Hagan and Green 1994). |
|---|---|
| **Increasing demand for 'counselling' services** | Surveys conducted on behalf of the Defeat Depression Campaigns (MORI 1992; MORI 1995) report that 80 per cent and 85 per cent of respondents (respectively) considered 'counselling' to be the treatment of choice for depression.<br><br>Feedback from users and user groups for the NHSE review of psychotherapy services suggested that 'talking treatments' are highly acceptable and many prefer them to physical interventions (Department of Health 1996). |
| **Limited access to NHS therapy service providers** | The NHSE strategic review (Department of Health 1996) identified that demand for all psychotherapies outstrips supply, with a shortage of clinical psychologists and long waiting lists for psychiatric and psychology services. Many services have difficulty reaching patients' charter standards for first appointments being within 13 weeks of referral.<br><br>In a survey in Pontefract concerned with people's views about statutory mental health service provision, five key problems were identified: services were inaccessible, unacceptable and untargeted, with inappropriate usage and variable quality in service provision (Hagan and Green 1994). |
| **Proactive counselling in primary care development initiatives** | Three specialized texts have been published to promote the benefits of counselling to primary care practice (Corney and Jenkins 1993; East 1995; Keighley and Marsh 1995).<br><br>In 1991 the Counselling in Primary Care Trust was set up as 'a proactive organisation, committed to the establishment of a competent professional counselling service in primary health care' (East 1995: 23).<br><br>Voluntary sector initiatives such as the Counselling in Primary Care Project (Rain 1996) have actively, and directly, promoted counselling to primary care practice, advocating the benefits as: optimizing practice staff time and reducing staff strain, and providing on-site mental health expertise; more appropriate referral; help at the point of need; and health care cost savings (Rain 1996).<br><br>The Counselling in Medical Settings division of the British Association of Counselling has been cited as the fastest growing division within BAC (East 1995), with a membership of over 2000. |

**Table 9.2**   Restraining forces to the growth of counselling in primary care

| | |
|---|---|
| **No agreement as to what constitutes 'counselling' or a 'counsellor'** | Despite the considerable growth of provision, there is evidence that many GPs do not have an understanding of the training and qualifications in the field of 'counselling' and the term 'counsellor' is used interchangeably to refer to mental health professionals and counsellors with very limited mental health experience (Department of Health 1996).<br><br>In a BMJ survey of GPs published in 1993, 31 per cent of practices had a 'counsellor' with no other job in the practice. Of these practices 80 per cent of GPs were unaware of the counsellors' qualifications and 42 per cent of the 'counsellors' whose qualifications were known to the GP had had no training in 'counselling' (Sibbald *et al.* 1993). This has led some to question the appropriateness of such provision (Illman 1993). |
| **No appropriate training, supervision, support or evaluation for counsellors** | Many counsellors contracted to provide a service within primary care do so devoid of any specific training preparing them to work in the general practice setting (Einzig *et al.* 1992), and in many cases work without job descriptions, accreditation or professional association, indemnity insurance, supervision or any form of quantitative audit or evaluation (Sedgwick Taylor 1996). |
| **Inability of GPs to make appropriate referrals** | Those responding to the strategic review survey (Department of Health 1996) expressed concern that counsellors are being asked to see patients whose mental health problems are inappropriate for primary care interventions, or for their level of skill. |
| **No evidence of cost effectiveness** | No differences in attendance rates or psychotropic drug prescription have been found between patients who had received counselling, and a matched comparison group who received no counselling (Martin and Martin 1985). |
| **No evidence base for clinical effectiveness** | A review commissioned by the DoH concluded that 'counselling for mental health problems in primary care settings is an increasingly common but poorly researched therapeutic technique. Very few investigations demonstrate any consistent benefit to patients from counselling, and no studies show generic counselling to add to standard general practice care' (Roth and Fonagy 1996: 261).<br><br>Since December 1993 the DoH has recommended that purchasers should not invest in certain procedures that are still being evaluated (National Health Service Executive 1996: 2.13). |

Table 9.2  (*cont'd*)

| Opposition to growth by mental health professionals | According to recent media stories, British psychiatrists are becoming increasingly concerned that scarce resources are being diverted away from the seriously mentally ill, and instead spent on unnecessary and inappropriate services such as counselling ('Worried well force aside mental illness', *Independent on Sunday*, 10 December 1995). Clinical psychologists feel that the growth of counselling in primary care will result in only difficult to treat (and therefore, perhaps overtly costly) referrals being made to psychology, harming the relationships between psychology and general practice. 'It is important to challenge vigorously the idea that it should be another profession that does what we are trained to do . . . it is hazardous to suggest that counsellors with only a narrow range of knowledge should be performing these tasks' (Blakey 1996: 38). |
| --- | --- |

and potentially unsafe service provision. Set in context, this phenomena occurs in a climate in which there is a call for increased clinical effectiveness (National Health Service Executive 1996) and where *The Health of the Nation* (Department of Health 1992) policy has set statutory health and social care sector services the objective to reduce ill health and death caused by mental illness, and targeted the reduction of suicide rates and the improvement of the health and social functioning of the mentally ill.

I conclude that the provision of counselling in primary care is a domain of mental health care provision that has seen considerable growth despite a paucity of information on the structure of the provision (the counsellors), the processes involved (the counselling), the problems treated (the counselled), and the outcomes gained (effectiveness). Whereas a more recent national survey into the structures, processes and outcomes of CPC (Mellor-Clark 1998) has begun to challenge some of the 'myths' created by previous research, here we focus on the outcome effectiveness agenda, where the current lack of evidence is wholly at odds with an NHS committed to the promotion, development and maintenance of evidence based practice.

## Clinical effectiveness and evidence based practice

It is evident that the zeitgeist of the NHS drives a quest for contained costs, clinical effectiveness, and evidence based practice. One of the many documents aiding the move towards the adoption of evidence based practice is *Promoting Clinical Effectiveness* (National Health Service Executive 1996). This is designed to help NHS Trusts develop ways of promoting greater clinical effectiveness in both primary and secondary sectors of care. Here, the maxim of 'effective' practice rests on a core triad of *informing* decision making, *changing* practice where appropriate, and *monitoring* the associated outcomes. This promotes a strategic approach to service development solely based on information from research evidence (National Health Service Executive 1996: 2.2). The (ranked) types of evidence commended by the NHSE include: randomized controlled trials; robust experimental or observational studies; and more limited evidence reliant on the advice of expert opinion or respected authorities (3.17). Mental health and the primary/secondary care interface are both targeted as areas where information on effectiveness and cost effectiveness are urgently needed. The single largest programme is in health technology assessment (2.3) and, as this is written, both systematic reviews and controlled trials are about to be published.

In the former, the Universities of York, Manchester and Leeds, working closely with the Cochrane Centre, have undertaken a review of the efficacy and cost effectiveness of counselling in primary care. In the latter, the Royal Free Hospital Medical School in association with the National Primary Care Research and Development Centre at the University of Manchester, have conducted a controlled trial of counselling in general practice. At the time of writing, the results of neither of these initiatives are publicly available. However, no matter – paradoxically, the *Promoting Clinical Effectiveness* document recognizes that information is used more effectively if it is made acessible at the time and point at which the decision is being made (2.21). This recognition sits somewhat uncomfortably with the rapid expansion of counselling in primary care over the past five years, and with the nature of controlled trials that take several years not only to conduct, but potentially several more to disseminate as guidelines for 'best' practice. Furthermore, there is recognition that 'sound information' is an essential prerequisite for promoting clinical effectiveness (2.24), and as such, 'should be presented in ways which meet the needs of busy clinicians and managers, and in ways that can be understood by patients and the public' (2.24). The next section of this chapter considers these paradoxes, highlights additional problems impacting on the reliance on controlled trials as the sole evidence base for promoting clinical effectiveness in counselling in primary care, and concludes with the presentation of a case for the urgent adoption of 'methodological pluralism' (McLeod 1994; Aveline *et al.* 1995; Black 1996).

## Randomized controlled trials and evidence based practice

There is growing recognition from a variety of stakeholders connected to the field of mental health that the randomized control trial (RCT) should not be the *sole* evidence base for promoting clinical effectiveness, as it may be severely limited. These advocates include stakeholders concerned with psychological therapy research in both the USA and UK (for example Bergin and Garfield 1994; McLeod 1994; Aveline *et al.* 1995), generic health and social policy (for example Black 1996) and policy directly associated with therapy service provision (for example Roth and Fonagy 1996). Here the propositions of Black and Roth and Fonagy are summarized.

Black (1996) advocates that the RCT, as the 'gold standard' for health care evaluation, is not a panacea for all enquiry, and the denigration of observational methods as having no value is unjustified, limiting our potential to evaluate and hence to improve the scientific basis of how to treat individuals and how to organize services. Using well known examples from a broad range of health research, Black argues that complementary observational methods are needed to address the limitations of experimentation, which may prove unnecessary, inappropriate, impossible or inadequate.

Roth and Fonagy (1996) in their critical review of psychotherapy research take a stance cautioning us against the wholesale adoption of both systematic reviews and RCTs. Addressing the former, they warn against the temptation of turning to findings of systematic reviews as though they provide some definitive blueprint for service delivery, as this creates a dilemma. Where purchasers yield to the temptation to design 'managed-care programmes' and 'first line' treatments based on the evidence of systematic reviews, the reaction of providers is to become suspicious of the moves (towards) and demands (of) evidence based practice. The argument maintains that this creates a potential position in which, on the one hand, there is a risk that practitioners will reject research and, on the other, the possibility that purchasers will embrace research findings uncritically, leading to a 'cookbook' approach to planning. Clearly, systematic reviews are also no panacea for service planning.

In addition to addressing systematic reviews, Roth and Fonagy address RCTs and maintain that although RCT findings can identify potentially effective interventions, they say little about how effectively and efficiently such interventions are implemented in any particular setting. Without this, not only may effectiveness and efficiency be poor, but other domains of quality service delivery may remain poor (such as acceptability, appropriateness, accessibility and equity). Table 9.3 attempts to match some of the strengths and opportunities that have been claimed by researchers engaged in health technology assessment (HTA) funded RCTs in CPC, against some of the potential weaknesses and threats associated with a sole reliance on such a methodology.

## Challenges imposed by the reliance on RCTs as the CPC evidence base

The three 'challenges' of the HTA funded programme to promote clinical effectiveness in the provision of counselling in primary care are emphasized in Table 9.3 using constructs published by Aveline et al. (1995). These include prematurity, informativeness and representativeness. In this section each of these 'challenges' are considered sequentially, and drawing on the limitations of RCTs posited by Black (1996), medical examples are offered where appropriate.

### The challenge of prematurity

The principal challenge of the reliance on the RCT as the evidence base for promoting clinical effectiveness in counselling in primary care relates to the

**Table 9.3**  SWOT analysis of RCTs for promoting clinical effectiveness in counselling in primary care

| Strengths* | Weaknesses |
|---|---|
| The controlled trial of counselling in primary care uses the methodology enjoying unique standing in clinical research, claiming unrivalled power to sustain causal inference and being the methodology of choice for all health research. For health service planners (that is NHSE) this maximizes credibility. | Being within the zeitgeist of funding doesn't maximize the potential for use. The methodology is prohibitively expensive, using relatively small numbers of patients, unrepresentative providers, concentrating on a specific single disorder (depression), receiving an unrepresentative treatment. |
| In each treatment group (CBT, non-directive counselling, routine GP care), the motivation of patients is taken into account using a 'patient preference model' (Brewin and Bradley 1989) allowing choice of preferred treatment. This maximizes the potential for participants to comply with treatment and minimizes attrition potential. | By using a patient preference model, it may prove difficult to find enough patients agreeing to be randomized and/or entering the routine GP care arm of the study. Although power calculations for statistical inference would need a 50–50 split between treatments, the take-up of routine GP care may be less common than the take-up of psychological treatments. |
| Each of the available treatments are 'manualized' and taped for later adherence rating to allow all three intervention treatments to be standard (within groups) and replicable. | The manualized forms of treatment are biased in favour of CBT as the manualization of person centred counselling is oxymoronic and can only serve to delineate the philosophy and boundaries of a person centred approach. |
| Considerable care is taken to match treatment groups by stringent inclusion criteria to allow outcome differences to be causally attributed specifically to the treatments. | Stringent inclusion criteria compromises the generalizability of the treatment due to the un-representativeness of the problem treated. |

| Opportunities** | Threats |
|---|---|
| Planning on the basis of demonstrated efficacy of one treatment over another is essential if time and money are not to be wasted. | RCTs are so costly and technically difficult that an adequate evidence base can never be wholly reliant on them. In the absence of more information on what represents current practice, there may be considerable *prematurity* in a reliance on RCTs in advance of a similar level of resources distributed over a variety of pluralistic methodologies. |

Table 9.3   (cont'd)

| Opportunities** | Threats |
|---|---|
| RCT findings will show whether non-directive counselling and/or CBT is more cost effective than usual GP care in the treatment of depression in general practice. | The *informativeness* of the RCT is confined to addressing a globally framed hypothesis about effective interventions. The contribution to treatment effects of the characteristics and behaviours of treatment providers (and receivers) may be obscured by restricted number and types of patients and providers and the uniformity of treatment delivery imposed by standardization. |
| These findings will enable purchasers at general practice or district level to make rational choices in providing services with the greatest benefit for the treatment of minor mood disorders in primary care | The standardization and uniformity (manualization) imposed by the rigour of the RCT produces a set of 'purified' treatments, patients, providers and problem characteristics seldom seen in routine practice. Together with the knowledge of a trial potentially producing atypical psychological processes within providers and patients, *representativeness* is severely threatened. |

*Source: King 1994, 1995, 1998
**Source: King 1998

prematurity of a substantial investment in RCTs to the exclusion of altern-ative complementary methods. Aveline *et al.* (1995) argue that in the domain of physical medicine, RCTs are the third phase in new drug verification, following extensive developmental work building empirical observational data (phase I) which suggest the specific treatments likely to prove effective in a given disorder (phase II). A similar notion is characterized by Salkovskis (1995) using an hourglass metaphor. Here, RCTs belong to an intermediate stage of development represented by the narrow stem of the hourglass. This is preceded by broader theoretical developments and closely observed case series, prior to broadening out again to more naturalistic studies in everyday settings. Given the paucity of activity in either broader domains of the hourglass, it appears, using this model, that there is a strong argument that major investment in RCTs may be, at best, a premature expenditure. This contrasts dramatically with King's assertion that planning based on demon-strated efficacy is essential if time and money are not to be wasted (King, 1998), which in turn addresses the 'informativeness' of the RCT methodology.

## The challenge of informativeness

The cited RCT in counselling in primary care sets out to present findings that will show whether non-directive counselling and/or CBT intervention are/is more cost effective than usual GP care in the treatment of depression in general practice (King 1998). This, it claims, will have considerable utility to inform policy makers and purchasers of the cost effectiveness of counselling in primary care. However, the contrary position, outlined in Table 9.3, maintains that such findings may be inadequate in answering the 'effectiveness' question because paradoxically the 'rigour' imposed by the design dilutes the 'informativeness' of the findings. At best, given the focus of the study, information will be available on the treatment of a set level of 'pure' depression, treated by two specific forms of manualized therapy, delivered by a benchmarked group of providers, in a tightly controlled experimental setting. The limitations therefore are self-evident. Information will be available for the treatment of depression by a set criteria of provision (structure), delivering a standardized form of counselling/therapy to a defined level of problem presentation (process), having clinical effectiveness assessed via short-term cost effectiveness (outcome). Many of the criticisms of this logic are addressed in the subsequent consideration of 'representativeness'; here, limitations of the informativeness of the programme are considered (briefly) in respect of sample size, outcomes, and information utility.

*Sample size*
The sample size, allocating 70–80 patients to each of the six arms (CBT preferred/randomized, person centred counselling preferred/randomized, routine GP care preferred/randomized), is too small to measure more infrequent adverse outcomes. Black (1996) cites the example of benoxaprofen (Opren), a drug launched in 1980, which despite trials on 3000 patients, had to be withdrawn in 1982 due to serious side effects that included 61 fatalities.

*Outcomes*
Firstly, Howard *et al.* (1995) maintain that it is virtually impossible to avoid missing data in RCTs, either through incomplete instrumentation returns (data attrition) or failure to complete treatment (subject attrition). The consequence is that this severely weakens the strength of the methodology and reduces its status to poorly designed quasi-experimentation. Secondly, even where there is complete treatment data, the outcomes of interest may be far into the future and therefore outside the life-cycle of the RCT. Again, Black (1996) cites the example of the long-term consequences of oral contraception, which may not be manifest for decades. Might not the same be true for the treatment of depression?

*Information utility*
The utility of the information obtained from the trial will take several years to be collated and disseminated. In the meantime, GPs will continue to see an increasing number of patients requiring or requesting psychological intervention and will have to continue to make decisions about purchasing and supplying services. This is in contradiction to *Promoting Clinical Effectiveness*, which recognizes the need to have information at the point of decision making (National Health Service Executive 1996: 2.21). Faced with long waiting lists for traditional secondary and tertiary services, the prediction is that the provision of counselling in primary care is likely to continue to grow. Potentially this is likely to be both in spite of and ultimately, despite, an evidence base.

*The challenge of representativeness*

The final challenge of the HTA programme is that of representativeness. The RCT programme claims that the findings from the study will enable rational purchasing and provision of maximally beneficial services for the treatment of minor mood disorders (King 1998). However, again there is a contrary position challenging such a claim. This maintains that RCTs are, by their very nature, *unrepresentative* of everyday practice and consequently, non-generalizable. Once again this presents a paradox. In maximizing the internal validity and replicability of the study, the hypothetico-deductive research model (Howard *et al.* 1995) dilutes the external validity or generalizability of the findings. It is critical to remember that RCTs provide information about the value of an intervention shorn of all context, despite the fact that contextual factors may be critical in determining the success of the intervention (Black 1996). More specific considerations of the problems of representativeness (and hence potential inadequacies) point to the need for consideration of atypicality in health care participants, patients' problems and counselling treatments.

*Health care participants*
Two tiers of health care participants are engaged in the RCT study – GPs and providers – and in both cases they are atypical for having a vested interest in the outcome. GPs are being provided with a quality, accessible service to which they would not normally have such direct access. At the same time, the providers partaking in the study know they are under scrutiny for the effectiveness of their profession and naturally have a vested interest in providing the best possible care. Clearly, this is far removed from the everyday context of clinical practice for all participating health care professionals. Indeed, it can be equated to an example given by Black (1996) in which he cites a study of glue ear where all the out-patient and surgical care was performed by a highly experienced consultant surgeon. In real life, in both domains of care, most of such work is provided by much less experienced individuals, in very different contexts, with very different motivations.

*Patients' problems*
The patients' problems under investigation in the RCT are atypical of presenting problems in primary care. This is due to the fact that the exclusion criteria are so restrictive that the patients eligible for inclusion in the study potentially represent a fraction of patients being treated in real practice. The more testing exclusion criteria for King's RCT include: patients scoring more than 14 on the Beck Depression Inventory (Beck *et al.* 1988); those with any substance abuse (known to be highly associated with depression); and patients currently receiving any other psychiatric and counselling care. In addition, many practitioners would argue that few individuals present with such 'clean' psychological problems and much depression is associated with other more circumstantial problems such as interpersonal difficulties and adjustment to long-term illness. As co-presentation is not considered in the King trial this presents a further limitation of the generalizability of the findings for 'enabling rational purchasing and provision'. In summary, there appears

to be considerable evidence to believe that there is significant potential for these limitations to equate to Black's cited health care example that only 4 per cent of patients currently undergoing coronary revasculation in the UK would have been eligible for inclusion in the trials conducted in the 1970s (Black 1996).

### Counselling treatments

Linked to the health care professionals engaged in the trial, the problem here is that patients who agree to participate in the trial may receive 'better' or 'best' treatment, irrespective of which arm they are allocated to. Thus the treatments available offer what can be achieved in the most favourable circumstances and are thus not generalizable to everyday treatments offered in routine practice, many of which might plausibly be much more eclectic or systemic to deal with the co-presentation of a multitude of cause–effect relations. This suggestion leads to another problem, in that King considers only two forms of treatment (person centred counselling and CBT) among what has been estimated as over 400 different theoretical models (Fonagy 1995). Little is known about how representative these treatments are in respect of those offered in practice.

In summary, this section has reviewed a variety of arguments against the sole reliance on the RCT as providing *the* evidence base for the promotion of clinical effectiveness of counselling in primary care. However, throughout this chapter, there have been a number of clues as to how complementary research might rise to the challenge of enhancing the evidence base for CPC:

- Authors writing on generic health policy (for example Black 1996) have argued against the denigration of *observational methods*, maintaining that such attitudes limit our potential to evaluate and hence to improve the scientific basis of how to treat individuals and how to organize services.
- Authors writing on psychological therapy research (for example McLeod 1994; Aveline *et al.* 1995) have called for a recognition of the urgent need for *methodological pluralism* in the development of knowledge and subsequent enhancement of practice. This has seen RCTs belonging to an intermediate stage of knowledge development represented by the narrow stem of an hourglass, preceded by broader theoretical developments and closely observed case series, prior to broadening out again to more naturalistic studies in everyday settings (Salkovskis 1995). This is the model of evidence based practice proposed by the Department of Health (1996) and Roth and Fonagy (1996), which, in part, calls for the standardization of service auditing and outcome benchmarking.
- Authors writing on psychological therapy service development (for example Roth and Fonagy 1996) have maintained that although RCT findings can identify potentially effective interventions, they say little about how effectively and efficiently such interventions are implemented in actual practice settings. Furthermore, they add that without such enquiry, not only may service effectiveness and efficiency be poor, but other domains of *quality service delivery* may remain poor.

This summary of propositions begins to give shape to complementary methods of research enquiry that would help meet the need to provide an evidence base for CPC. The aim is not only to meet the dictates of *Promoting Clinical Effectiveness* (to purchase services with scientific and other sources of *evidence*), but more importantly, to secure information that is *usable* by busy clinicians and managers and *understandable* to patients and the public (National Health Service Executive 1996: 2.24), having an aim to enhance service delivery. This has led to an initiative that recognizes the urgent requirement for a complementary evidence base for the provision of counselling services within primary care that comprises the following key features:

- consensus as to the determinants of a 'quality' counselling provision (Mellor-Clark and Barkham in press);
- measurement by a standardized set of evaluative audit measures that have both clinical credibility and research reliability and validity capable of monitoring service quality (Barkham *et al.* 1998);
- coordination by a centralized body, summarizing and disseminating comparative data with other domains of service provision to maximize and operationalize both informativeness and generalizability (CORE System Group 1998).

This initiative sets out to address the calls for: rigorous and independent audit (Roth and Fonagy 1996); methodological pluralism (McLeod 1994; Aveline *et al.* 1995); enhanced service delivery (Black 1996; Department of Health 1996); and information addressing how effectively and efficiently (counselling) interventions are implemented in any particular setting (Roth and Fonagy 1996).

Collectively, this supports what Vivienne Ball and Rosyln Corney advocated in the first text dedicated to counselling in primary care (Ball and Corney 1993). These authors maintained that in setting up and developing counselling in primary care, ongoing evaluation is absolutely essential. This was not only to ensure that service aims are achieved, but to secure and contribute to the professional development of all those deployed in the field. In the conclusion to the text they advocate that evaluative research needs should be coordinated to create standards and protocols for psychological care in general practice. In this text there has been an attempt to rationalize, contextualize and operationalize the need to swiftly realize that vision, instead of relying on RCTs as the sole evidence base. In other texts, ways in which progress has been made, quality data that have been gathered, and their potential impact on both research and clinical practice have all been addressed in comprehensive detail (see Mellor-Clark and Barkham 1997; CORE System Group 1998; Mellor-Clark & Barkham in press).

## References

Aveline, M., Shapiro, D.A., Parry, G. and Freeman, C. (1995) Building research foundations for psychotherapy practice, in M. Aveline and D.A. Shapiro (eds) *Research Foundations for Psychotherapy Practice*. Chichester: John Wiley.

Ball, V. and Corney, R. (1993) The future of counselling in primary care, in R. Jenkins and R. Corney (eds) *Counselling in General Practice*. London: Tavistock Routledge.

Barkham, M., Evans, C., Margison, F. *et al.* (1998) The rationale for developing and implementing core outcome batteries for routine use in service settings and psychotherapy outcome research, *Journal of Mental Health*, 7: 35–47.

Beck, A.T., Steer, R.A. and Gabin, M.G. (1988) Psychometric properties of the Beck Depression Inventory. Twenty-five years of evaluation, *Clinical Psychology Review*, 8: 77–100.

Bergin, A.E. and Garfield, S.L. (eds) (1994) *Handbook of Psychotherapy and Behaviour Research*, 4th edn. Chichester: John Wiley.

Black, N. (1996) Why we need observational studies to evaluate the effectiveness of health care, *British Medical Journal*, 312: 1215–18.

Blakey, R. (1996) Some thoughts on the development of clinical psychology in primary care, *Clinical Psychology Forum*, 97: 37–9.

Brewin, C.R. and Bradley, C. (1989) Patient preference and randomised controlled trials, *British Medical Journal*, 299: 313–15.

CORE (Clinical Outcomes in Routine Evaluation) System Group (1998) *CORE System (Information Management) Handbook.* Leeds: CORE System Group.

Corney, R. (1994) Unpublished survey.

Corney, R. and Jenkins, R. (eds) (1993) *Counselling in General Practice.* London: Tavistock Routledge.

Curtis-Jenkins, G. (1995) Effectiveness in counselling services: recent developments in service delivery, in G. Curtis-Jenkins (ed.) *Information Booklet: Supplement No.1.* London: Counselling in Primary Care Trust.

Curtis-Jenkins, G. (1996) The cost of counselling in primary care – or the lack of it. Who pays the price? Paper presented at Leeds MIND conference, Leeds, 14 June.

Department of Health (DoH) (1990) *National Health Service and Community Care Act* (E 2 cap 19). London: HMSO.

Department of Health (DoH) (1992) *The Health of the Nation: A Strategy for Health in England.* London: HMSO.

Department of Health (DoH) (1996) *NHS Psychotherapy Services in England: A Review of Strategic Policy.* London: DoH.

Department of Health (DoH) (1997) *The New NHS: Modern – Dependable*, Cm 3087. London: The Stationery Office.

Dowrick, C. (1992) Improving mental health through primary care, *British Journal of General Practice*, 42: 382–6.

East, P. (1995) *Counselling in Medical Settings.* Buckingham: Open University Press.

Einzig, H., Basharan, H. and Curtis Jenkins, G. (1992) The training needs of counsellor working in primary medical care: The role of the training organisation, *CMS News*, 33: 9–13.

Fahy, T. and Wesley, S. (1993) Should purchasers pay for psychotherapy? *British Medical Journal*, 307: 576–7.

Fonagy, P. (1995) Is there an answer to the outcome research question – waiting for Godot?, *Changes*, 13: 168–77.

Goldberg, D. and Huxley, P. (1980) *Mental Illness in the Community: The Pathway to Psychiatric Care.* London: Tavistock.

Hagan, T. and Green, J. (1994) *Mental Health Needs Assessment: The User Perspective.* Department of Public Health: Wakefield Health Centre.

Howard, K.I., Orlinsky, D.E. and Leugar, R.J. (1995) The design of clinically relevant outcome research: Some considerations and an example, in M. Aveline and D.A. Shapiro (eds) *Research Foundations for Psychotherapy Practice.* Chichester: John Wiley.

Illman, J. (1993) Are counsellors any use at all? *GP Life & Leisure*, 21 May 1993.

Keighley, J. and Marsh, G. (eds) (1995) *Counselling in Primary Health Care.* Buckingham: Open University Press.

King, M. (1994) Controlled trials in the evaluation of counselling in general practice, *British Journal of General Practice*, 44: 229–32.

King, M. (1995) Evaluating the benefit of general practice-based counselling services, in M. Aveline and D.A. Shaprio (eds) *Research Foundations for Psychotherapy Practice*. Chichester: John Wiley.

King, M. (1998) Evaluating the effectiveness of psychotherapy in general practice. Paper presented to the Department of Psychiatry Seminar Series, Leeds University, 30 April.

McLeod, J. (1994) *Doing Counselling Research*. London: Sage.

Martin, E. (1988) Counsellors in general practice, *British Medical Journal*, 297: 637.

Martin, E. and Martin, P. (1985) Changes in psychological diagnosis and prescription rates in a practice employing a counsellor, *Family Practitioner*, 2: 241–3.

Mellor-Clark, J. (1998) Results of a National Survey of Counsellors Working in General Practice. Psychological Therapies Research Centre Memo, Leeds University.

Mellor-Clark, J. and Barkham, M. (1997) Evaluating effectiveness: needs, problems and potential benefits, in I. Horton and V. Varma (eds) *The Needs of Counsellors and Psychotherapists*. London: Sage.

Mellor-Clark, J. and Barkham, M. (in press) Quality evaluation: methods, measures and meaning, in C. Feltham, and I. Horton (eds) *The Handbook of Counselling and Psychotherapy*. London: Sage.

MORI (1992) *Attitudes Towards Depression*. Research study conducted for the Defeat Depression Campaign.

MORI (1995) *Attitudes Towards Depression*. Research study conducted for the Defeat Depression Campaign.

National Health Service Executive (1996) *Promoting Clinical Effectiveness: A Framework for Action in and through the NHS*. Leeds: NHS Executive.

Rain, L. (1996) *Counselling in Primary Care: A Guide to Good Practice*. Leeds: Mind.

Roth, P. and Fonagy, A. (1996) *What Works for Whom? A Critical Review of Psychotherapy Research*. New York: Guilford.

Salkovskis, P.M. (1995) Demonstrating specific effects in cognitive and behavioural therapy in M. Aveline and D.A. Shaprio (eds) *Research Foundations for Psychotherapy Practice*. Chichester: John Wiley.

Sedgwick Taylor, A. (1996) *Clinical Psychology and Counselling in Primary Care: The Partnership Scheme*. Final report to Severn NHS Trust.

Shepherd, M. (1966) *Psychiatric Illness in General Practice*. Oxford: Oxford University Press.

Sibbald, B., Addington-Hall, J., Brenneman, D. and Freeling, B. (1993) Counsellors in English and Welsh General Practices, *British Medical Journal*, 306: 29–33.

Wesley, S. (1996) The Rise of Counselling and the Return of Alienism, *British Medical Journal*, 313: 158–60.

# ⑩ Complementary medicine and primary care: towards a grassroots focus

Jon Adams and Philip Tovey

## Introduction

The relationship between the institutions and practitioners of conventional medicine and those of the disparate group that is taken to constitute complementary medicine[1] (CM) is one that defies simplistic assessment. In recent years this complexity has been seen at a number of levels. For instance, while the position of the BMA continued to be based on the dismissiveness of the mid-1980s report (British Medical Association 1986), *ad hoc* programmes of interaction were developing apace at the level of individual practitioners (Saks 1992). However, this itself needs to be seen against a background of continuing reticence about collaboration among large sections of practitioners, notably hospital based clinicians (Tovey 1997b). And where groups from both sides claim authority for practice – as in homeopathy – the relationship between legitimate and illegitimate practice remains as complicated as ever (Cant 1996).

Why it is important to make this clear at the outset is to underline the point that in talking about the integration of complementary medicine into the practice of primary care we are neither talking about a complete process nor, indeed, about one in which the continuing adoption of 'alternative' practices is a predetermined outcome of this process. Still less are we making a case one way or another about this trend; that is a separate issue bound up with questions of efficacy, an evidence base and the like.

But intersection is occurring; in key specific sites new forms of practice are being forged. That it is uneven and incomplete emphasizes the need to understand the specific *character* of the examples of collaboration, cooperation or integration that *are* being established; they provide a new research focus and a new set of research questions to be tackled.

### Institutional context and individual action

Although in no sense constituting a new or uniformly positive consensus, a number of recent developments have provided something of a supportive context for intersection. The shift (away from overt dismissiveness) in the institutional position of the BMA in the early 1990s (British Medical Association 1993) has understandably received substantial coverage. Meanwhile, the RCGP has consistently shown support for the use of certain therapies in general practice (Honigsbaum 1985); the British Holistic Medical Association, although not set up exclusively to promote CM, supports the idea of a multi-disciplinary primary care team, of which CM forms a part; research that 'tests' the claims of therapies is (slowly) developing (for example Chan *et al.* 1997); and the path to professionalization being pursued by the representative bodies of some therapies (notably osteopathy) brings an increased level of structural similarity between 'professions' across the divide.

But concentration on changes at the institutional level has limited potential for extending our understanding of how change is evolving on the ground and how the nature of that change is being negotiated and formulated at the micro level. Given their current retention of therapeutic control and (substantial) autonomy, it is the growing number of GPs either interested in, referring to, or personally practising complementary therapies that is particularly important (Reilly 1983; Dale 1996). This focus embraces an interest in the networks that are evolving between some GPs and non-medically qualified practitioners (Adams 1998), the *ad hoc*, small scale, yet significant, pilot schemes/projects such as the Marylebone Clinic (Pietroni 1992a; Reason *et al.* 1992), as well as more individually based action. The shape of intersection in the primary care setting hinges on the actions of GPs (and their engagement with others).

It is on this new terrain of GP centred intersection that our attention can profitably be focused. Although developments at the level of institutions are real enough, *change is being constructed in practice at the level of the practitioner*, and for this reason can be seen to form the key feature of the 'complementary medicine issue' for primary care.

*About this chapter*

Although a chapter concerned with CM could have been written with a range of quite differing emphases – with a concentration on matters relating to the evidence base of therapies, to the most appropriate ways of measuring effectiveness, to change at the level of institutions and legislation, and to many more issues besides – these are assigned an essentially supportive role in our coverage.

Bypassing this wide range of policy and practice related issues, we are able to focus directly on the integration of CM into the world of primary care, and the questions raised by it. Our concern is that while numerous examples of intersection are occurring (Sharma 1992), we know very little about them. Our task is to seek out a means of making sense of this integration, to consider what is going on and why. As a consequence, there is a need to look closely at the kinds of questions that require answers, and to consider whether the approaches that have formed the basis of research strategies to date are suited to this project.

Specifically, then, the main components of this chapter are:

- a concise critical engagement with the existing literature on CM and primary care (and orthodox medicine more widely) with a view to demonstrating both the current state of knowledge and, crucially, its limitations in addressing the 'new terrain' of intersection;
- identification of the kinds of questions that have been raised by existing work but that, as yet, remain unanswered and indeed unexplored; and the argument that it is through empirical attention to the key site of intersection – the grassroots – that such answers will be found;
- argument for a renewed or re-emphasized research agenda geared towards an exploration of this intersection, and the case for the use of the concepts and framework of a largely overlooked approach – social worlds theory (SWT) – as one means by which the complexities of change in grassroots practice can be explored;
- identification of elements of a future research agenda and the means by which these can be examined.

Thus, our concern is to highlight a gap in our understanding and to argue for a means of overcoming this. As a result, the chapter is rather more about raising questions than answering them; those answers lie in future empirical work, which the proposed approach will facilitate.

## Complementary medicine and primary care

### Forms of integrative practice

The sporadic development of integrative practice, involving the use of both unconventional and conventional medicine, has been identified across a

**Table 10.1** Models of integration of complementary therapies within general practice

| Models of integration | Character of integration |
| --- | --- |
| Referrals | Direct referrals under NHS budget or encouragement of 'self-referral' of patient. May be to lay therapists or to medical colleagues who practise a form of CM (other GPs, practice nurses, and so on). Can be to practitioners within NHS or private practice. |
| Multidisciplinary integrative primary care teams | Have been largely *ad hoc* experimental developments where lay therapist and GP (and others) are based in one 'clinic' with the aim of developing collaborative treatments. GP may retain lead role or practice may be established on a more egalitarian basis. |
| Direct integrative practice | This is based upon the use of one or more therapy by GPs themselves and requiring no direct input from other practitioners. |

number of medical sites (Rankin-Box 1988; Booth 1993; Perkin *et al.* 1994; Dale 1996). However, we would concur with the view that it is in primary care that 'complementary medicine is making its presence felt' (Peters 1994: 171). Indeed, the past 15 years have seen a range of studies reflecting the growing interest and involvement of GPs with a range of complementary therapies (Reilly 1983; Nicholls and Luton 1986; Wharton and Lewith 1986; Anderson and Anderson 1987; Swayne 1989).

Drawing on this previous research it is possible to identify three distinct models of integration within general practice. These are outlined in Table 10.1.

These different models harbour both potentially contrasting power relationships between the different practitioners involved, and different constructions about the role of the GP (Pietroni 1992a; Peters 1994). For the purposes of this chapter we will focus specifically upon direct integrative practice, and illustrate the points made by reference to work in progress (Adams 1998). Our exploratory case study is intended to provide a theoretical framework that may be adapted for the study of integration in this field more broadly.

*Existing research on unconventional therapies and integration*

CM has been increasingly written about over the past 20 years, and much of this work – including that produced by some social scientists – has been criticized for adopting a conventional medical perspective (see Saks 1995; Power 1997 for such critiques).

More recently there have been attempts to establish a symmetrical approach to the medicines (Saks 1995; Cant and Sharma 1996; Power 1997). This approach responds to the call to study alternative medicine in context, taking the 'margin' and the 'centre' together rather than in isolation (Sharma 1993), and acknowledges the 'contested' nature of the 'truths' promoted by different medical groups.

In problematizing the ideology of the medical profession this symmetrical approach illustrates how the legitimacy and status of unconventional medicine in Britain are the result of social and political processes (Nicholls 1988; Saks 1995; Cant and Sharma 1996). In turn, it can be argued that the marginal or excluded status that these therapies have acquired is neither consistent with other earlier circumstances (Cooter 1988), nor necessarily characteristic of future relationships (West 1992). This suggests that the boundaries between conventional and unconventional medicine are not fixed but are, at least in part, produced, maintained and reconstituted through the activities of medical groups. In the light of this, some work has emphasized the importance of boundary maintenance and reconstruction between the two medicines (Saks 1995, 1996; Cant and Sharma 1996) and this chapter builds on such a focus. However, our adaptation of SWT leads to a rather different approach to issues of boundaries and their construction and maintenance: one that is both sensitive to intra- and interprofessional 'movements' (Bucher 1962, 1988) while at the same time linking the structural organization of medicine to the concrete work activities of practitioners in actual practice settings.

Sociologists interested in the interface between conventional and unconventional medicines have characteristically produced monolithic accounts of the medical profession. Yet the profession is 'a broad church' (Cant and Sharma 1996) and there exist divisions and rivalries between, and within, the different specialisms. For instance, there have been numerous attempts from within general practice to expand the role and identity of the profession away from the shadow of hospital ideology. In the face of the lack of a unique body of knowledge some within general practice have laid claim to treating the 'whole person', attempting to extend their approach beyond a strict biomedical model of illness (Armstrong 1979; Bowling 1981; Jefferys and Sachs 1983; Calnan and Gabe 1991). The case for their generalism to be accepted as the basis of specialist status is also made (Stacey 1988). An appreciation of such *inter-* and *intraprofessional* tensions is central to exploring the working sites of integration between the two medicines.

Work to date has also tended to display an overriding concern with the attitude of the elite of the medical profession towards unconventional medicine. Shifts in the approach of the medical elite – such as the one to an 'incorporativist' stance by the BMA (Saks 1995) – are certainly of importance to sociological analysis and they have been the concern of a number of interesting works to date (Saks 1992, 1995, 1996). And while some recent research has begun to explore alternative and complementary medical knowledge in local practice settings, and its transformation between and within groups, although not specifically relating to sites of integration (Johannessen 1996; Power 1996), most writers have continued to pitch their analysis at the level of formal rhetoric and the approach of collective bodies, while neglecting the concrete work activities of practitioners.

This approach encourages a conceptualization of legitimization processes exclusively within structural terms (or at an organizational level). Yet the research mentioned earlier has highlighted *grassroots practice* as being of fundamental importance to an understanding of the situation, given that it is this level that constitutes the key site of enthusiasm for developing integrative practice (Wharton and Lewith 1986; Anderson and Anderson 1987, and so on). As has been pointed out with specific regard to the non-medically qualified, there has been little research examining what these therapists actually do (Sharma 1994), a situation that corresponds to the study of GPs who are also practising these therapies. Through our formulation of a Social Worlds framework we aim to redirect the researcher's gaze upon the concrete work activities of grassroots practitioners. This is not an attempt to reveal the individual motivations of doctors – we are concerned with approaching such practitioners as representatives of social worlds – but, in contrast, it reveals our conviction that the study of this professional community should be based upon integrating an examination of structural units with an empirical investigation of everyday work activities within actual medical settings.

So although previous writers have raised a number of pertinent questions about the practice of unconventional medicine by NHS GPs (Taylor 1985; Sharma 1992, 1994), due to the nature of the approaches used, these have yet to be systematically addressed. These have included such questions as the following. In what way does the NHS environment affect the practice of unconventional therapies? What 'style' of practice is produced? And how does this practice differ from that of lay therapists outside the NHS? Adopting an SWT framework will help in the attempt to answer these and related questions, because of the altered orientation it demands of the researcher.

## Sketching a new theoretical approach

Given that SWT has received little attention to date (even within its parent discipline), a brief sketch of its central concepts – as they are relevant here – is presented at this point.

The concept of *social worlds*, as developed within SWT, refers to 'groups with shared commitments to certain activities, sharing resources of many kinds to achieve their goals, and building shared ideologies about how to go about their business' (Clarke 1991: 131). The concept of a social world can be applied to any substantive topic of social life: banking, art, stamp collecting and so on. Social worlds may involve only a handful of individuals or may be comparatively large, even spanning countries or continents. Some are loosely bound with easily penetrable memberships, while others have a much tighter control of entrants.

Where a number of worlds congregate and place attention upon one activity an *arena* is formed. All worlds are involved in ongoing claims and debates with other worlds within *arenas* about *legitimacy* and *authenticity*. Processes of *legitimacy* relate to issues like who can do a certain activity, when they can do it, where, and in what way. Meanwhile, *authenticity* processes are concerned with who and what are to be deemed authentic members in the world itself. Another important process of social worlds is *segmentation*. This refers to the way in which groups within worlds are always 'emerging, evolving, developing, splintering, disintegrating or pulling themselves together, or parts of them falling away and perhaps coalescing with segments of other groups to form new groups' (Strauss 1978: 120–1). One such mode of segmentation is based upon the intersection of two previously opposed social worlds.

The process of authenticity is a crucial concept in that it highlights the centrality of individuals and their interactions within worlds. Worlds are sustained through co-members repeatedly judging the authenticity of others within moment by moment interaction. Divergent acts or products are contained through the threat or actual mobilization of distancing processes: 'people who step out of bounds too frequently will either be considered mavericks and disregarded or may become candidates for informal or formal excommunication' (Strauss 1982: 188).

However, these mechanisms of 'self reference' (Bloor 1996) do not dictate the actions of individual members; more specifically, they act to constrain and coordinate behaviour. SWT is fundamentally an anti-determinist approach to collective action; at all times members possess the potential to create new meanings and introduce new practices.

Building on the work of Clarke (1990a) – which has further developed a social world approach, combining elements from the interactionist study of work (for example Freidson 1976) with a social world framework – we centre analytical focus upon the concrete work tasks and activities within worlds. Such an approach reveals, among other things, 'the complex organisation of work tasks and activities, and the negotiation of the actual division of labour (rather than, for example, professional claims-making about it)' (Clarke 1990a: 21–2).

The following section outlines some of the ways in which this particular version of SWT can be applied to the topic of direct integrative practice in primary care. Quotes are drawn from an ongoing study that is studying GPs who include CM as part of their practice. They are selected from in-depth semi-structured interviews (Adams 1998).

### SWT and the integration of unconventional therapies within primary care

At the risk of oversimplification we can note that writers to date have identified two parent medical worlds (orthodox and complementary), which are built on contrasting constructions of aetiology, nosology and treatment, as well as of therapeutic relationships and responsibilities (Taylor 1985; British Medical Association 1986; Spence 1990; Pietroni 1992b; Douglas 1994; Peters 1994; Sharma 1994). Moreover, the languages of these different worlds reveal the use of different and often contrasting 'modes of thought' (Pietroni 1992b).

So we might begin to talk in terms of the 'unconventional medical world' and 'conventional medical world'. But, to leave the analysis at this point is to leave a monolithic vision of the medical profession (and unconventional medicine too) intact. Previous work on intersection (Tovey 1997a,b) has demonstrated how these two parent worlds are not homogeneous medical communities; we need to 'segment' these worlds further into 'subworlds' (Strauss 1984).

### Identifying the subworlds of general practice and unconventional therapies

General practice itself can be taken to constitute a particular subworld; that is to say, it has developed its own particular activities, ideologies and knowledge claims from within the wider medical profession. This subworld can be analytically dissected further: there are competing visions of general practice (see pages 9–23) promoting a 'multiplicity of perspectives' with regard to the role, responsibilities, and identity of the profession. General practice, like any other professional community, is to be seen as a contested world housing many different 'professional movements' and the *authenticity* of practitioners and activities are issues that are constantly negotiated, debated and fought about within the ranks of the profession.

Turning to the unconventional medical world we can detect similar subdivisions and factions. The therapies often have different underlying philosophies, origins and historical relationships to the medical orthodoxy (Saks 1992; Cant and Sharma 1996), and research has illustrated some of the differences among non-medically qualified therapists with regard to their

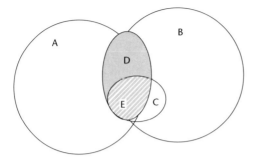

A:       Unconventional medical world
B:       Conventional medical world
C:       Subworld of general practice
D⬜ : Potential sites of intersection
E ▨ : Intersecting subworld within general practice developing around integrative
         practice

**Figure 10.1**  Analytical framework: unconventional medicine, conventional
medicine, intersection and appropriation

perceptions of their role and identity (Cant and Calnan 1991). As such, we
can identify subworlds based upon the character of therapies themselves. In
addition, it also follows, as in the case of general practice, that these subworlds
are themselves contested sites where *authenticity* is not to be seen as fixed or
resolved, but as the ongoing topic of negotiation and dispute.

Based on the concepts of medical worlds and subworlds, we can produce
an analytical framework for this case study (outlined in Figure 10.1).

Complementary therapies have become an arena of common interest. Different worlds and subworlds of medicine have increasingly laid claim to the
practice of them. Here we have a picture of competing and jostling constructions and claims as to the therapies' 'authentic' nature, location and role
within medicine.

Adopting these social world concepts we can interpret the development of
unconventional therapies within general practice as representing an emerging and evolving subworld (subworld E in Figure 10.1). This subworld, constituted upon the boundary between the conventional and unconventional
medical worlds (see Figure 10.1), is represented at an institutional level by
such bodies as the British Medical Acupuncture Society, the British Society of
Medical and Dental Hypnosis and the Faculty of Homeopathy.

Like the wider worlds referred to earlier, this particular subworld houses
further divisions. For instance, some GP acupuncturists might distance their
use of CM from that of GPs who use hypnotherapy or homeopathy, and vice
versa. As one GP acupuncturist notes,

> I feel that unlike homeopathy, where I find it difficult to understand why
> homeopathy works, I can see why acupuncture works. I still feel that a
> lot of [homeopathy] is psychotherapy, they have long consultations which
> makes me wonder if it's just that patients are listened to for a change.

And similarly, a number of GPs practising hypnotherapy have been found to present their role and identity as GP therapists as being distinct from GP acupuncturists. One GP practising homeopathy, hypnotherapy and neurolinguistic programming comments thus:

GP:            These things introduced me to the idea that there's other powers beyond us and in my various reading to expand my knowledge of hypnosis and NLP (neurolinguistic programming) is always this suggestion that what's very important are the messages that you give yourself; that if you think badly of someone else and want revenge on someone else you'll end up with that revenge coming to you . . . now you start even telling some of the doctors who do acupuncture that.

Interviewer:   What do you think their reaction is going to be?

GP:            Oh, they'd have you certified!

What makes this subworld particularly interesting is that it involves GPs adopting styles, activities and technologies that are essentially associated with, and found within, the unconventional medical world (parent world A in Figure 10.1). Such adoption produces tension for the subworld and its members. As Strauss explains, 'there is a pull towards being distinct from neighbouring (subworlds), but not so distinct as to be defined as outsiders altogether' (Strauss 1984: 128). The development of unconventional therapies within general practice would seem to remain a point of controversy within the profession (Spence 1990) and the members of this subworld would seem to be involved in *processes of appropriation* (of concepts and activities from world A to subworld C in Figure 10.1) through which the therapies can be justified to others in their medical world (Sharma 1996).

### Theoretical refinement for primary care

The concept of *intersection*, which is central to SWT, is extremely useful for interpreting and investigating these developments. However, we suggest that the study of the emerging subworld of CM in general practice requires attention to the *degree* of intersection (Strauss 1993). Indeed we go further by introducing additional refinements to this concept: *strong intersection* and *weak intersection*.

We would argue that the majority of empirical social world research has tended to concentrate upon areas of *strong* intersection. This is where prolonged, and often well established patterns of cross-discipline or cross-professional practice and collaboration can be identified (Clarke 1990a,b; Garrety 1997). Some forms of integration between general practice and unconventional medicine (Models 1 and 2 in Table 10.1) may be interpreted as clear examples of such strong intersection between two parent medical worlds. Multidisciplinary integrative practice clearly involves different degrees of collaboration and cooperation between GPs and lay therapists. In addition, while referrals to the non-medically qualified may involve a somewhat more 'distanced' interface between the two medical groups, these developments are, at least potentially, sites for developing networks and communication between therapists and doctors.

However, direct integrative practice does not necessitate, nor appear to lend itself to, collaboration or communication between the worlds of conventional and unconventional medicine. Research (Adams 1998) has revealed that many GP therapists demarcate their practice of the therapies from that of the non-medically qualified, regarding their own use of unconventional therapies as supplementary to a biomedical base and their practice of conventional treatments. They frequently regard lay therapists as being engaged in a different style of therapy. This style is often defined as 'alternative' and is presented by these GPs as dangerous, more rigidly based upon ungrounded philosophical and theoretical models, and invariably affected by the self-interest of the therapist seeking and retaining patients in a competitive free market. As one GP describes his practice of acupuncture and how it differs from that of non-medically trained acupuncturists:

> the yin and the yang and the circulation of Chi and things like that . . . are concepts that I don't need to worry about – they seem a bit woolly to me. If you're going to switch into a Chinese model it's a totally different concept from Western medicine, so, *if you're doing it as complementary rather than alternative* I think in real life you cannot sit here and see the patient at ten-minute intervals doing Western medicine and then switch for two minutes into Chinese medicine, so . . . you've got to make you're choice if you're doing it the way I do it.

Another GP acupuncturist explains what he sees as the difficulty of accepting an 'alternative' model of medicine within his general practice:

> you have to forget everything you know about Western medicine and just re-orientate your mind totally to the Chinese model of thinking, and it has no relation to anything that we have ever learned in medical school . . . I would suspect that it's all nonsense but I've decided not to go . . . down that path.

And in the case of a GP homeopath, her 'complementary practice' is perceived as 'safe' in relation to lay practice. She says:

> I would like to think that I wouldn't miss serious pathology, that I wouldn't be treating someone with a homeopathic remedy who should be, you know, having their cancer removed. I would say that's a safe-guard for the patients in the respect that there is pathology that goes on which needs traditional medical and surgical treatment and it may be that a non-medically qualified homeopath may miss symptoms which should be properly investigated.

As such, we suggest that direct integrative practice represents an example of *weak* intersection where the cooperation between worlds may be reluctantly undertaken and relatively brief in nature. The processes of distancing and demarcation would appear to have become predominant. The development of informal networks and practice contact between these GPs and their lay counterparts is minimal, and is often rejected with many of these GP therapists referring patients only to other medical colleagues for complementary treatment that they see as relevant (Adams 1998). Formal positions have mirrored this point. Many of the professional organizations that claim to represent medical therapists deny membership to non-medically qualified therapists, and some have opposed the practice of their particular therapy by others outside the medical profession (West 1992).

In line with these circumstances, we would argue, *appropriation* has become the central process to be examined in relation to direct integrative practice. To date, no work has attended to how the appropriation of these therapies is achieved by GPs through their construction of clinical work, and there is a need to move beyond the representations and claims of professional groups, and to investigate how unconventional therapies are actively integrated within the GPs' surgery.

Concentrating our attention upon social worlds and subworlds, and examining concrete work and its organization, enables us to understand some of the tensions, limitations and opportunities faced by doctors who are integrating unconventional therapies into their practice regime. Questions that need investigating here include the following. How do GPs construct the therapies in practice? How do they construct their own role in the practice of unconventional medicines? How do they construct the role of the patient receiving unconventional therapy? How, if at all, are these constructs different from those found in their conventional medical practice? And how do they differ between therapies?

What is important, we would suggest, is that work attempting to answer these questions, rather than relying upon claims detached from the actual medical sites of integration, should instead base analysis upon what practitioners actually do: examining integration *in process* within the doctor's surgery. In this way we analyse constructions of the therapies and related issues that are negotiated in interaction and are situationally bound within the consultation itself.

## Concluding comments

Our principal concern in writing this chapter has been to highlight the benefits to be derived from a shift in focus in the way we address the often complex intersection between CM and established forms of primary care. At the heart of our approach has been a stress on the need for a greater attention to grassroots activity. We have further proposed a framework (based on SWT) as a means by which this can be undertaken. The use of this theoretical framework provides a means by which we can focus in on the micro level without reducing the analysis to mere description of isolated events and practices.

In essence, therefore, our task has been to outline the potential of this revised focus to explore important questions (often implicitly or explicitly raised by previous research work). We do not pretend to be in the business of providing answers at this stage. Our discussion of this little known sociological framework should also be seen as an illustration of the potential contribution to be made by mainstream sociology to the much touted multidisciplinary approach to primary care research; one that can extend beyond the decontextualized use of qualitative methodology, which can sometimes appear to be the accepted extent of 'sociological' involvement.

Throughout the chapter we have emphasized that it is what is actually going on in primary care that should take centre stage. Formal (institutional) statements of policy might provide the context but understanding must proceed on the assumption that what is said to happen (or what should happen) and what actually happens do not necessarily coincide. Our attention, therefore, becomes drawn to the level of the practice. And what results from that emphasis on day to day activity is the necessity to engage fully with examples of intersection, an appreciation of the strength and character of that intersection, conflicts over the legitimacy of participants (and the bodies of knowledge they use) and so on. As we have seen these are the very processes that the concepts of SWT have been developed to elucidate.

Moreover, and inextricably linked with these aspects of the framework, there is a capacity built into SWT to not merely accept ever multiplying subdivisions but to actually *anticipate* their formation. This is important for the study of CM because of the range of beliefs about its character that exist among both conventional and unconventional practitioners. Lip service is frequently paid to the heterogeneity of the two sectors, but in SWT we have a framework that has been specifically developed to track splinter groups and diversity of opinion rather than to try and squeeze them into all-embracing camps.

This is of paramount importance for our task of establishing knowledge about grassroots activity because, by making local action the focus of attention, we are able to get away from talking about the integration of a 'sector', and can instead begin to consider the nature of the integration (or otherwise) of practices in quite specific settings, against a background of individual circumstances. The unevenness of intersection – a feature of the current situation that we flagged up earlier – is, therefore, able to remain central to analysis and be explored as an ongoing and integral feature of the situation rather than being glossed over as a side issue.

Furthermore, once differentiated subworlds are identified we are given the opportunity to access information on a specific arena from a number of angles. For instance, we have based our chapter on the example of GPs who use CM. This is certainly important, but we could just as appropriately examine numerous other 'worlds' that are of direct relevance to an understanding of how intersection is occurring in primary care; an example of which is nurses, nursing and CM (Tovey 1997b). And once we begin to broaden the gaze to embrace multiple 'takes' on the same circumstance we can begin to explore issues that reach well beyond the descriptive. For instance, there are very real issues of power involved here. The world of primary care nursing and the world of general practice are, in many ways, quite distinct and bring with them quite different expectations, authority to implement change and so on. It is therefore reasonable to explore the possibility that the integration of objectively similar practices will be imbued with quite different meanings and implications for the various groups and that the interpretation of practice consequences, or indeed the practice consequences themselves, will be similarly diverse.

In addition, the changing roles of these groups means that the capacity to track that change, which is inherent in SWT, is crucial. The emphasis in the approach on fluidity, constant evolution and the continual redefining of groups means that an overly static and rigid interpretation of roles and collaborations in the practice setting is avoided.

One further benefit of the approach is that it permits greater attention to be paid to the impact, significance and consequences of developments at practice level than might ordinarily be the case. For instance, the realization that a certain number of collaborative ventures are up and running actually tells us very little of interest. It is, for example, the extent to which these can be regarded as being in the vanguard of change, or as being isolated and peripheral, that needs to be explored. This can only be achieved by looking at how these emerging practices fit into, or help reconfigure, pre-existing (medical) worlds.

All this brings with it implications for the way in which research is conducted, and in particular for the methodologies adopted. There is a need to find the best means of accessing that all-important level of activity (rather than rhetoric). And although it would be naïve to assume that any setting can be accessed without the mediation of researcher interpretation, the detailed observation integral to ethnography (Hammersley and Atkinson 1983) provides a necessary starting point for investigations of the sort required. For instance, how established patterns of power and authority impact on the legitimacy ascribed to certain therapies, and to the practitioners of those therapies, is one aspect of the emerging research agenda that could be explored in this way. Another is the way in which CM is actually conceptualized in various quarters, and how it then becomes operationalized as a result. This last issue is rather more than the purely academic interest it might at first appear to be; not least because of the practical implications that result from a conceptualization of therapies as either specialisms or generalisms. To date the appropriation of therapies has tended to rest on an interpretation of them as specialisms (Peters 1994); however, should therapies come to be regarded as competing generalisms (as may be the case with, say, homeopathy) a very different dynamic may be established, especially as the division of labour is still up for grabs (Abbott 1988).

As unconventional therapies continue to be integrated into primary care practice the range of issues relating to applicability, position, ownership and more will remain matters of debate and contestation. And given that private CM is inevitably beyond the reach of many, the local practice constitutes a key interface between patients and therapies. The way in which GPs and other primary care practitioners negotiate and resolve tensions between sections of these interpenetrating medical worlds will be pivotal to the way in which a service embracing, modifying or appropriating CM may evolve.

## Note

1 The issues of nomenclature, and what is, and what is not, a therapy which should be seen to be a part of the 'sector', have been discussed frequently (Saks 1992;

Sharma 1992) and need not be repeated here. In this chapter, we use 'complementary' as the principal label largely as a reflection of its current predominance in practice. It is, though, used interchangeably with other terms, such as unconventional.

## References

Abbott, A. (1988) *The System of Professions*. Chicago, IL: University of Chicago Press.

Adams, J. (1998) Complementary therapies in general practice. Paper presented at the 4th Qualitative Health Research Conference, University of British Columbia, Vancouver, February 19–21.

Anderson, E. and Anderson, P. (1987) General practitioners and alternative medicine, *Journal of the Royal College of General Practitioners*, 37: 52–5.

Armstrong, D. (1979) The emancipation of biographical medicine, *Social Science and Medicine*, 13A: 1–8.

Bloor, D. (1996) What is a social construct? Paper presented at the London School of Economics, All London History and Philosophy of Science Meeting, 'the role of constructivism in current studies of science', May 10.

Booth, B. (1993) Fringe benefits, *Nursing Times*, 89, 17: 34–6.

Bowling, A. (1981) *Delegation in General Practice*. London: Tavistock.

British Medical Association (BMA) (1986) *Alternative Therapy: Report of the Board of Science and Education*. London: BMA.

British Medical Association (BMA) (1993) *Complementary Medicine: New Approaches to Good Practice*. Oxford: Oxford University Press.

Bucher, R. (1962) Pathology: a study of social movements within a profession, *Social Problems*, 10(1): 40–51.

Bucher, R. (1988) On the natural history of health care occupations, *Work and Occupations*, 15(2): 131–47.

Calnan, M. and Gabe, J. (1991) Recent developments in general practice: a sociological analysis, in J. Gabe, M. Calnan and M. Bury (eds) *The Sociology of the Health Service*. London: Routledge.

Cant, S. (1996) From charismatic teaching to professional training: the legitimation of knowledge and the creation of trust in homeopathy and chiropractic, in S. Cant and U. Sharma (eds) *Complementary and Alternative Medicines: Knowledge in Practice*. London: Free Association Books.

Cant, S. and Calnan, M. (1991) On the margins of the medical marketplace? An exploratory study of alternative practitioners' perceptions, *Sociology of Health and Illness*, 13(1): 39–57.

Cant, S. and Sharma, U. (eds) (1996) *Complementary and Alternative Medicines: Knowledge in Practice*. London: Free Association Books.

Chan, J., Carr, I. and Mayberry, J. (1997) The role of acupuncture in the treatment of irritable bowel syndrome: a pilot study, *Hepato-Gastroenterology*, 44: 1328–30.

Clarke, A. (1990a) A social worlds research adventure: the case of reproductive science, in S. Cozzen and T. Gieryn (eds) *Theories of Science and Society*. Bloomington, IN: Indiana University Press.

Clarke, A. (1990b) Controversy and the development of reproductive sciences, *Social Problems*, 37(1): 18–37.

Clarke, A. (1991) Social worlds/arenas theory as organizational theory, in D. Maines (ed.) *Social Organisation and Social Processes: Essays in Honour of Anselm Strauss*. New York: Aldine de Gruyter.

Cooter, R. (ed.) (1988) *Studies in the History of Alternative Medicine*. Oxford: Macmillan.

Dale, J. (1996) Practising acupuncture today: a postal questionnaire of medical practitioners, *Acupuncture in Medicine*, 14(2): 104–8.

Douglas, M. (1994) The construction of the physician: a cultural approach to medical fashions, in S. Budd and U. Sharma (eds) *The Healing Bond*. London: Routledge.

Freidson, E. (1976) The division of labor as social interaction, *Social Problems*, 23(3): 304–13.

Garrety, K. (1997) Social worlds, actor-networks and controversy: the case of cholesterol, dietary fat and heart disease, *Social Studies of Science*, 27(5): 727–73.

Hammersley, M. and Atkinson, P. (1983) *Ethnography: Principles in Practice*. London: Routledge.

Honigsbaum, F. (1985) Reconstruction of general practice: failure of reform, *British Medical Journal*, 290: 823–6.

Jefferys, M. and Sachs, H. (1983) *Rethinking General Practice*. London: Tavistock.

Johannessen, H. (1996) Individualized knowledge: reflexologists, biopaths and kinesiologists in Denmark, in S. Cant, and U. Sharma (eds) *Complementary and Alternative Medicines: Knowledge in Practice*. London: Free Association Books.

Nicholls, P.A. (1988) *Homeopathy and the Medical Profession*. London: Croom Helm.

Nicholls, P.A. and Luton, J. (1986) *Doctors and Complementary Medicine: A Survey of General Practitioners in the Potteries*, occasional paper no. 2. Department of Sociology, Staffordshire Polytechnic.

Perkin, M.R., Pearcy, R.M. and Fraser, J.S. (1994) A comparison of the attitudes shown by general practitioners, hospital doctors and medical students towards alternative medicine, *Journal of the Royal Society of Medicine*, 87: 523–5.

Peters, D. (1994) Sharing responsibility for patient care: doctors and complementary practitioners, in S. Budd, and U. Sharma (eds) *The Healing Bond*. London: Routledge.

Pietroni, P. (1992a) Beyond the boundaries: the relationship between general practice and complementary medicine, *British Medical Journal*, 305: 564–6.

Pietroni, P. (1992b) Towards reflective practice – the languages of health and social care, *Journal of Inter-professional Care*, 6(3): 7–16.

Power, R. (1996) Considering archival research in one's own practice, in S. Cant and U. Sharma (eds) *Complementary and Alternative Medicines: Knowledge in Practice*. London: Free Association Press.

Power, R. (1997) The whole idea of medicine, *Medical Sociology News*, 23(2): 39–50.

Rankin-Box, D.F. (ed.) (1988) *Complementary Health Therapies: A Guide for Nurses and other Caring Professions*. Kent: Croom Helm.

Reason, P., Chase, H.D., Desser, A. *et al.* (1992) Towards a clinical framework for collaboration between general and complementary practitioners: discussion paper, *Journal of the Royal Society of Medicine*, 85(3): 161–4.

Reilly, D.T. (1983) Young doctors' views on alternative medicine, *British Medical Journal*, 287: 337–9.

Saks, M. (ed.) (1992) *Alternative Medicine in Britain*. Oxford: Clarendon Press.

Saks, M. (1995) *Professions and the Public Interest: Medical Power, Altruism and Alternative Medicine*. London: Routledge.

Saks, M. (1996) From quackery to complementary medicine: the shifting boundaries between orthodox and unorthodox knowledge, in S. Cant, and U. Sharma (eds) *Complementary and Alternative Medicines: Knowledge in Practice*. London: Free Association Books.

Sharma, U. (1992) *Complementary Medicine Today: Practitioners and Patients*. London: Routledge.

Sharma, U. (1993) Contextualizing alternative medicine. The exotic, the marginal and the perfectly mundane, *Anthropology Today*, 9(3): 13–18.

Sharma, U. (1994) The equation of responsibility: complementary practitioners and their patients, in S. Budd, and U. Sharma (eds) *The Healing Bond*. London: Routledge.

Sharma, U. (1996) Situating homeopathic knowledge: legitimation and the cultural landscape, in S. Cant, and U. Sharma (eds) *Complementary and Alternative Medicines: Knowledge in Practice*. London: Free Association Books.

Spence, S.A. (1990) Meaning in medicine: A tao of healing? *Holistic Medicine*, 5: 81–6.

Stacey, M. (1988) *The Sociology of Health and Healing*. London: Unwin Hyman.

Strauss, A. (1978) A social world perspective, *Studies in Symbolic Interaction*, 1: 119–28.

Strauss, A. (1982) Social worlds and legitimation processes, *Studies in Symbolic Interaction*, 4: 171–90.

Strauss, A. (1984) Social worlds and segmentation processes, *Studies in Symbolic Interaction*, 4: 125–39.

Strauss, A. (1993) *Continual Permutations of Action*. New York: Aldine De Gruyter.

Swayne, J. (1989) Survey of the use of homeopathic medicine in the UK health system, *Journal of the Royal College of General Practitioners*, 39: 503–6.

Taylor, R. (1985) Alternative medicine and the medical encounter in Britain and the United States, in J.W. Salmon (ed.) *Alternative Medicines: Popular and Policy Perspectives*. London: Tavistock.

Tovey, P. (1997a) Autonomy and practice: the case of UK alternative practitioners, *International Journal for Quality in Health Care*, 9(1): 55–9.

Tovey, P. (1997b) Contingent legitimacy: UK alternative practitioners and inter-sectoral acceptance, *Social Science and Medicine*, 45(7): 1129–34.

West, R. (1992) Alternative medicine: prospects and speculations, in M. Saks (ed.) *Alternative Medicine in Britain*. Oxford: Clarendon Press.

Wharton, R. and Lewith, G. (1986) Complementary medicine and the general practitioner, *British Medical Journal*, 292: 1498–500.

# Postscript

Philip Tovey

This book has been written at a particularly interesting time in the evolution of primary care in the UK. As has been seen, change at the level of organization and delivery is being accompanied by the emergence of new issues relating to practice, and by the need to re-visit perennial problems, albeit in a modified temporal context. This is a time of challenge to: established practices; existing roles and responsibilities; and prevailing conceptions of health and illness among practitioners as well as patients.

However, this is not just an interesting time for primary care itself but also for the academic study of it. There are three (largely interrelated) reasons why this is so. Firstly, during the past few years it has been recognized that primary care has, to date, been under-researched (Mant 1997; Medical Research Council 1997). Secondly, and as a logical progression of the first point, work in this field is becoming increasingly prioritized. And, thirdly – and this is of some importance – partly as a result of this lack of attention, and partly as a result of the changing nature of primary care organization and practice, there are many issues and themes, often of fundamental importance to the everyday functioning of primary care, about which we know very little. Indeed, a number of contributors to this book have made explicit reference to gaps in knowledge, or the need to extend the scope of research, in their own areas of interest.

So what is the nature of the questions that will dominate the agenda in this period of increased attention to primary care? Perhaps, above all, what binds such questions is that they are rarely amenable to unequivocal or one dimensional answers; often these questions emerge from issues that are grounded in contingency, complexity and intrinsic uncertainty. So, for instance, patient experience and presentation of medically unexplained symptoms, by their very nature, present limited intervention options, and invite all manner of debate about the limits of medical knowledge, the role of personal narrative in understanding illness and so on; and appreciation of varying levels of compliance with medical regimens takes analysis beyond the surgery towards individual life processes, family relationships and cultural influences.

As attention becomes focused on the need to counteract the current lack of evidence on these multifaceted issues, it becomes increasingly apparent that the social location of patient experience and professional action, and the individual mediation of bodily sensations have to be central to analyses. The current involvement of a range of disciplines in the research process is one way in which a broadened perspective can be encouraged. In the present volume, contributors were drawn from anthropology, clinical psychology, disability studies, public health, and sociology, as well as general practice and other primary care professions. And while the approaches taken by authors should not be seen to represent *the* view of their discipline on particular issues (differences within disciplines are, of course, frequently more pronounced than those between them) they do incorporate what the contributors themselves take to be the key themes, useful theory or important debates in those disciplines. Thus, as has been seen in this volume, while it may well be the case that primary care issues are ultimately played out in the surgery setting, they can be approached from very different angles that can reach well beyond the immediate context of the practice, and in so doing establish very different types of (research) questions. For instance, in the case of disability, working from the political perspective of disabled people directs attention towards disabling practices rather than medical action; and, placing socio-economic inequality at the heart of analysis necessarily establishes a structural dimension to researching the health problems of disadvantaged groups.

In short, the challenges of an ever changing primary care system require a research agenda that is able to embrace the centrality of socially located personal experience (of illness and of being a patient), in tandem with (and indeed as part of) pursuit of effective practice level care and treatment options. An enhanced critical focus is called for; and a *theoretical*, as well as a methodological pluralism is pivotal to the achievement of that.

### References

Mant, D. (1997) *R&D in Primary Care.* Leeds: NHS Executive.
Medical Research Council (1997) *Primary Health Care.* London: MRC.

# ⬤ Index

## UNDERSTANDING THE CONSULTATION
EVIDENCE, THEORY AND PRACTICE

**Tim Usherwood**

The general practice consultation is one of the most challenging encounters in medicine. It demands of the doctor not only a high degree of technical knowledge and skill, but also considerable interpersonal competence and self-knowledge. Many books have been written about the consultation, but most are informed by a limited range of theoretical perspectives. The aim of this book is to help the reader gain a deeper understanding of the encounter between patient and doctor by examining it from a number of different points of view. Topics that are addressed include:

• information sharing and decision making in the consultation
• theories of the patient-doctor relationship
• the social context of illness

The research evidence is described, and practical implications for patient care are explored. Verbal and non-verbal communication, the care of patients with chronic illness, and management of emotional and psychosocial problems are discussed in detail.

*Understanding the Consultation* will be of particular interest to trainee general practitioners, but should also be of interest to established general practitioners and senior medical students.

### *Contents*
*The consultation in context – Information sharing in the consultation – Empathy and rapport – Psychodynamic insights – The transactional perspective – Discourse in the consultation – The family and chronic illness – Emotional and psychosocial problems – Somatization and somatic fixation – The consultation back in context – References – Index.*

160pp     0 335 19998 4 (Paperback)     0 335 19999 2 (Hardback)

# COUNSELLING SKILLS FOR DOCTORS

## Sam Smith and Kingsley Norton

- What are intrinsic counselling skills?
- How can doctors deploy them to help optimize the outcomes of clinical transactions with their patients?
- Can such skills be taught and learned?

This book is about the doctor-patient relationship. It is not about counselling *per se* but about certain counselling skills intrinsic to the medical consultation or clinical transaction. Together with other clinical skills, intrinsic counselling skills are needed to achieve clinical goals, satisfactory to both patient and doctor and appropriate to the clinical transaction and to the wider systems of healthcare.

Clinical transactions can be intellectually, emotionally and sometimes physically demanding. Success depends on doctor and patient adequately fulfilling the obligations and responsibilities of their respective roles. But evidence shows that success also depends on doctors and patients forming a personal relationship of a quality capable of sustaining the sometimes arduous and distressing clinical work. Such a relationship depends on good communication, adequate mutual trust and the ability of doctors to empathize sufficiently with patients and their predicaments. Intrinsic counselling skills are those deployed in the essential task of harmonizing professional and interpersonal aspects of the clinical transaction.

This book is recommended reading for doctors and medical students, postregistration vocational trainees and medical educators within medical schools.

### Contents
*Introduction – Consulting skills – Intrinsic counselling skills and the clinical transaction – Making a diagnosis: examination and investigation – Managing the problem – Health promotion – Clinical teams and systems of health care – Implications for training – Closing comments – References – Index.*

144pp    0 335 20014 1 (Paperback)    0 335 20015 X (Hardback)

**PRIMARY CARE**
MAKING CONNECTIONS
**Noel Boaden**

- How should the professional career in primary care be seen in light of the intentions for a primary care-led NHS and what changes does this suggest in professional education?
- How might primary care be organized to provide the right context for such professional careers and a framework which can facilitate the formal politics and public participation which give it legitimacy?

This book looks at primary care in a broad way which goes beyond the idea that it is only about general practice. It explores the linkages involved in that extended view through an examination of the history of development in healthcare and through the application of a systems analysis to that process.

In light of that discussion it then examines the current organization and management of primary care and the fragmented professional staffing in relation to the demands of a primary care-led NHS. These chapters lead on to consideration of new forms of organization in primary care and the development of the professions involved and their education and training. Recommendations are made about both aspects as a framework for a consideration of the politics of primary care both institutionally and in relation to emerging ideas about citizen participation.

*Contents*
*Introduction – Health and health care in society: missing links – A new departure in the 1980s: forging new links – Primary care today – Seeing connections: models of systems – Professional divisions – Organization and management – Integrating education for primary care – A new organization for primary care – The politics of the new primary care – Conclusions – Bibliography – Index.*

176pp      0 335 19748 5 (Paperback)      0 335 19749 3 (Hardback)